THE HOMELESSNESS OF BEING

THE HOMELESSNESS OF BEING

HEIDEGGER
AND THE
MEANING OF
EXISTENCE

PRASHAN RANASINGHE

UNIVERSITY of ALBERTA PRESS

Published by

University of Alberta Press
1-16 Rutherford Library South
11204 89 Avenue NW
Edmonton, Alberta, Canada T6G 2J4
amiskwaciwâskahikan | Treaty 6 |
Métis Territory
ualbertapress.ca | uapress@ualberta.ca

Copyright © 2024 Prashan Ranasinghe

LIBRARY AND ARCHIVES CANADA
CATALOGUING IN PUBLICATION

Title: The homelessness of being : Heidegger
   and the meaning of existence /
   Prashan Ranasinghe.
Names: Ranasinghe, Prashan, 1977– author.
Description: Includes bibliographical
   references and index.
Identifiers: Canadiana (print) 20240316991 |
   Canadiana (ebook) 20240317033 |
   ISBN 9781772127683 (softcover) |
   ISBN 9781772127768 (PDF) |
   ISBN 9781772127751 (EPUB)
Subjects: LCSH: Heidegger, Martin, 1889–
   1976—Criticism and interpretation. |
   LCSH: Sociology—Philosophy.
Classification: LCC B3279.H49 R36 2024 |
   DDC 193—dc23

First edition, first printing, 2024.
First printed and bound in Canada by
Houghton Boston Printers, Saskatoon,
Saskatchewan.

All rights reserved. No part of this
publication may be reproduced, stored in a
retrieval system, or transmitted in any form
or by any means (electronic, mechanical,
photocopying, recording, generative
artificial intelligence [AI] training, or
otherwise) without prior written consent.
Contact University of Alberta Press for
further details.

University of Alberta Press supports
copyright. Copyright fuels creativity,
encourages diverse voices, promotes free
speech, and creates a vibrant culture. Thank
you for buying an authorized edition of this
book and for complying with the copyright
laws by not reproducing, scanning, or
distributing any part of it in any form
without permission. You are supporting
writers and allowing University of Alberta
Press to continue to publish books for
every reader.

This book has been published with the
help of a grant from the Federation for the
Humanities and Social Sciences, through
the Awards to Scholarly Publications
Program, using funds provided by the Social
Sciences and Humanities Research Council
of Canada.

University of Alberta Press gratefully
acknowledges the support received for its
publishing program from the Government
of Canada, the Canada Council for the Arts,
and the Government of Alberta through the
Alberta Media Fund.

Contents

Acknowledgements VII
Abbreviations for Works by Heidegger XIII
Introduction XV

1 | Anxiety and the Revelation of Nothingness 1
2 | Profound Boredom 33
3 | Ontological Homelessness and Revelation 77
4 | Dwelling in Ontological Homelessness 101

Conclusion 127
Notes 145
Bibliography 153
Index 167

Acknowledgements

THE SEEDS OF THIS BOOK WERE SOWN, if memory does not fail me, toward the waning stages of writing my previous book, *Helter-Shelter*. Drawing and building upon that work, an ethnography of an emergency shelter, I had planned to undertake a detailed and systematic ethnography of homelessness, focusing specifically on those who are houseless and living on the streets (knowing full well, of course, that the literature on homelessness is as vast as it is nearly exhaustive). The idea was to contribute to this literature through the philosophy of Martin Heidegger, particularly his take on dwelling, a project that was in some ways like mixing oil and water. That project never came to fruition for a variety of reasons, but mainly because it became nearly impossible to secure funding. It soon became obvious to me that despite all their proclamations about the intellectual exploration of ideas, the social sciences broadly (and sociology and criminology in particular) are, with a few exceptions, quite averse to engaging with ideas, especially when grounded philosophically, and are dogmatically mired in the business of reproducing facts, mostly the same ones with a different gloss. Whether the philosophy of Heidegger was offensive or confounding to those who read the funding application will never be clear, but these efforts were generally met across the board with little to no enthusiasm or approval, and the place of the philosophical endeavour was often questioned vis-à-vis the business of fact finding.

Frustrated with seeking funding and dissatisfied with the myopia of the social sciences, I moved to engage with the subject on a purely theoretical level, a direction in which my interests were already leaning after *Helter-Shelter*. All this turned out to be a blessing in disguise and in thinking deeper about/through the work of Heidegger and its relation to understanding humanity, focus was cast upon the status of ontological homelessness, the subject of this book. Shelving any pretense of the empirical, my attention was strictly grounded in the theoretical, and with it in the philosophy of Heidegger.

As such, over the course of some six years, which included a sabbatical, I engaged slowly, patiently, and deeply with many of Heidegger's texts, which are, simply put, difficult to work with/through. The more I read, however, the more convinced I became that there is something profoundly revelatory about the Heideggerian project, even for (or dare I say, especially for) the social sciences. This slowly began to shape the text to which these comments are attached. Slowly as the ideas grew and became clearer, and started coming together, I was able to see the picture that I have sought to paint here, and over the course of three years or so, the text was completed.

Writing a book is not easy—at least for me—and writing one that engages Heidegger makes matters even harder, especially in trying to find a home for it. At University of Alberta Press, I found this home and folks willing to take a chance on a book that cannot necessarily be categorized in a straightforward manner: not properly philosophy, not sociology or social science, but some strange sort of intellectual attempt to engage with a particular set of ideas.

The road to UAlberta Press itself, as with everything in my life, came about by the grace of God. Douglas Hildebrand, who now heads UAlberta Press, commissioned *Helter-Shelter*. When he left his previous post to take up the post at UAlberta Press, he extended an invitation that if I wrote another book, that I should keep him in mind (interestingly, on the very day he e-mailed me to let me know that the first copy of *Helter-Shelter* was sitting on his desk, he mentioned his departure and news about his new post). In some ways, the possibility of working with UAlberta Press was a product of a request I had made to Doug before I signed the contract for *Helter-Shelter*: that he amend the Right to First Refusal in the contract, which he did (at that point somewhat reluctantly). It was this that permitted a simple and straightforward path to UAlberta Press (as I look back, I now see the Lord's providence in this as well).

My email to Doug to pitch this book was met warmly and we chatted virtually (during the pandemic). Doug had invited Mat Buntin to the meeting as he would be shepherding the project. Mat turned out to be a blessing: he is patient and kind and was very skilful in softening my rather abrasive approach and writing, especially when it came to responding to critiques and so forth (the time he took to edit many of these letters is duly appreciated).

In that sense, I am thankful to both Doug and Mat for taking a chance on a book that I believe not many publishers would because it cannot be properly or neatly slotted into an existing category. I think this is a good thing, but in a world where everything is commoditized and must be sold, I am grateful to them for willing to push for and foster intellectual curiosity over the rigidity of boundaries.

As noted, writing a book like this is not easy: saying that it is hard is also not necessarily true because this was an exhausting process—certainly rewarding, but exhausting. While engaging with Heidegger itself is taxing, life, as always, only complicates matters. When I began the project, my older son was less than a year old. By the time writing was ready to commence, my wife was pregnant with our younger son, and most of the writing was undertaken and completed with him in our lives. Writing is hard enough; writing with two young children is challenging and exhausting. The grace of God, as always, has upheld me.

There are many folks who need to be thanked for their support or for simply putting up with me and this project. First, as noted, I appreciate UAlberta Press for taking a chance on this project, and I was blessed to be able to work with Mat, whose patience, more than anything else, I appreciate. I am grateful to my colleagues Jon Frauley and Steven Bittle who kindly read and commented on a draft of the introduction and did so during a very busy time in the academic term. I am also thankful to the Faculty of Social Science, University of Ottawa, which provided funds to help offset production costs of the book, and especially so for a book that does not fit within the mandate of the social sciences, certainly not criminology. Additionally, the funds received from the Aid to Scholarly Publications Program through the Social Sciences and Humanities Research Council have been a welcome source of support.

I am immensely thankful to the three reviewers who read the manuscript, and I owe very much to two of them. Two reviewers read the original submission, provided helpful comments and guidance, and did so in a very timely manner that was and is truly appreciated. One, who would also read the revised version, was exceptionally generous and caring, providing extremely thoroughgoing, thoughtful, and helpful comments and suggestions: I truly believe that the reviewer read the text as if it were his/her own, and I will forever be indebted to this reviewer. It took some nine months to complete the revisions, owing both to what was recommended/needed and, simply put, life (I was on parental leave for some of this time and then took a reduced workload for one year to help with childcare at home. This meant that the writing process was slower than usual). When the time came to submit the revised text, I was dealt an unexpected blow: one of the reviewers declined the request to read the revised text. This, however, turned out to be a great blessing, and is yet another example of God's imprint upon the entirety of this project. The new reviewer who came into the project was professional in engaging with the text. Both reviewers who read the revised text provided extremely generous, thoughtful, and erudite comments, engaging with the text thoroughly and carefully. I have taken the additional comments they provided seriously, and these have made their way into the final version. In sum and put simply: I am grateful to the three reviewers who read the text and for undertaking what is essentially a thankless task. I am forever grateful to the two reviewers who read the revised text and did so with care, compassion, and a great deal of erudition. I do hope that I will be able to communicate with them to be able to forge some sort of intellectual, even working, relationship. Until then, from this end, thank you dearly.

Support, as always, came from my parents, who in the midst of all this moved from Ottawa to Edmonton, where my brother resides (who is also a source of support), citing a conviction that the Lord was calling them to move. In faith they left, and delighting in this faith, a gift from the Lord, I watched them leave. Numerous men from the church I attend, whom I consider not merely friends but brothers, were extremely supportive and upheld me in prayer during difficult times, especially in relation to completing the book: I am thankful to the Lord for them and how they have been a blessing to my walk in Christ. I appreciate my wife for putting up with me—and my demands and difficulties—as I tried to complete this book. My sons have been an immense blessing and a source of happiness and inspiration in my life, and I cherish them dearly. The time I spent writing meant time away from them—even though they were a mere stone's throw away, and I could often hear them or their footsteps—but every time I would finish and come out of the office, I would be greeted by the sound of their feet running toward me. These were (and are) truly blessed times and I am grateful for every moment I get to spend with them, most of it doing the most ridiculous, mundane, and banal things (such as playing "goohava" under the bedsheets or "hakada-bakada styles").

Finally, and most importantly, it is my faith in Christ, my hope and salvation, that sustains all this, including this book, from its very start to finish. It has His imprint firmly upon it. I have leaned on Him in every way imaginable and it is through Him, and only Him, that there is an is (John 1:3). This book has nothing to do with acumen or erudition or curiosity or intellectualism, but is a gift from Him to me (Psalm 127:1-2). As such, let Colossians 3:16, and Psalm 119:11, 105, and 114 be the anthem of my life and those of my family, especially my sons.

In faith, I look forward to the next project, which is already ingrained upon my mind (two, in fact) which, if He is willing, will see the light of day (when I will most likely hear the footsteps of my children running away from, rather than toward, me). So goes life.

Abbreviations for Works by Heidegger

BDT   Heidegger, Martin. 1954/2008. "Building Dwelling Thinking." In *Basic Writings*, revised and expanded ed., edited by David F. Krell, translated by Albert Hofstadter, 347–363. London: Harper Perennial.

BT   Heidegger, Martin. 1927/1962. *Being and Time*. Translated by John Macquarrie and Edward Robinson. New York: Harper and Row Publishers.

FCM   Heidegger, Martin. 1929–1930/1995. *The Fundamental Concepts of Metaphysics: World, Finitude, Solitude*. Translated by William McNeill and Nicholas Walker. Bloomington: Indiana University Press.

I   Heidegger, Martin. 1942/1996. *Hölderlin's Hymn "The Ister."* Translated by William McNeill and Julia Davis. Bloomington: Indiana University Press.

IM   Heidegger, Martin. 1935/2000. *Introduction to Metaphysics*. Translated by Gregory Fried and Richard Polt. New Haven: Yale University Press.

IP   Heidegger, Martin. 1944–1945/2011. *Introduction to Philosophy—Thinking and Poetizing*. Translated by Phillip

XIII

Jacques Braunstein. Bloomington: Indiana University Press.

LH Heidegger, Martin. 1947/2008. "Letter on Humanism." In *Basic Writings*, revised and expanded ed., edited by David F. Krell, translated by Frank A. Capuzzi and J. Glenn Gray, 217–265. London: Harper Perennial.

NW Heidegger, Martin. 1943/2002. "Nietzsche's Word: 'God is Dead.'" In *Off the Beaten Track*, edited and translated by Julian Young and Kenneth Haynes, 157–199. Cambridge: Cambridge University Press.

OM Heidegger, Martin. 1954/1993. "Overcoming Metaphysics." Translated by Joan Stambaugh. In *The Heidegger Controversy: A Critical Reader*, edited by Richard Wolin, 67–90. Cambridge, Massachusetts: The MIT Press.

OTB Heidegger, Martin. 1962/2002. *On Time and Being*. Translated by Joan Stambaugh. Chicago: The University of Chicago Press.

QCT Heidegger, Martin. 1953/2008. "The Question Concerning Technology." In *Basic Writings,* revised and expanded ed., edited by David F. Krell, translated by William Lovitt, 311–341. London: Harper Perennial.

WIM Heidegger, Martin. 1929/2008. "What Is Metaphysics?" In *Basic Writings*, revised and expanded ed., edited and translated by David F. Krell, 93–110. London: Harper Perennial.

Introduction

MARTIN HEIDEGGER has left an undeniable legacy and imprint not merely in philosophy but in intellectual life more broadly. Heidegger's philosophical oeuvre and endeavours can be—and have been—characterized and labelled in myriad ways. Despite the eclecticism of Heidegger's writings, certainly evident in form, especially when juxtaposing the early phase of his work with the middle and later phases, it is fair to claim that the concern over being (often penned in English translations as Being), grounds and animates Heidegger's philosophical endeavours. As such, Heidegger's work is said to be focused directly on what supposedly has, or at least ought to have, concerned the core of philosophy, namely, the meaning of existence, taking head-on one of the more profound questions that has occupied philosophical inquiry since its very inception.

As a result, and unsurprisingly, Heidegger's writings have often been located within some of the more foundational fields of philosophy, namely, metaphysics and epistemology. Given Heidegger's preoccupation—perhaps obsession—with being, this makes sense. At the same time, Heidegger's writings can be reread as articulating a philosophy that is also social in nature. This is not simply in relation to ethics and values, in the way that Robert Nichols (2014), for example, creatively reads Heidegger's *Being and Time* and some of his other early works as being profoundly concerned with freedom. Rather, it is to claim that beyond metaphysics, epistemology and ontology—fundamental ontology, as Heidegger puts it in his early phase—Heidegger's concerns, at their very centre or core, are focused upon the human being, and it is the being of this human being that grounds, and has always grounded, Heidegger's inquiry. More straightforwardly, Heidegger's oeuvre concerns being, a point generally accepted without controversy. That said, this concern about being and its inquiry necessitate, at its heart, a human being who cannot be extricated from nor minimized in any analysis of/about being. Given that human beings are inherently social in the sense that they cannot be extricated from the social world or else the very meaning of being human would be nullified, it is fair to claim that beyond metaphysics, epistemology, and ontology, which are important cogs of Heidegger's work, a profound concern about the social via the human being both grounds and animates Heidegger's writings. In that sense, the corpus of Heidegger's work can also be thought of as a social philosophy that aids in understanding not merely the human being but the relation of this being to the social world.

It is perhaps for this reason that more recently, especially in the past decade or so, that Heidegger's writings have slowly—and it is a *very* slow progression—gained some attention in the social sciences, especially in sociology. It is important to stress that such attention only occupies the margins of the social sciences, and when Heidegger is invoked it is often in passing. There is nevertheless some recognition of Heidegger's intellectual contribution among a handful of scholars who have sought to excavate his ideas and insights to shed new light upon myriad subjects of inquiry. In some circles in criminology (see Crewe 2009; Polizzi 2011), as in geography (see Harrison 2007; Rose 2012), Heideggerian insights have found their way into explanations of the essence of crime or the nature of space.[1] Interestingly, while Heidegger said next to nothing about formal or official law (see LH, 262, for an exception), legal studies and legal theory have also drawn upon his work to shed light upon various aspects related to law and the legal system (see Ben-Dor 2007; Papacharalambous 2022; Ranasinghe 2019b). And, as noted, in a very small circle in sociology, there is an effort to bring to life the import of Heideggerian philosophy, especially concerning the import of ontology to social inquiry.

Notwithstanding the foregoing, it is important to underline that, to date, Heidegger has been quite poorly received outside of philosophy, even though, as noted, Heidegger's philosophy can be, to some extent at least, reread as a social philosophy. There are myriad reasons for this. One important reason—and this is not something simply relevant to the social sciences, but all intellectual and scholarly inquiry—is that Heidegger's insights are often muddled because of the form of his writings. Such views and claims emanate not just from outside the discipline, but from within philosophy itself, where Heidegger was at home. Paul Edwards' (1989, 449) reference to "Heidegger's obfuscating jargon" is, in fact, the kindest remark he makes about the philosopher. Edwards proceeds, in forceful vitriol, to unravel his sheer disdain for Heidegger, accusing him, among other things, of "bogus Greek and German etymologies…and all kinds of gimmicks" along with "huge masses of hideous gibberish which must be unique in the history of philosophy" (468). Edwards concludes his diatribe with a warning, perhaps an exhortation, that "[m]ore sober and rational persons will continue to regard the whole Heidegger phenomenon as a grotesque aberration of the human mind" (469).

While Edwards' comments might be aberrant—and at least in their vitriol second only to Theodor Adorno's (1973/2003) polemic *The Jargon of Authenticity*—there is general consensus that Heidegger's writings (both in form and substance) are exceedingly difficult (excruciating, in fact) to work with/through, even among scholars who warmly embrace Heidegger's intellectual brilliance and acumen and who have claimed that his work was pioneering for the twentieth century philosophy. Robert Mugerauer's (2008) tome on Heidegger's quest for homecoming states early that "the question of how to understand what he [Heidegger] says is all the more pressing. That his individual works are notoriously difficult because of their apparent subject matter and his complex (often idiosyncratic) language is compounded by the fact that he seems to write in a number of different styles…This makes it difficult to discern what he actually intends to say" (3). The "bewildering complexity" (5) of the work only exacerbates matters. Partly, the problem is that Heidegger's work has "multiple voices" (6) and speaks "polyphonically" (5), a criticism that the acclaimed sociologist Pierre Bourdieu also levels against Heidegger, accusing him of being "the master...of double talk" (Bourdieu and Wacquant 1992, 150; see also Bourdieu 1988/1991, 47). Similarly, Brendan O'Donoghue (2011, 9) admits that "Heidegger himself is aware of the abstruse nature of thinking that on occasions defies comprehension," a point echoed by Simon Lumsden (2015, 20). Stephen Erikson (1966, 492) similarly states that "Heidegger uses a complex language and offers few clues as to the way it is to be construed." Scores of other complaints could be levelled, but the point is that it is an understatement to say that Heidegger's language, style, and presentation are unclear: Heidegger is difficult to read—and this is putting it kindly—and in some instances nearly impenetrable, and the chorus of criticism against his work and writing only continues to grow even among those who are ardent admirers of his work.

Beyond Heidegger's writing, there are several other important matters that cannot be glossed over. The most obvious is Heidegger's connection to fascism and Nazism, a point attended to in more detail in a later section. More pertinently for sociology and the social sciences, it has been noted that the "lack of attention to capitalist social relations" in Heidegger's "account of the human" (Nielsen and Skotnicki 2018, 114) may have significantly contributed to many sociologists dismissing his work as failing to provide insights into the nature of humanity vis-à-vis social relations. Given that much of sociology has been grounded upon the place and effects of capitalism as an explanatory lens for/of social relations, as postulated by Emile Durkheim, Max Weber, and certainly Karl Marx, this reasoning is quite plausible. Heidegger is—correctly or incorrectly—viewed within sociology as a metaphysician, and metaphysics is a "loathed enemy" of sociology (Aspers and Kohl 2013, 494) largely because of its supposed affinity toward grand theory and explanations grounded upon universal truths.

Despite these significant issues, there is, as already noted, slowly beginning to emerge, even if only in the margins, a call to recognize Heideggerian philosophy as more relevant to the social sciences, and sociology in particular, than previously accepted and acknowledged.

This relevance is viewed from specific lacuna that can, supposedly, be filled via Heidegger's insights. Such a premise is birthed from a simple but nonetheless contentious position in some camps of sociology, namely, that sociology desperately needs an ontological foundation to sustain its claims, especially given that the theoretical resources available to sociology from within have been, apparently, exhausted without much success. Within this perspective, philosophy is viewed as capable of being a trustworthy ally of sociology (see Smith 2013, 14), even though the two are grounded upon very different assumptions and forms of inquiry (Bourdieu 1988/1991, 36–37). Specifically with respect to the apparent lack of ontological foundation, the argument presented in these camps of sociology, essentially paralleling the very criticism that Heidegger would launch against philosophy itself (detailed below and in the next chapter), is that while sociology claims to probe the subject matter ontologically, what it ends up examining, and working with/in, is the ontical.

While given fuller consideration and elaboration later in this chapter and again in chapter two, for present purposes it is worth briefly distinguishing the ontic from ontology, which is an important distinction not merely in Heideggerian scholarship but also in terms of what is developed here. The term *ontic* (or *ontical*) refers directly to entities be they things (e.g., tables or chairs) or living beings (e.g., human beings or animals). Because an ontical inquiry is concerned with entities, it is focused upon facts about/of entities, which is to say that its focus is upon specific features of/about entities, and these features aid in understanding what makes an entity the particular entity that it is. This is perhaps best evinced in how the sciences approach the study of an object, though, taken at a more basic level, to say that the ontic is concerned with the features of an entity is to say, as an example, that the concern about a table is what features a table has (or must have) to make that entity, the table, a table. The specific features of the table aid in making intelligible the table as a table, or what makes a table a table, as opposed to a bed or a horse.

Such a way of approaching, thinking about, and understanding entities, while important, necessary, and beneficial, has a significant limitation: because the focus of an ontical inquiry is cast upon, and only upon, features, which is to say that the interrogation goes no further than the features of the particular entity, deeper reflection or questions about that entity, that is, about its being, for example—are precluded and foreclosed. An ontological inquiry, however, permits going deeper into the entity by going beyond the features of an entity. Here, the focus is upon the meaning of that entity vis-à-vis its social world, and by meaning what is specifically meant is the meaning of its existence, that is, what makes that particular entity possible to begin with. As such, in consideration of a table, it is not merely the features of that entity that are relevant to understanding what makes the table a table, but upon what it means for a table to be a table in its existence in the world. Heidegger's novel contribution to twentieth century philosophy, and perhaps to philosophy as a whole, is that the intelligibility of the entity must be explored and deciphered not merely by thinking about the entity, but also by practically engaging with the entity, a point that firmly grounds him as locating the import of beings (and their things) in the world they live in. This is ontology, what can essentially be termed the meaning of existence.

A somewhat recent criticism of sociology's failure to engage and work with the ontological is found in Patrik Aspers and Sebastian Kohl's (2013) exhortation that Heidegger be taken seriously, or at least be acknowledged, in sociology. For Aspers and Kohl, sociology "lacks a truly social foundation" (488) because of its failure to explore ontology and to do so "based upon a person who is in the world" (499) (a similar argument based upon the lack of personhood in sociology and its disinterest in it can be found in Christian Smith's [2010] concerns as well). Borrowing from and heavily influenced by Heidegger, Aspers and Kohl posit a socio-ontology of/for sociology that seeks to ground sociological inquiry in the ontological. In so doing, their focus is to rescue sociology from its focus upon the ontical and, via Heidegger, to draw attention to the ontological as the basis upon which to come to terms with what it means to be human and the relation between being human and social relations.

Such claims are situated in the polemic that sociology, while professing to be interested in engaging with the ontological, is grounded upon the ontical (Aspers and Kohl 2013, 496). Aspers and

Kohl boldly write, for example, that "virtually all social science theories" are "ontically rooted theories" (500) and thus are "only capable of reflecting ways in which being is 'acting,' but do not reflect essence of being" (501). To some extent at least, such claims are not bereft of foundation and veracity. Existential sociology can be cited as one example. Close to fifty years ago, Jack Douglas and John Johnson (1977) brought together a collection of essays under the banner of existential sociology. Their focus was to study human experience in the world that is driven and grounded by philosophical inquiry (vii–viii). However, the form of the inquiry was, whether intentionally or unintentionally, a sociology of emotions. In his lengthy essay titled "Existential Sociology," Jack Douglas (1977, 3) speaks of "brute being," by which he referenced the "core of feeling and perception that is our innermost selves, our beings." This theme was similarly carried into Richard Brown's (1977) essay in which he described humanistic sociology as a discipline that examines and explores the problematics of feeling and the meanings surrounding such feelings (77). What is clearly revealed is that existential sociology, with its focus on humanism and social experience, is grounded upon human emotion. There is nothing necessarily problematic with such an approach, but it cannot lay claim to being ontological; it functions, and can only function, at the ontical. This is the concern raised by Aspers and Kohl more generally about sociology (they do not necessarily engage with existential sociology) and, interestingly, by Heidegger himself, who, in "Letter on Humanism," critiques humanism in his concerns about the ontical being given primacy over the ontological. Any doubt on this matter can be allayed by turning to what might be called the more updated version of existential sociology. Some twenty-five years after Douglas and Johnson's work, Joseph Kotarba and Johnson (who was part of the original existential sociology text), brought together a collection of what can be called *postmodern existential sociology* (Johnson and Kotarba 2002). In introducing the field, Kotarba (2002) notes that existentialism concerns the view that individuals are central to social life and inquiries about it, and that it is a "sociology of emotions" (vii). As such, existential sociology and its updated (perhaps improved) version, postmodern existential sociology, are defined without any doubt as sociologies of/about emotion. In that same volume, Candace Clark (2002), who draws upon the original concept of "brute being" formulated by Douglas (1977), presents it, yet again, as a sociology of emotion. Existential sociology, as such, is a sociology premised upon human emotion and, as such, its contours are framed within the ontical. Despite its name, existential sociology is not a sociology of the ontological.[2]

There is nothing necessarily problematic with focusing upon emotions nor with grounding an entire approach on it (in fact, the argument can be made that such approaches are necessary to understanding human nature). The point, rather, is that such an approach cannot—because it is not equipped to—lay claim to be premised upon the ontological. This is the important point that Aspers and Kohl (2013) bring to light or at least provide as a reminder: that sociology, to a large extent, is an inquiry of the ontical, not the ontological, despite its claims to be otherwise. Heidegger, as such, would not necessarily appeal to sociologists (and this very well might explain his absence in sociological inquiry). Yet, as Aspers and Kohl argue, Heidegger's ontology is an important framework through which sociology can become richer. Such a view is also echoed by Richard Swedberg (2011, 41) who claims that sociology can benefit from the type of profound thinking engaged by Heidegger. The point, then, is not necessarily whether what these authors posit is correct or not; the point, rather, is that such a claim about the impoverished nature of sociology *has* been made, even if it only exists on the margins of the discipline.

Despite the (dis)connection between Heidegger and sociology (and the social sciences more broadly), it is hard to deny one important aspect about Heidegger's exploration of beings and being: many of Heidegger's concepts, especially Dasein, are social (Aspers and Kohl 2013, 490; Dreyfus and Rabinow 1993, 38–39). Being-in-the-world, an important aspect of Heideggerian philosophy, is inherently social, which is to say that it concerns social practises and experiences (Dreyfus and Rabinow 1993, 38). Dasein, in other words, cannot be extricated from its social world (the very world in which Heidegger places and locates Dasein), and if so done, then, Dasein will not be Dasein, which is to say that Dasein would lose any explanatory significance. In this sense, Heidegger's central concern—as will become apparent—is and has always been about what it means to be human, and what it means to be human is and has always been meaningful *only* in relation to the fact that beings are social creatures (Nielsen and Skotnicki 2018, 112; the same point is made by Smith [2010], though he has little to no interest in Heidegger and is instead galvanized by critical realism; that said, Smith's focus is to reclaim a space for a personhood of being in sociology).

As such, and while perhaps polemical to some, perhaps many, Heidegger's interests and concerns are sociological at least in the sense that he is operating from the presupposition that human beings—which is probed via Dasein—are social, and that it is not only impossible but also fatuous to strip beings of their social essence. This is important because when focus turns, in the next two chapters, to the moods of anxiety and boredom, it will become clear that these moods are centred in the fact that beings are social beings. However, while the focus, in that sense, is on emotions and as such is ontical, Heidegger does not terminate his inquiry at this point. Rather, for Heidegger, the ontical is the preparatory stage for profound interrogation into the ontological (explicated in the next chapter). As such, Heidegger utilizes the ontical to probe the ontological. In other words, the focus is not merely upon the emotions of anxiety or boredom, but what each reveals about the broader and deeper meaning of existence. Thus, it is critical to point out that while Heidegger's inquiry shares much with sociology in that he is focusing upon human beings and presupposing that human beings are social and that they cannot be extricated from their social world, his endeavour moves beyond the ontical. To take the example of existential sociology in juxtaposition to Heidegger's discussion of moods, both focus upon emotions. Heidegger, however, draws upon these emotions not to explicate emotions but to probe what it means to be human and what it means to exist. He draws, then, upon pertinent matters that make humans human, but does so to go the one additional step further that some sociologists accuse sociology of failing to explore. This is the ontology of what it means to be, the focus of Heideggerian philosophy from its inception to its twilight.

This book is grounded upon the two previously discussed points. Heidegger's philosophy is, to some extent at least, a social philosophy insofar as the explanatory tool to probe the meaning of existence, Dasein, is inherently social: to extricate Dasein from the social or to deny Dasein its social status and character would be to render Dasein meaningless. As such, Heideggerian philosophy is, from the very outset, social. This might not be the point that the sociological literature pointed to above necessarily seeks to underline (though it would countenance it), but this point connects to this literature: many of Heidegger's premises are sociological and, as such, can be viewed in that manner. Given, then, what appears to be the inherently social nature of Heidegger's philosophy that is neglected in philosophy and the underlining of his "sociology" within sociology, this book enters this discussion to contribute to these two areas. The premise is as simple as it is straightforward: to shed light upon and clarify important aspects of and around Heidegger's thoughts on the meaning of existence in a detailed and systematic manner. To do so, the book casts its attention and focuses specifically upon a key theme that grounds much of Heideggerian philosophy, what can be referred to as ontological homelessness. Rereading Heidegger's conceptualization of the ontology of homelessness, this book argues that ontological homelessness can be reread to shed light on the meaning of existence as nothingness, which speaks to the indeterminacy of what it means to be (human). To be human, in other words, is to traverse an indeterminate, essentially unfinished, state that this book theorizes as nothingness.

As such, this book is a contribution both to Heideggerian philosophy and a sociology that seeks to excavate Heideggerian insights to its endeavours. The book seeks to bring to light and clarify several important concepts utilized by Heidegger which are here reread and theorized to underline that the ontology of homelessness that Heidegger engages in can be reread as nothingness. While the concept of nothingness has occupied an important place in Heideggerian scholarship, it has been the subject of much confusion. Rereading nothingness through ontological homelessness as an indeterminacy, this book seeks to bring attention to these somewhat neglected concepts but, more importantly, bring clarity to a state of affairs that has otherwise been confounded. It is in this manner that this book casts its gaze upon Heideggerian philosophy. The book is also, in some ways, a response to the calls within some camps of sociology for an Heideggerian-centred focus upon existence. To that end, heeding the call of this literature, the book examines the meaning of existence as postulated by Heidegger and argues that, at its core, this is a program that can be understood as person-centred. As such, the book argues that the nothingness that constitutes the meaning of existence helps shed light upon what it means to be human. The book does not engage with *how* to do Heideggerian sociology. It is strictly concerned with the meaning of existence according to Heidegger which, as noted, can be thought of socially. This is its ambit. As such, the book is strictly a theoretical reflection on the meaning of humanity and aims to give colour to and is grounded upon Heideggerian philosophy.

Ontological Homelessness and the Essence of Being

This book, as noted, seeks to articulate Heidegger's concept of ontological homelessness which is reread as an indeterminacy of being referred to as nothingness. Ontological homelessness, this book argues, speaks to the very essence of what it means to be human: to be human is to be homeless.

One fruitful way to situate ontological homelessness is to briefly compare it with what can be thought of as material homelessness. Material homelessness refers to the state of being homeless given the absence of (permanent) housing, be it through ownership, rental accommodations, or some other form, and thus subject to housing conditions that can be best described as precarious (e.g., shelters). The term *houselessness*, rather than *homelessness*, better describes what is at stake here, though the vast and virtually exhaustive literature on the subject tends to describe the phenomenon as homelessness (see Ranasinghe [2017, 4–5] for an overview). It is, to put it somewhat crudely—and in rather cliché fashion—to be without a roof over one's head, perhaps best illuminated, at least in folklore, in the outstretched hand of a beggar who solicits from passersby (see Ranasinghe 2010, 2011, 2015). The phenomenon of material homelessness is a significant and important issue facing the human condition, and the attention it has generated both in academic and policy circles is warranted. The plight of the millions who struggle to survive the streets is as serious as it is sobering and sad. This, however, is not the focus of this book. As such, what is focused upon in this book is not meant to be an affront to the condition of material homelessness (nor to the myriad activists and scholars working in this area). Nothing of this sort is intended, and this is important to keep in mind because Heidegger is sometimes accused of neglecting the material conditions of life (the ontical) for the ontological. Yet, a close reading of his ideas on home and homelessness cannot substantiate such a conclusion (as chapter four especially points out).

Returning to the example of the beggar, it is worthwhile comparing this status, of one subject to precarious housing and thus materially homeless or houseless, to a person who is housed, what this book refers to as being homeful. The plight of the former can, without controversy, be described or labelled as one constituting, and constituted by, homelessness. Such a label, however, would only extend to and capture the material homelessness of the beggar. Lost in this labelling is the homelessness in the ontological sense. Here, ontological homelessness is effaced in the narrative of and about the beggar's houselessness because ontological homelessness cannot be reduced to a material condition or status nor dismissed as simply an absence of/about the material. Conversely, if attention is cast upon the homeful, it is equally without controversy that such persons are not thought of as homeless precisely because their material condition and status foreclose the possibility of seeing and appreciating homelessness. Shelter, then, comes to stand *for* home and, as such, those with shelter are (at) home and said to be fulfilled—homeful. What such a narrative fails to reveal, however, is that the homeful are still homeless, and fundamentally so. This is a homelessness of an ontological nature, a homelessness that speaks to the very existence of life, of what it means to be human.

Ontological homelessness concerns the very essence of humanity: to be human, at its core, is to be homeless. This homelessness is profound and has nothing to do with housing and crises generated from the lack of material conditions. It is a homelessness that has everything to do with an absence, or more accurately an emptiness, but this is not predicated upon the lack of materiality. Rather, the absence in question emanates from within, that is, from the very core or essence of one's being, which this book refers to as an indeterminate nothingness. As such, beings are, by the very nature of being human, bound and constituted by a state that is simultaneously both full and empty. It is essentially an unfinished state. In this state, to be homeless means to be distanced and separated from one's essence or nature. To understand and come to terms with the essence of humanity, then, it is necessary to grapple with the indeterminacy of nothingness.

In the broad sense that speaks to and captures the essence of what it means to be human, what this book aims to highlight and explicate is a simple but nevertheless agonistic point: that humans are, by virtue of being human, homeless, and this homelessness pertains to the very distancing and separation of the self from itself. Thus, both the beggar on the street and the homeful are equally homeless in the ontological sense, that is, in terms of their essence. In other words, regardless of whether one is housed or not, and whether that housing is precarious or stable, humans are, as a matter of being human, ontologically homeless. This is what Heidegger's concerns about being, this book claims, reveal and this is brought to light through the indeterminacy that grounds beings, referred to here as nothingness.

The Heideggerian Project and Ontological Inquiry

As noted, Heidegger's writings are grounded upon an eclecticism, both in form and substance. Despite this eclecticism, Heidegger's work, most commentators appear to agree, is united by a singular focus, that of being (cf. Sheehan 2013). Heidegger uses the term *being* in juxtaposition to *beings*. The latter refers to entities, be they humans or things. The former refers to an ontological status about entities, that is, the being of an entity. The difference between being and beings Heidegger refers to, at least in his early works, as the ontological difference (Slaby 2021, 551). Throughout the corpus of his work, Heidegger frequently references the "being of beings" when speaking of the ontological status of beings (e.g., WIM, 104, 108; *IM*, 38, 141; *I*, 87), by which he means the meaning of existence. As such, Heidegger's project—though undergoing several metamorphoses, as noted below—has always (or largely) been concerned with being in this ontological sense, that is, the meaning of existence or what it means to be (human).

The concept of ontology engaged with in this book is Heideggerian, which is to say that the concept of ontology registers differently not simply across fields but also within a specific field itself. In the social sciences, ontology generally refers to what is called social reality (e.g., Berger and Luckmann 1966; see also Dreyfus and Rabinow 1993; Smith 2010), and this can be traced to some of the pioneering works of Durkheim and Weber, to name just two examples. In the philosophical tradition, there is not a necessarily settled meaning of ontology (and certainly not so in terms of engaging in ontological inquiry) and it ranges and differs depending upon the tradition of the thinker. Thus, for example, the ontology of Marx differs from Walter Benjamin's, as does Friedrich Nietzsche's from Heidegger's (see Rae [2021] for one example pertaining to the differential ontology of Gilles Deleuze vis-à-vis the fundamental ontology of Heidegger).

The clearest path to engaging with Heideggerian ontology is to return to his concept of the being of beings, as it speaks directly to an ontological inquiry that is capable of revealing an ontological status. By the "being of beings," Heidegger means, in the simplest sense, the meaning of existence. What is at stake here, then, is the meaning of the existence of a particular entity, that is, what it means to be. In terms of a human entity, this can be thought of as the human way of being (Dreyfus 1991, 14). According to Taylor Carman (2013, 84; emphasis omitted), "Being is that in virtue of which entities are entities; it is what makes (in a noncausal sense of 'makes') entities[,] entities." In other words, being "is neither an entity nor the totality of entities nor a property of entities...It is simply what we understand in our understanding of being, what we know when we know—however tacitly and obscurely—that entities are, and (more or less) what they are" (85; emphasis omitted; see also Rae 2021, 360–365). Put simply, for Heidegger, ontology, referenced in the being of beings, is concerned with the meaning of existence. This is what an ontological inquiry proper, what he, in his early works, calls fundamental ontology, ought to be interested in, namely, disclosing the ontological status of an entity, the meaning of its existence.

If the ontology of being concerns the meaning of existence, then, the path toward uncovering this meaning is as specific as it is precise, and the way Heidegger grapples with a methodology vis-à-vis being reveals this. According to Heidegger, an ontological inquiry cannot be approached directly. Rather, it first requires a preparatory discussion or analysis by way of an ontical inquiry. If, as noted above, ontology is concerned with being, that is, the meaning of existence, an ontical inquiry—what Carman (2013, 84) refers to as "Heidegger's jargon"—is concerned with the "particular features entities happen to have" (Carman 2013, 94). The features of an entity pave the way—or prepare the way, as Heidegger puts it—*into* or toward an ontological inquiry of and about that entity. Gavin Rae's (2021, 361) explication is worth reproducing for its lucidity: "Being is not an entity and so is always tied to entities and must be thought in its own terms, but Being is always the Being of an entity and so is always tied to entities and must be thought through them." In other words, being "can only be revealed through an analysis of" entities (361; see also Nichols 2014, 29–31), or what is here referred to as the ontical. This is the Heideggerian method, if it can be so put, to engage with and explore the being of beings.

The Being of Beings and the Turn: Homelessness and Dwelling

Heidegger's exploration of the being of beings undergoes important metamorphoses throughout his intellectual career, commonly referred to as "the turn." The turn—or more precisely turns, given three important shifts (Sheehan 2013)—reveals the preoccupation with ontological homelessness, one, however, that is given different emphasis, even language, in and through the concept of dwelling. Heidegger's work is generally said to fall into the early, middle, and late stages, with the early period consisting of his output up until the early 1930s,[3] the middle period from about the early 1930s until the mid-to-late 1940s (even 1950s), and the later period from then onward (see Sheehan 2013). In some instances, however, and perhaps for the sake of simplicity, his work is compartmentalized into an early and later stage, what is referred to as the young versus mature Heidegger (see Carman 2008, ix–x). Regardless of how many phases or turns there are said to be or the precise time frames when these are said to have taken place (cf. Thomson 2021, 521), what is important to underline for present purposes is that incontrovertible fact that there was a shift—the turn—in the *emphasis* and *form* of his scholarship, where ontological homelessness, still the preoccupation in his quest to reveal the being of beings, is translated into the language and concept of dwelling.

This shift in emphasis and form sheds light not only upon the place of homelessness to Heidegger's thinking but also how he engages with it. There is an important continuity between what was commenced in *Being and Time*—in the nascent stages of his career—and his later work, especially as found in *On Time and Being*. The inversion of being and time between the late 1920s and early 1960s, as found in the titles of the two texts, clearly shows a change in emphasis, which had already seen Heidegger draw less from philosophical avenues and settle more upon the literary, in the form of the poetic. Partly, as well, this shift signals the important place reserved for time and temporality in Heidegger's thinking, as chapters one and two make clear. Yet even in this later work, Heidegger clearly notes and acknowledges the connection between the two works and phases, separated by some forty years, writing that *On Time and Being* is "the continuation of the thinking of *Being and Time*" (*OTB*, 43).

This continuation, however, is as precise as it is specific. It is not a continuation in the sense that Heidegger had initially wished or conceptualized, that is, as a completion of the final division of *Being and Time*, known as Division III. As Julian Young (2015, 332) shows, the contemplated turn in Heidegger's work was originally planned for this last—uncompleted—part of *Being and Time*. Yet, as Young notes, "going through the page proofs of *Being and Time* with Karl Jaspers at the end of 1926, he [Heidegger] became convinced in the course of 'friendly arguments' that Division III as it stood was 'unintelligible', so...the decision was made to abandon its publication." According to Young, what became unintelligible was "Heidegger's dawning recognition of the fact that the proposed Division III would need to square the circle." Heidegger had recognized that a new way of thinking about the subject of being was necessary, and this was so even in the very early phase of his work. Thus, the turn, in some ways at least, was already occupying Heidegger's thoughts even before it officially happened (or is said to have happened).

What is key, then, is that in *Being and Time*, as Heidegger envisages it, Dasein—essentially Heidegger's means for engaging with fundamental ontology (see Haugeland 2013; Rae 2021, 366)—is homeless; and, as noted, Heidegger is unable to find a way for Dasein's homecoming in the language of philosophy (precisely why, as Young puts it, he would have needed to square the circle). The turn, then, signals a shift in emphasis and form, into the poetic, especially through the poet Friedrich Hölderlin, with and through whom Heidegger is able to find a way home for Dasein. This entails, however, a shift in emphasis, *from being to dwelling*. It is in dwelling that the homeless can (come to) be at home *in* homelessness. Thus, it is not that the meaning of existence is lost or thought to be irrelevant; rather, it is merely that the shift in conceptual language, from being to dwelling, permits the meaning of existence to be extrapolated and grounded.

Heidegger's invocation of ontology puts this into perspective. In *Being and Time*, he underlines the import of ontological inquiry as a way to ground metaphysics. Thus, he repeatedly excoriates philosophers who preceded him, noting that while they proclaim to engage in an ontological inquiry that focuses upon being, what they end up examining is beings. In his later work, notably the essay "Letter on Humanism," Heidegger directly attends to this so that rather than simply grounding metaphysics (as in his early work), he could seek to overcome it. His point is that a shift in conceptual language—away from metaphysics—is necessary because the history of philosophy has been a history of metaphysics and this has had the unfortunate effect of rendering the status of ontology to (and as) the ontical (perhaps an unintended effect), so that what philosophy has always examined has been beings, not being. Heidegger's critique of Nietzsche in "Nietzsche's Word: 'God is Dead'" shows that while Nietzsche thought that an overturning of metaphysics was sufficient to resurrect being, this was a gross error on Nietzsche's part, because an overturning of metaphysics is still metaphysics. What is needed is an over*coming* of metaphysics (see OM). Thus, when, in the "Letter on Humanism," Heidegger writes of an apparent dissatisfaction with ontology, it is not that he is seeking to abolish an inquiry of fundamental ontology as he calls it, but rather to underline the very need for a shift in conceptual language, one that still very much holds to the import of ontology (LH, 258–260). It is in this way that Heidegger sought to "overcome" metaphysics, by which he had in mind a reframing of its contours and not necessarily a wholesale renunciation of it. The point, then, is that despite the different emphases and the transformations of the form of inquiry, Heidegger's fundamental concern has always been being, that is, the meaning of existence, of what it means to be human or what is the human way of being.

This human way of being, as this book makes clear, is homelessness. To be human is to be homeless. There is, however, an interesting paradox, an indeterminacy as articulated in this book, that underpins the being of beings: it is not merely that beings are homeless, an inescapable fate, but that this homelessness is the very condition—in fact, the only condition—of being (at) home. In other words, to be (at) home, is to be homeless, such that one is (and can only be) home in one's homelessness. To put it another way, one's homelessness is one's status and condition of being home.

Two profound matters arise from the preceding statements, each essential to forming the core of the book, and thus each deserving attention even at this introductory stage (one issue is taken up in this section and the other in the section to follow).

First, to claim that one can only be at home when one is homeless—and, in fact, when one comes to terms with and embraces homelessness—is, at first glance, a statement that appears to be not merely paradoxical but certainly also counter to modern culture, specifically a culture of property that glorifies material products, especially in the form of houses. Heidegger's claim, thus, appears to invert this traditional, even commonsensical, take on life: if one is housed, how is it possible—even conceivable—that one is (or can be) homeless?

This requires conceptual transformation: as such, Heidegger elides the language of being for something suitable and appropriate to let his point (perhaps polemic) resonate. This is the concept of dwelling. In and through dwelling, Heidegger can first show and then prepare the way for the grounding of homelessness: that one is not only at home in one's homelessness—and, as well, that one cannot be at home in any other way—but also that one can and ought to embrace this homelessness as one's very being, that is, as one's very core or essence. This, however, requires that Heidegger convincingly make the case that one can only be (at) home if one dwells. This means that while beings traverse the world, they will inevitably be constituted by multiple statuses—being housed is one important aspect—but what they are still not privy to is the fundamental need to dwell. It is only via dwelling that beings can be (at) home. Thus, this book argues that any meaningful attempt to conceptualize home requires engagement with dwelling. The modern condition of humanity—of being housed and at home—requires an understanding that beings are and will forever be homeless unless they are capable of dwelling. To dwell, as Heidegger shows, is to not merely recognize the homelessness of humanity and that home is (and can only be) in this very homelessness, but to also embrace and come to terms with this fact and fate: to be (at) home is to dwell in homelessness. As such, the argument presented here is that one can not only dwell without being housed, but that one must learn to dwell irrespective of whether one is housed. This, then, leads to the second point alluded to above, pertaining to the very indeterminacy of being which the book reads as nothingness.

Nothingness, Ontological Homelessness, and the Being of Beings
Technically, there is nothing paradoxical about Heidegger's claim that for one to be (at) home, one must be in/with one's homelessness. Essentially, then, what is at stake is this: humans are homeless despite being housed, and this homelessness is not merely a by-product of being human, but central to it. To be human is to be homeless. There is no escaping this fact, or rather fate. To put this differently: if one is not homeless, one is not—and cannot be—human. If Heidegger's arguments are extended to their rightful conclusion, this means that what constitutes beings is an indeterminacy (see Klooger 2013): beings are housed and thus at home, but are nevertheless homeless, though, and rather perplexingly, it is in this very homelessness that they are (and can be) home. This indeterminacy is read from the concept of nothingness that can be extrapolated from Heidegger's

work, especially his early phase, as will become evident in the first two chapters. What is contended here is that the homelessness of beings *is* nothingness, a term that is meant to capture the indeterminacy that constitutes beings.

Nothingness and nothing are not the same and should not be read as interchangeable. While they are related, they are profoundly different. Heidegger's invocation of nothingness has been, like much of his work, subject to confusion (Heidegger also refers to nothing, though technically, as will become apparent, it is *no-thing* that he speaks of, and this only serves to add to the confusion). Edwards (2004, 105), for example, even while embracing the import of nothing and nothingness not only for Heideggerian scholarship but also for philosophical inquiry more broadly, candidly admits that "nobody with the slightest intellectual honesty can be satisfied that Heidegger has adequately explained what he means by *nicheten*, the 'nothing-ing' in which Nothing is supposedly engaged." While perhaps bordering on the caustic, the statement nonetheless flags an important point about a difficult and contentious concept in Heidegger's work that this book tackles head-on.

It is important, however, to recognize that Heidegger's invocation of nothingness is as specific as it is, in some ways at least, precise. Nothingness is differentiated from nothing to underline that being is *no-thing* (that being is not a thing, that being cannot be found nor located in a thing). In other words, when Heidegger says that being is not a thing, that is, not an entity, he is underlining, as already explicated in the previous sections, that being is not reducible to an entity. Thus, when Heidegger references being, he is speaking of the being of a particular entity, not that being has its own being. It is in this sense that he refers to nothing, that is, no-thing, to underline being: being is not a thing.

Besides philosophical inquiry (e.g., Gusman 2018; Richmond 2007), and Heidegger in particular, it has been natural science, particularly physics, that has shown interest in the concept of nothingness but via a related concept, namely, nothing. This literature refers to nothing as a total or complete absence, essentially drawing upon the concept of a vacuum (e.g., Barrow 2001; Close 2009; Genz 1999). While this literature is useful as far as it goes, which is to say that it is grounded upon a desire to reveal nature, two significant matters immediately give pause for concern. First, the subject of inquiry in the natural sciences (and physics)—e.g., vacuums and blackholes—are not merely irrelevant for the human sciences but are also not of a common language to be useful. This point, of course, was cogently made more than a half-century ago by Peter Winch (1958) in his penetrating analysis of the inapplicability of the science of nature to the study of human life (see also Arendt 1969, 22–24). Second, there is a rather uncritical tendency to conflate and confound nothing and nothingness (e.g., Barrow 2001; Close 2009; Genz 1999; for more nuanced and sophisticated analyses, cf. Barad 2012, 2017). Ronald Green (2011) provides some bases to distinguish the two, though many of these are derived from false constructions, including subjecting Heidegger's readings of nothingness to unnecessarily harsh criticisms that are often either factually incorrect or superficial (see 217–218, 241–243). Green distinguishes between two types of absences: the absence of something, which is referred to as nothingness, and the absence of everything, which is referred to as nothing (132). Such attempts from the natural science—or in critiques of this literature—have paved the way for the exploration of nothingness in the social sciences, endeavours that are as impoverished as they are scarce. A good example is Susie Scott's (2019) attempt to exhort sociology to recognize nothing as a subject worthy of exploration (which, perhaps unwittingly, tends to conflate nothing and nothingness). While the engagement is cursory and vague, fails to adequately theorize the subject (cf. Feng [2021] for an example of a failure to even attempt to define the term), and makes numerous passing and superficial, even erroneous, references to Heidegger and other philosophers, including Jean-Paul Sartre, the text at least underlines that nothing (or nothingness) is an important subject worthy of consideration (see also Croissant 2014). This book, then, is intended not merely to underline the import of nothingness to the essence of humanity, but also seek to engage it in a theoretically profound manner via Heidegger, and in so doing, seek to bring clarity to an often-confounded concept in Heideggerian philosophy.

In this book, nothingness is invoked not to capture nothing, but *a sense of nothing*: a presence of an absence or emptiness, and, thus, nothing (given an absence), but a nothing that already speaks to the presence of something missing, a missing-ness that is also a something. Precisely what this nothing-something is, however, is difficult—perhaps impossible—for the subject to decipher (the moods of anxiety and profound boredom, discussed in chapters one and two respectively, illuminate the something-nothing nexus). In other words, the contention here is that nothingness refers to the hybridity of *something* and *nothing*, which coexists in the same breath as simultaneity. Nothingness, then, is related to nothing but is not reducible to it, just as it is related to something but is similarly not reducible to it. Drawing upon and rereading Heidegger's premise that beings are homeless and further extending this homelessness to a state of indeterminacy, this book argues that beings are constituted by nothingness. Nothingness, then, captures the being of beings: to be human, this book claims, is to be in and traverse this indeterminate phase, an unfinished state where a permanent sense of homelessness constitutes beings, which, in fact, and rather perplexingly, is a status of being (at) home, a state, however and unfortunately, that is often read as the antithesis of home. Whether beings realize this and are willing to come to terms with it are, of course, different sets of questions and issues.

To claim that beings are—and can only be (at)—home *in* homelessness seems peculiar. It violates many sacred contemporary and historical presuppositions that laud the import of property (underwritten, in fact, into the very ethic of historical and contemporary law and legal institutions) (e.g., Waldron 1991; Essert 2022). Yet, such peculiarity is a product of a particular manner in which the concept of the home has been viewed historically, one inextricably tied to the material structure and site of a house. What is needed, then, is a reorientation of the conceptual language that is drawn on to explore the being of beings. This requires, as explicated in the previous section, that the concept of dwelling be given priority and examined alongside the nothingness that constitutes the being of beings.

This book presents Heidegger's concept of dwelling as a status, not as a status tied to materiality (e.g., a house, so that one dwells because one is housed), but as a status of one's being: to be, in other words, is to dwell (cf. Tonner 2018; Ben-Dor 2007, 353–398). Dwelling, then, is not just about being but is a way of being. This book also argues that beings can dwell authentically or inauthentically. Authentic dwelling refers to the realization that beings are, perennially, homeless, that their status of being *is* homelessness (to be distanced and separated from their essence—hence the unfinished nature of beings). Additionally, and importantly, authentic dwelling refers to embracing this ontological status and living in (not just with) homelessness. As such, dwelling *in* homelessness ensures that beings are (at) home. Dwelling concerns the status of being vis-à-vis the essence of humanity, namely, the nothingness of beings: beings traverse an indeterminacy in search of home while in homelessness which, interestingly (even paradoxically), is home. It is an abyss that is nevertheless full. Inauthentic dwelling, conversely, is either the failure to realize and come to terms with the homelessness that is being or the refusal to accept this homelessness and the fact that it is in homelessness that one is and can be (at) home. In inauthentic dwelling, dwelling takes place *against*—and in refusal of—the homelessness of beings in order to counteract it (the incessant desire to overcome boredom, especially prevalent today, is, as discussed in chapter two, an apt example of the refusal to come to dwell in homelessness and is instead a desire to seek refuge and home in something outside the essence of what it means to be).

The foregoing speaks to an important—and in some cases polemical—set of concepts in Heideggerian philosophy, namely, authenticity and inauthenticity. This necessitates further attention given the contentious issues surrounding these terms; the next section seeks to unpack these terms as they are mobilized in this book.

Authenticity and Inauthenticity

In the early phase of Heidegger's scholarship, especially in *Being and Time*, the concepts of authenticity and inauthenticity play a significant role in the explication of the meaning of existence. According to Heidegger, something fundamental about humanity grounds its existence as it is in the world. This fundamental aspect of/about humanity is inauthentic existence or inauthenticity. Inauthenticity characterizes being human insofar as beings are in the world. This can be thought of as being lost in the world (Heidegger refers to it as fallenness) where beings are lost in—that is, immersed in or fallen into—what Heidegger calls the "they-self" and what has also been called "the anyone" (Käufer 2021, 72). The they-self represents the site of fallenness of beings and, as such, the already social nature of humans as they are in the world (what Heidegger calls "being-in-the-world") is plainly evident. Accordingly, and as many scholars have noted, for Heidegger, it is inauthenticity, not authenticity, that "is phenomenologically more prominent" and, thus, "the most common mode of existing" (71).

It is important to underline, despite appearances to the contrary, that Heidegger is not necessarily making a value judgement in claiming that being-in-the-world is constituted by inauthenticity (*BT*, 68). This is because beings have no choice but to be in the world and the overwhelming or all-consuming nature of the they-self swallows the essence and identity—read individuality, if preferred, though this is not precisely what Heidegger has in mind—of beings. Robert Nichols (2014, 53–54) speaks of "the they" as a depersonalizing or depersonalization of the self that is quite accurate and in keeping with what is claimed here: in being-in-the-world, beings are depersonalized, which means that they are brought into the fold of the they-self. As such, the they-self speaks *for* beings and any possibilities open to beings are foreclosed, which is to say that beings are unable (perhaps because they are unwilling) to see any other possibility than what grounds them.[4]

As such, in inauthenticity the possibilities open to beings are foreclosed, foreclosed not in the sense that they are unavailable, but rather that beings are uninterested in them or unable to see them (for example, in and through anxiety, discussed in chapter one, beings are able to *see* the insignificance of their lives—what Heidegger calls "utter insignificance"—while in profound boredom, discussed in chapter two, an indifference not just about other beings and things, but also about the very subject him/herself, overcomes the subject and leaves him/her indifferent to everything).

Accordingly, authenticity refers to the ability or capacity to take back—in some ways rescue—oneself from the they-self (Käufer 2021, 71–72). This does not mean that one ceases to be social, that is, that one extricates oneself from being-in-the-world, as this is an impossibility. Rather, it means that one understands one's place in being-in-the-world and comes to terms with it. As such, "[a]uthenticity...shows that the self cannot be separated from the world it engages" (73), which is to say that it speaks to a "self-awareness of possibilities within a set of relations to other beings" (Nichols 2014, 54). Authenticity speaks to the fact that one is no longer depersonalized (53–54). As noted, to be depersonalized is to lack the essence of oneself, which is essentially folded into or is an amalgam of the they-self. That is, that one's person—and one's personality—is in and a product of the they-self. As such, it is the realization that being-in-the-world renders one homeless—homeless because one's self "resides" with/in the they-self and, as such, does not belong to one's own. Thus, it becomes necessary to be cognizant of this homelessness and come to terms with it because it is from this very homelessness that the possibility of coming home is to be located and grounded. This is the crucial aspect of authenticity. Thus, "[a]uthentic existing" refers to "a modification of the way we exist" (Käufer 2021, 72), and as noted, this modification speaks directly to coming to terms with the homelessness that grounds beings as they are in the world. This is a homelessness not of the material sort—to lack material shelter—but a homelessness of one's very self, where that self is separated and distanced from its essence simply by the fact it is (and finds itself) in the world.

The failure to come to terms with homelessness and/or the desire to overcome homelessness via the they-self grips beings in inauthenticity. As noted, authenticity means to understand and come to terms with the homelessness that constitutes life. It is both the cognizance of homelessness and being right or aligned with homelessness—what Heidegger calls dwelling *in* homelessness, as explicated in chapter four—that renders beings authentic, something "prompted by rare and difficult experiences" (Käufer 2021, 72; see also Nichols [2014, 48–50], who refers to this cognizance as a self-awareness of one's possibilities). Anxiety and profound boredom, as chapters one and two will show, serve as two examples of such rare and difficult experiences that can bring beings face-to-face with homelessness.

The significance of authenticity is not simply that beings are brought in line with their essence—an important matter in its own right. Additionally, and practically speaking, authenticity is also significant because it is the basis of freedom; that is, to be authentic is to be free, which also means that inauthenticity is unfreedom (see Nichols 2014; Käufer 2021, 77). Nichols (2014) has developed the place of freedom to Heidegger's writings that can be extrapolated through the concept of authenticity. As such, there is no need to rehash this position. That said, for what is developed here, it is worth underlining the connection between authenticity, freedom, and homelessness because it is this connection that is particularly developed in this book: it is the failure to come to terms with and dwell in homelessness that renders beings inauthentic and thus inherently unfree. This unfreedom renders beings enslaved to the they-self so that it is not merely that beings are in the world, but that there is no room nor place for their essence. As such, it is impossible for beings to be (at) home because there is no space made for the essence of beings to reside, to be. To be free, then, is to be in one's homelessness, to dwell in homelessness.

It is important to underline that homelessness is not—nor does it equal or mean—unfreedom. Homelessness, rather, is freedom in the sense that to be in the world is to be homeless and, as such, to be and dwell in and with homelessness is freedom. It is when beings seek to overcome homelessness via the they-self that they remain trapped in unfreedom. For example, the incessant desire, prevalent in today's culture, to combat boredom (see the essays in Gardiner and Haladyn 2017, for example) is an apt example of the unfreedom that permeates beings. As such, the desire to put boredom to sleep, as Heidegger puts it (discussed in chapter two), distances beings from their very selves and grips them in inauthenticity and unfreedom.

It also needs recognition that despite what Heidegger says, that the concepts of authenticity and inauthenticity are not meant to impute value, certainly pejorate, it must be acknowledged that there is value judgement imbued into the very words *authentic* and *inauthentic*, if not for any other reason than the fact that they are held up, and only meaningful, in opposition to each other (*BT*, 68). In fact, in *Being and Time*, authenticity "functions as an evaluative ideal" and Heidegger is unequivocal that authentic Dasein is "free, lucid, immediate and concrete. It is honest, courageous, and truthful. It faces fate and does not feel or cover up its possible collapse" (Käufer 2021, 77; see also Nichols 2014, 39). As such, "authentic Dasein is characterized by a kind of freedom that inauthentic Dasein lacks" (Käufer 2021, 76). Nichols (2014, 50) echoes this point in writing that this unfreedom is a self-estranging or estrangement from oneself. There is no doubt, then, that for Heidegger, it is in and through authenticity that freedom is possible. One is not free, nor can one be free, unless one is authentically situated (to underline once more: authenticity is dwelling in homelessness and, as such, homelessness is not, by any means, unfreedom but rather the basis of/for freedom). As such, it is possible to conclude that for Heidegger, authentic existence is better than inauthentic existence, and thus more valuable, even though authentic existence is far more difficult to obtain (Käufer 2021, 77) because inauthenticity is the norm of being-in-the-world. This "better" is premised upon its capacity to make beings free, and as this book seeks to unpack, making beings free connects to the homelessness of beings, which is theorized as the nothingness of being given the myriad indeterminacies that constitute what it means to be in the world, all of which are to be embraced rather than shunned.

Perhaps the best way to bring this to light is to tackle head-on what is perhaps the most vitriolic of all criticisms levelled against Heidegger, and this comes from Adorno. Engaging with this polemic helps situate the Heideggerian project as it is conceptualized in this book so as to tightly frame the contours within which Heidegger's concepts are both brought to life and given colour to in this work.

Reframing the Authentic vis-à-vis the Inauthentic

Adorno's *The Jargon of Authenticity* (1973/2003) is, arguably, a caustic criticism of Heidegger's ontological project. What follows does not engage with Adorno's criticisms in an exhaustive, even systematic, manner, but it does draw upon it in some detail to bring to light several matters of import for what is developed here. Adorno accuses Heidegger of a plethora of issues—some in relation to Heidegger's intellectual integrity and honesty, even referring to ontology itself as fraudulent (c. 1963/1998, 11)—ranging from the substitution of truth for ideology, the arbitrary distinction between authenticity and inauthenticity, the relegation of the ontic to the intellectual dustbin to spare and laud the import of the ontological, and the extrication of the social (society or culture as two examples) from fundamental ontology. Most, even all, of these accusations are, if not untrue, then at least grossly exaggerated and misplaced. What appears to have birthed and grounds Adorno's polemic is a paranoia—or at least a robust fear—of the expert over the layperson and expert knowledge over lay knowledge that is said to be the death of progression, which would give rise to tyranny (fear over fascism, specifically Nazism, reign heavily as undertones in Adorno's concerns). Specifically, Adorno laments expert vocabulary, which is dismissed as "jargon," as the dilution or erosion of truth. While such is certainly plausible, whether it describes Heidegger's work, specifically *Being and Time*, is a different matter altogether.

Before proceeding, it is worth considering whether labelling and describing Adorno's criticism of Heidegger and his work as paranoid or fearful can be read as harsh, even unwarranted. While such a reading might be harsh in terms of upsetting, even unsettling, certain sensibilities (especially those who are pro-Adorno or anti-Heidegger), it is, nevertheless, fair. To some extent at least, Adorno engages in certain fear tactics to heighten the reader's sensitivities toward Heidegger's supposed programme: "In the higher ranks of the hierarchy of authenticity...negativities are also served. Heidegger even requisitions the concept of destruction which is tabooed in the lower ranks, together with the blackness of fear, sorrow, and death" (Adorno 1973/2003, 20). Additionally, Adorno's essay on the place of philosophy for contemporary theorizing lays at the root cause of Heidegger's involvement with Hitler's fascist programme, a "philosophy that equated Being with Führer" (Adorno c. 1963/1998, 10). These are serious, even caustic, claims, and as Adorno sees it, Heidegger's philosophy was, at its very core, from its very inception, a philosophy of and about oppression and darkness, that was bred by and further reproduced blackness (of fear, of death, of hierarchy, and so on). The point, then, is that Adorno's criticism of Heidegger draws upon the very fear mongering tactics he accuses Heidegger of to buttress his position and give colour to it, while being all the while a criticism that is itself premised and grounded upon a fear of what such a philosophy could and would inevitably lead to if left to its own course. To some extent this is understandable given what Adorno witnessed unfolding around him, but that does not—and cannot—erase the fact that there is, at a minimum, an element of fear that adorns Adorno's scathing polemic against Heideggerian philosophy, especially considering that he is explicit that "the thinking of Being" ought to be confronted "for all the fraud it propagates" (Adorno c. 1963/1998, 11).

According to Adorno (1973/2003, 59–62; 79–81), philosophies of authenticity are inward-focused philosophies, which means that they, apparently, strip the outside world of any bearing upon their premises. As such, it is not so much that Adorno is concerned with jargon but with authenticity. In fact, it is more than authenticity that concerns Adorno, because authenticity merely points to or masks something more dangerous, namely, the ontological project. That said, jargon, authenticity, and ontology are, for Adorno, clearly and inextricably linked in the Heideggerian project, and they coalesce into oppression and darkness. It is important, thus, to keep these three concepts in mind when considering Adorno's critique of Heidegger.

For Adorno, the ontological project is replete with danger because it is simply a philosophy of as-is—or, better, as-if (Adorno 1973/2003, 23)—and inward focused. According to Adorno, ontology takes the world as given, reading into it supposed timeless truths that it fabricates, and in so doing, the project strips any pretense of history that grounds the making and sustaining of reality and truth. Trent Schroyer (1973/2003), who penned the "Foreword" to the English translation of *The Jargon of Authenticity*, writes that Adorno would view ontology as "an ideology of the simple," with all its intended pejoration: "In the universal of transcendental subjectivity into Dasein, the empirical is totally lost and, as Adorno claims, an essence-mythology of Being emerges" (Schroyer 1973/2003, xv).

According to Adorno, Heidegger's being is ahistorical (or unhistorical), and beings are stripped of their concreteness. Being sustains itself mythically and draws its basis upon an understanding of beings that is equally mythical. As such, from its very inception, the ontological project for Adorno is a project designed to fail because it is grounded upon and further reproduces falsities. Heidegger's supposed reading of anxiety in a strictly ontological register (as opposed to an ontical one premised on emotions) is, for Adorno, evidence of the immense danger that lurks because such a reading fails to locate and appreciate the profound fear and anxiety that grounds people in their everyday lives (Adorno 1973/2003, 27). For Adorno, "philosophy should be the binding commitment to non-naïveté" (Adorno c. 1963/1998, 12), and ontology is at best naïve and at worst fraudulent (11).

The concept of authenticity (witnessed in thinkers beyond Heidegger but of which Heidegger is perhaps the most important spokesperson) is, as Adorno views it, the representation of the naïveté of the ontological project in action. Authenticity, for Adorno, amounts to nothing other than jargon; in fact, for him, authenticity itself is jargon, and jargon is immensely dangerous because it masks many issues and problems under the guise of intellectual thought. Adorno refers to the entirety of the ontological project as "the jargon of ontology" (c. 1963/1998, 8) and notes, in his author's note to *The Jargon of Authenticity*, that this "jargon has become an ideology unto itself" (Adorno 1967/2003, xix) that masquerades as philosophy. This is the danger that Adorno seeks to expose and takes Heidegger to task on.

With respect to Heidegger's work, especially his early phase, there is no basis to substantiate such claims. The very premise of being-*in*-the-world which Dasein finds itself—or, to put this differently, where Heidegger deliberately locates or places it—and from where it cannot be extricated, conclusively shows this. Virtually all scholars in sociology or the social sciences who have drawn upon or critiqued Heidegger recognize that Dasein is inherently social (e.g., Bourdieu 1988/1991; Aspers and Kohl 2013; Nielsen and Skotnicki 2018; Dreyfus and Rabinow 1993, 38–39). As such, the argument that Heidegger's ontology is blind to the social world is untrue. Heidegger's concern with the being of beings, which is the meaning of existence, is *inherently* social, and this means that the tool he uses to probe being, Dasein, is always in the social world. Partly, the criticism Adorno levels against Heidegger's apparently inwardly constructed philosophy is, as noted above, based upon trepidation, even paranoia, where Adorno claims that the expertise of the thinker that Heidegger lauds (detailed in chapter three), is grounded upon the substitution of truth with ideology (Adorno 1973/2003, 123–126; 132). This, according to Adorno, has the effect of stifling the progress of society, perhaps best evinced in his rather off-handed comment that one of the consequences of jargon thriving or at least not being critiqued is that "suffering, evil, and death are to be accepted, not to be changed," a blackness, as he refers to it (53). As such, Adorno points to "Heidegger's arrogance toward the merely ontic" which leads to "the unfulfillment of life" (92), perhaps best evinced in Adorno's rather veiled accusation that shelter is rendered secondary to the ontological status of being, a point taken up below.

Heidegger has certainly been accused of such things, especially his alignment with fascism. Yet, to claim that the Heideggerian quest for the meaning of existence promotes evil and suffering via its jargon is a different issue—and whether Heidegger's discourse is jargon itself needs rethinking, especially given the esoteric nature of intellectual discourse as a whole. For example, Heidegger's essay "Building Dwelling Thinking" (discussed in chapter four) is often cited as evidence that Heidegger is more interested in the ontology of being than the suffering of those without shelter (see Bourdieu 1988/1991, 127n15). Such claims cannot survive a close reading of the text, as chapter four demonstrates. Pierre Bourdieu (1988/1991), for example, who is somewhat sympathetic to Adorno's reading of Heidegger, while unequivocally noting that Adorno misses the mark on several significant matters (see 3, 83), provides a more nuanced reading of the philosopher vis-à-vis his Nazism, noting that neither the early nor the later Heidegger was a Nazi ideologue despite enrolling, for a short period, in the party (103–105).[5] In that sense, Bourdieu provides a historical-intellectual critique of Heidegger without succumbing to the fear, even paranoia, that adorns Adorno's polemic. As such, while Bourdieu claims, and rightfully so, that it is important to "abandon the opposition between a political reading and a philosophical reading, and undertake a simultaneously...*dual reading*" (3; emphasis in original), he does so by nevertheless preserving the "pure thought" (3) of Heidegger, that is, Heidegger's thoughts in their essence or their own terms, without adulterating them with an ideology of fear. Indeed, it is quite ironic that Adorno's accusations of Heidegger's work as pure ideology end up being, in Bourdieu's account, that very thing: ideology.

The clearest way to illustrate this is to return to the concept of authenticity that Adorno (and Bourdieu) critique. Adorno's position, explicated somewhat already, is that authenticity is essentially an ideology to suppress the masses and laud and glorify the experts. It suppresses the truth in favour of elitism. (Bourdieu [1988/1991, 78–79] appears to echo this when he speaks of the duality between the elite and the masses in Heidegger's framing of authenticity.) More specifically, Adorno claims that the distinction is arbitrary and that the only reason Heidegger draws upon it is to promote his ideological endeavour, which can only be presumed to be fascism or the promotion of elitism (Adorno 1973/2003, 78). Before engaging with this argument, it is worth underlining, again, that Adorno's reading of Heidegger is not only unfair but quite superficial to begin with and tends to excoriate him for the promotion of ideology all the while being blind to the very ideology—one grounded upon fear and paranoia—that underpins his critique (really criticism). Perhaps the best example of this is Adorno's reading of Heidegger's concept of death (113–114, 121–128), where he says that, for Heidegger, it is via death that authenticity can be achieved. Adorno thus writes that Heidegger is "smitten with death" (125) and claims that in *Being and Time*, "death is maneuvered into the position of the authentic" (113–114). According to Adorno, "[a]uthenticity is death" (125).

The problem, however, is that Heidegger speaks of death (discussed in the next chapter) in a very specific sense that has nothing to do with perishing or demise (what is thought of as death in the orthodox sense) but rather as a status where beings face the possibility of no further possibilities in terms of their everyday lives and experiences. In that sense, Adorno must read into Heidegger's analysis of authenticity premises that are absent. Perhaps a fairer critique of Heidegger and authenticity can be drawn from Bourdieu—who, recall, is sympathetic to Heidegger but certainly critical of him. For Bourdieu (1988/1991, 86), authenticity "is not a naïve designation…" as Adorno's reading appears to portray it, but rather "indicates a universal potential—as does inauthenticity." Already, then, Bourdieu's reading appears to delve into the heart of Heidegger's analysis without necessarily imparting value judgments, a point that Heidegger underlines quite forcefully: "inauthenticity of Dasein does not signify any 'less' Being or any 'lower' degree of Being" (*BT*, 68). Though there is, as noted, an element of value that underpins the distinction between authenticity and inauthenticity that cannot be dismissed, the point, is that an explicit pejoration of the kind that Adorno is interested in levelling against Heidegger is absent in Heidegger's words. Bourdieu (1988/1991), it appears, is keen to stray from such a path. As such, for him, the potentiality of authenticity is "only accessible to those who manage to appropriate it by apprehending it for what it is, and by managing to 'tear themselves' away from 'inauthenticity'…" (86). In such a reading, authenticity is certainly valued as more desirable, but inauthenticity is not necessarily pejorated simply because it is a fact of being-in-the-world (cf. *BT*, 167). The point, very simply then, is that inauthenticity is of concern to Heidegger because it depersonalizes being, that is, it distances and separates being from its essence or nature and as such, being is without home, which is to say that there is no place or site for the essence of being to be because the very notion of what it means to be human is disengaged from beings. As such, authenticity is presented as the very recognition of the limits of being-in-the-world. No such pejoration or elitism in the way Adorno views it should necessarily be read into Heidegger's endeavours (though Bourdieu, it must be admitted, also does tend to criticize Heidegger for his apparent elitist language).

The concepts of authenticity and inauthenticity are mobilized in this book in a very specific manner, namely, in relation to the nothingness of being that is brought to light via the homelessness of being (in the world). As such, what is developed in the book is Heidegger's call to dwell in and with homelessness, which this book rereads as a need to be at one with the indeterminacy that constitutes being, which is read as nothingness. One way to put this into perspective is to return to Adorno's take on shelter, briefly noted before. The quest for authenticity, Adorno says, renders Heidegger to either neglect or downplay the import of material shelter, what Adorno refers to as "shelteredness" (Adorno 1973/2003, 26), to the existential status of coming to terms with one's being.

It is necessary to underline that Adorno's use of the term *shelteredness* can be read in two ways. First, and more abstractly, that is, "as an existential value" (Adorno 1973/2003, 20), it refers to a sense of protection in the sense of being shielded from things, specifically values or ideas. That said, Adorno's use of the term is meant to pejorate because it refers to a specific problematic. The oft-heard English phrase, in reference to a "sheltered life," where one has been sheltered from certain things, people, and ideas/values, aptly captures this sense of shelteredness that Adorno seeks to convey, one as alluded to, that references the negative or, at a minimum, a disadvantage. As such, Adorno is taking Heidegger to task not only for his apparent shelteredness, but also for promoting this very shelteredness as a way of thinking and being (Adorno 1973/2003; c.1963/1998), which Adorno sees as an overall reflection of Heidegger's philosophy, one sheltered from the everyday world and life experiences, one that substitutes ideology for reality.

The term shelteredness can also be read in reference to shelter in the material sense, as is read here. To fully appreciate this, it must be kept in mind that Heidegger's passing comment on housing, that ontological homelessness is of far more concern to the well-being and progress of humanity than material homelessness (or houselessness, properly put), has been met with severe criticism, even ridicule. Adorno's use of the term shelteredness, as such, meets Heidegger head-on to address his supposed failure to appreciate and underline the import of shelter as a basic necessity of life and living.

Adorno's reference to shelteredness, then, references both the material and the abstract. The material concept Adorno engages with in criticizing Heidegger is not plainly obvious, but it is certainly present. Adorno writes of the "[k]now-how and range of income" as "the only factors which determine whether one appears on the scene sheltered or has to start out without security" (Adorno 1973/2003, 22), a statement that appears to speak to the material, in the sense that the security spoken of here is tied directly to shelter, and the ability to be sheltered is tied to, among others, income. If this connection is not explicit, then, that Adorno also speaks to Heidegger's statement that the material is less concerning than the ontological is more directly evinced in the distinction Adorno carves between the literal and the figurative stating that the two are often interchanged in jargon (Adorno 1973/2003, 26). This suggests that in the quest to sustain an ontological programme, Heidegger misses the most important things facing humans in their daily lives. One example, noted before, is anxiety, which Heidegger, as Adorno reads it, fails to account for as a quotidian experience. Similarly, Adorno's comment on shelter evidences his belief that Heidegger places the absence of housing second to the meaning of life, so that while space is devoted to the reflection of existential matters, literal space is not carved out for one to live and exist in. It is true that Adorno (1973/2003, 25–26) draws directly from Otto Bollnow's reading of Heidegger's comments on housing to ground this point. Yet it ought not be lost that after reading Bollnow, Adorno himself underscores "the need for residences [a]s more serious than the pose of existential seriousness" to cement the supposedly erroneous position of Heidegger, specifically pertaining to Heidegger's "linguistic carelessness" (Adorno 1973/2003, 26), which upholds the abstract over, and as more important than, everyday struggles. The real plight and struggle of humanity, Adorno claims, is lost in the jargon of authenticity that gives primacy to ontology at the expense of life experiences.

Yet, this is not how Heidegger engages the subject (as chapters three and four show). It is true that Heidegger claims that the ontology of home(lessness) is more significant than the material condition of housing, and this is because of the inherent unfreedom that is a product of the failure to come to terms with homelessness, but this ought not be read as if material sheltering is unimportant. In emphasizing the ontological status of homelessness, Heidegger is eager to bring attention to the ontology of being homeless, which had, at that time, been given very little to no attention—in fact, the same can be said of the subject today. Heidegger's concern is to underline that shelter of the material type cannot and does not ensure dwelling. Thus, there are two very different issues that unfold. Adorno is claiming that Heidegger's position is that material structures are not important or relevant to being-in-the-world. This is very different from what Heidegger says: that these structures cannot guarantee dwelling. Heidegger's focus is to highlight the import of dwelling to being (and being-in-the-world), not to neglect or downplay material housing. It is dwelling, specifically dwelling in homelessness, that leads to authenticity. As such, Heidegger is merely using the example of shelter and housing to show that the very structures that are thought to be able to bring beings home cannot guarantee dwelling. Dwelling, as chapters three and four argue, is paramount to coming home, but coming home ultimately requires dwelling in homelessness, one that is an ontological status.

While it would be remiss to dismiss the concerns levelled against Heidegger and in particular his scholarship—in relation to authenticity, for example—such concerns also ought not foreclose upon the important, even ground-breaking, work undertaken by Heidegger. As this book seeks to make clear, there is unequivocally an aspect of the social in Heidegger that is at the forefront of his oeuvre that is worth recognizing, and in bringing this to light, the book speaks on two registers: both to the philosophical tradition that generally tends to place Heidegger within the major canons of the field (e.g., metaphysics) as well as to those on the margins of sociology who have called for attention to be paid to Heidegger's explication of the social. This book, thus, takes such a call seriously and seeks to, in a systematic and detailed manner, outline Heidegger's theory of the meaning of existence, which is here described as nothingness, one emanating from the fact that to be human is to be homeless. Thus, while the controversies surrounding Heidegger and his work will not abate, this does not mean that his insights cannot be extrapolated in a meaningful manner. This book, then, seeks to shed light upon and clarify Heidegger's being of beings, which is here read as an ontology of homelessness that speaks to the indeterminacy of being human, one theorized as nothingness.

The Organization of the Book

The substantive material of this book is contained in four chapters, and while they are not separated nor labelled as such, the chapters can be read as constituting two related parts: chapters one and two constituting one part, chapters three and four the other. A concluding chapter, which tends to depart from convention in that it functions substantively as well, seeks to give colour to the theoretical discussion of the four substantive chapters by putting into perspective what the concept of dwelling can illuminate about the nature of property relations. The book is, as noted, an exegetical rereading of several of Heidegger's important works. No effort is made to canvass or survey the corpus of Heidegger's voluminous literature. Instead, detailed focus is cast upon several important texts to reveal the ontology of homelessness as an indeterminate nothingness. The book is a theoretical endeavour to situate, ground, shed light upon, and clarify Heidegger's reading of what it means to be human.

Chapters one and two work in tandem. They focus upon the early phase of Heidegger's work, drawing heavily upon *Being and Time* and *The Fundamental Concepts of Metaphysics*. Chapter one examines *Being and Time* to disclose how Heidegger's invocation of the mood of anxiety, which is juxtaposed with fear, shines light upon the indeterminacy that constitutes the being of beings. The chapter explicates how beings are, in and through anxiety, forced to come to terms with an emptiness that is virtually impossible for the subject to conceptualize and contextualize. Beings, thus, are left to traverse an indeterminacy, and the chapter explicates how this indeterminacy can be read as nothingness. Chapter three continues this theme of the nothingness of beings by exploring yet another mood, or what Heidegger calls an attunement, namely, boredom. Drawing upon *The Fundamental Concepts of Metaphysics*, the chapter examines how profound boredom, which is juxtaposed to more superficial forms of boredom, prods beings to come to terms with the inner essence of their being. The chapter rereads the place of boredom to the essence of the meaning of life by moving from the taken-for-granted and commonly held beliefs that what is boring is inimical to life and instead reads profound boredom as emanating from the very core of one's being (as it is with rare anxiety). As such, the chapter explicates the nothingness of beings: that beings are constituted by an indeterminacy that they are forced to recognize, come to terms with, and live with and through. As such, chapters one and two take two common modes of feeling prevalent in modern culture (especially so since the pandemic) and rereads them to articulate more profound concerns about what it means to be human. Taken as a whole, chapters one and two lay the groundwork for the nothingness of the meaning of existence that is inherently tied to indeterminacy and argues that being human is nothingness.

Chapters three and four also work in tandem to explore the homelessness of beings as nothingness. These chapters focus on Heidegger's middle phase, the work that was produced after the so-called turn (or at least one turn). This turn, as explicated in the sections above, does not refer to a shift in the substantive focus of Heidegger's work given the consistent desire throughout his scholarship to expound the being of beings. Rather, the turn signals a shift in the form of inquiry, one that he believed was more suited to bring to light the homelessness of beings and lay a path and foundation for homecoming. What is clear, then, is that the phase(s) after the early period are less reliant on philosophical language and draw heavily upon the poetic. However, as already noted, this does not mean that Heidegger was renouncing philosophy as a whole, including ontological inquiry, but was seeking to find a more practical and appropriate path toward it.

Chapter three draws upon *Hölderlin's Hymn "The Ister"* to explore Heidegger's examination of the homelessness of beings. Focusing, among others, on Heidegger's reading of the flow of the river Ister, the chapter engages with Heidegger's claim that beings are not only homeless but are on a trajectory that further cements homelessness because the path travelled is both away from and against home, despite the obstinate belief that beings are, if not already home, then, at least homeward bound. Chapter four examines Heidegger's important and controversial essay "Building Dwelling Thinking," which underlines the significance of dwelling to humanity. The message of this essay is straightforward and sobering: material structures and the sites of houses and housing are insufficient for the purposes of dwelling, and beings are truly home and can only be so, when they dwell. Dwelling, as the chapter shows, involves reorienting the meaning of what it means to be (at) home, which necessitates accepting not merely that the being of beings is homelessness, but also that to be home, and the only way to be home, is to embrace and come to terms with this homelessness. This necessitates that beings learn to dwell in and through homelessness. Both chapters three and four read the status of ontological homelessness alongside the import of nothingness to show that the being of beings is an indeterminate nothingness pertaining to the place of home in homelessness.

The argument developed in this book is, in terms of its form, grounded upon the circular, something the reader may have already noticed in terms of how the argument is framed. This is perhaps best illustrated in the status of ontological homelessness which is read as indeterminacy, and this indeterminacy, then, is read as nothingness to explicate the meaning of existence. Similarly, the concept of dwelling is introduced to speak to the essence of being, namely, that to be is to dwell, and to dwell is to be, in homelessness.

While circularity is often decried in the social sciences, largely because of its apparent scientific tenor (cf. Winch 1958), this is not so in philosophy and certainly not in Heidegger's work. Heidegger, put simply, not only recognizes the circularity of/in his work, but warmly embraces it, among other intellectual faux pas such as tautology. The reason, as noted above, is that the fundamental ontology he engages in/with requires preparation by way of the ontical. That is, an ontological inquiry cannot be approached directly, which is to say that it cannot be easily accessed. It requires multiple, circuitous paths to unravel and reveal the essence of being. In *Being and Time*, for example, Heidegger writes that "[w]e cannot ever 'avoid' a 'circular' proof in the existential analytic, because such an analytic does not do any proving at all by the rules of the 'logic of consistency'. What common sense wishes to eliminate in avoiding the 'circle', on the supposition that it is measuring up to the loftiest rigour of scientific investigation, is nothing else than the basic structure of care" (*BT*, 363; emphasis omitted). Michael Gelven (1989, 101) points out that "[i]n no less than three separate sections Heidegger comments on the circular nature of his interpretation. The circularity of interpretation is of great importance when Heidegger applies this structure to the specific problem of what it means to be." Put simply, fundamental ontology requires preparatory work, and this preparatory work requires circularity to unravel and disclose the meaning of existence. As Heidegger sees it, without some element of circularity, fundamental ontology is not possible. This point is made, in a different context, in his critique of dialecticism as found in *The Fundamental Concepts of Metaphysics*: "The circular character of philosophical thought is directly bound up with its ambiguity, an ambiguity that is not to be eliminated or, still less, levelled off by means of dialectic. It is characteristic that we repeatedly find in the history of philosophy such attempts to level off this circularity and ambiguity of philosophical thinking through the use of dialectic, and most recently in a grand and impressive form. Yet all dialectic in philosophy is only the expression of an embarrassment" (*FCM*, 187). The circularity extant in this book, then, is a product of the form of its inquiry, a distinctly Heideggerian inquiry into the ontological status of the being of beings.

Anxiety and the Revelation of Nothingness

BEING AND TIME finds Heidegger spending considerable time discussing, among other matters, fear, which is then juxtaposed to anxiety. The discussion of these moods, as Heidegger calls them, is meant to demonstrate the revelatory aspect of anxiety that shines light upon human existence. This chapter rereads Heidegger's analysis of fear and anxiety in several stages beginning with an attempt to illuminate the ways that fear, while capable of revealing being, is only capable of doing so in an opaque manner. It is to anxiety that Heidegger turns to be able to reveal being fully and unadulteratedly, and the second phase of this chapter focuses on this. As this chapter argues, however, it is also possible to reread Heidegger's discussion of anxiety, especially if his premises and conclusions are extended further and followed to a logical conclusion, to see and appreciate that the being of beings can be read as nothingness. This is what this chapter sets as its focus. It draws upon the moods of fear and anxiety to illuminate the way the nothingness of being can be extrapolated from Heidegger's discussion. This chapter works in tandem with the next chapter to structure the theoretical basis upon which being can be read as nothingness and rereads Heidegger's discussion of anxiety and profound boredom (chapter two) toward this end.

This chapter begins with a somewhat brief overview of the Heideggerian project, one concerned with being. From here, the chapter explicates, again somewhat briefly, the role of moods or attunements in the Heideggerian endeavour. The bulk of the chapter situates Heidegger's discussion of fear and anxiety and explicates how the disclosures or revelations that emerge from anxiety can be read as the nothingness of being. The chapter concludes with the way the nothingness of being reveals and is revealed in the ontological homelessness of beings.

The Being of Beings and Fundamental Ontology
Being and Time is Heidegger's first important work and quite possibly his most famous, introducing the world to his philosophical program. The focus of *Being and Time* is straightforwardly introduced at the outset as an effort "to work out the question of the meaning of *Being* and to do so concretely" (*BT*, 19; emphasis in original).[1] It should be stressed that working out being is, for Heidegger, a reawakening of the question of being (Haugeland 2013, 221, 179). That is, the inquiry into being was, at some point in the history of philosophical investigation, considered an important matter, and Heidegger casts his philosophical endeavour on this "serious and vital question" (Haugeland 2013, 179). Being refers to the meaning of existence—what it means to be or exist, that is, what it means to be human, the human way of being—which Heidegger refers to throughout his various work as the "being of beings" (e.g., *WIM*, 104, 108; *IM*, 38, 141; *I*, 87). This is evident, for example, in his elaboration of the purpose of thinking: "The thinker thinks that which is. The thinker thinks beings. The thinker thinks beings in the sole consideration that beings are and what they are. What beings 'are', how they 'are', and the fact that they 'are', is what we call the being of beings" (*IP*, 36). In other words, and as Michael Gelven (1989, 7; emphasis omitted) clarifies, "there is a ... fundamental question that can be asked: What does it mean to exist at all? The question is not whether something does exist or how to characterize the existence of particular kinds of things, like material things or mental things, but simply to ask about the very meaning of Being."

Concern about the being of beings is an ontological question. According to Heidegger, fundamental ontology—an elevated and unadulterated version of ontology, an ontology proper—is the true course and direction of all philosophical inquiry. Unfortunately, Heidegger claims that the philosophical inquiry up to (and including) his time failed to fully come to terms and grapple with ontology despite its persistent belief that it was so doing. This is why Heidegger's endeavour can be thought of as an effort to reawaken the question of being (Haugeland 2013, 221, 179; Slaby 2021, 551). Thus, Heidegger writes that "all ontology, no matter how rich and firmly compacted a system of categories it has as its disposal, remains blind and perverted from its ownmost aim, if it has not first adequately clarified the meaning of Being, and conceived this clarification as its fundamental task" (*BT*, 31; emphasis omitted). An ontological inquiry, as Heidegger envisages it, "is concerned primarily with being" (*BT*, 31; see also Slaby 2021) and "is indeed more primordial" (*BT*, 31), which is to say that its inquiry is prior to and goes before facts and questions about facts or, put another way, questions about epistemology (see also Smith [2010] for a social-scientific approach to the debate between ontology and epistemology). It is the most fundamental question that can—and must—be posed and answered.

Ontology and ontological inquiry can be juxtaposed to an ontical inquiry. An ontical inquiry "is concerned primarily with entities and facts about them" as often framed and found in the positive sciences (*BT*, 31n3; emphasis omitted). Taylor Carman (2013, 94; emphasis omitted) distinguishes between the two by noting that ontic questioning has "to do with the particular features entities happen to have" while ontological inquiry concerns "what it is that makes those entities (intelligible as) [or meaningful as] the entities they are." Heidegger's claim is that philosophy up to and including his time, while professing to inquire into ontological questions, was (and is) really (or largely) posing and responding to ontical questions.

To undertake an ontological inquiry, Heidegger relies upon a particular methodological framework (Slaby 2021; Carman 2013, 94; Rae, 2001, 264; Nichols 2014, 29–31) to provide the appropriate opening to approach and engage with ontological questions.

Approaching ontological questions requires immense preparatory work which must be attended to patiently and which is then responsively disclosed via ontical inquiries (Thomson 2021, 524–525; Gelven 1989, 9). This is where Heidegger draws upon the concept of Dasein (discussed below). As Gelven (1989, 34) puts it, "the existential analytic must, according to Heidegger, begin from an account of Dasein in its everydayness." According to Heidegger, "by having regard for the basic state of Dasein's everydayness, we shall bring out the Being of this entity in a preparatory fashion" (*BT*, 38). "In short," as Robert Mugerauer (2008, 172) pithily explains, "preparatory thinking is understood by Heidegger as a way which belongs to growing and cultivation." For present purposes, growing and cultivation can be thought of as searching for, and finding, and then coming to terms with the essence of an entity. This coming-to-terms-with, as will be made clear in this work, concerns the nothingness of beings.

Heidegger's explication of Dasein, like many of his explications, is cryptic, riddled with ambiguities, and has the potential to cause some, if not much, confusion (recall the discussion in the introduction about Heidegger's convoluted, and abstruse style and jargon). Heidegger attempts to explain Dasein by noting that "[t]his entity which each of us is himself and which includes inquiring as one of the possibilities of its Being, we shall denote by the term 'Dasein'" (*BT*, 27; emphasis omitted). His more detailed explication, however, illustrates where confusion may take hold of the reader:

> Dasein is an entity which does not just occur among other entities. Rather, it is ontically distinguished by the fact that, in its very Being, that Being is an issue for it. But in that case, this is a constitutive state of Dasein's Being, and this implies that Dasein, in its Being, has a relationship towards that Being—a relationship which itself is one of Being. And this means further that there is some way in which Dasein understands itself in its Being, and that to some degree it does so explicitly. It is peculiar to this entity that with and through its Being, this Being is disclosed to it. Understanding of Being is itself a definite characteristic of Dasein's Being. Dasein is ontically distinctive in that it is ontological. (32; emphasis omitted)

On its face, this is confounding, especially when considering that the literal translation of Dasein, "being-*there*" (as in, "We name the being of man being-there, Da-sein" [*FCM*, 63; emphasis omitted]), is itself not without contention. For example, when Heidegger hyphenates Dasein, which is sometimes the case, evinced in the quote above, it is thought that a more appropriate translation should be being-*here* (see Fried and Polt 2000, xii). Perhaps more importantly, what precisely being-there means is unclear. For Leslie Paul Thiele (1997, 498), "[t]he 'there' of Dasein is not a geographic place but a phenomenological relationship, a way of being in and belonging to the world." Hubert Dreyfus (1991, 14; emphasis in original) claims that being-there ought to be thought of as Heidegger's interest "in the human *way of being*." In his introduction to a collection of Heidegger's essays, David Krell (2008, 32; emphasis added) comments that "Heidegger thinks of the being that raises questions. He names it Dasein, the kind of *being that is open to Being*." Gelven (1989, 28) describes Dasein similarly by noting that it is "that entity which is capable of inquiring into its own Being and, indeed, such an inquiry into Being is what makes Dasein what it is." An equally useful explanation is found in the translators' introduction to Heidegger's *Introduction to Metaphysics*, where Gregory Fried and Richard Polt (2000, xii) write, "[w]e can think of Dasein as a condition into which human beings enter, either individually or collectively, at a historical juncture when Being becomes an issue for them."

Despite what appear to be disparate explanations, there is unity and commonality to the foregoing treatments of the meaning of Dasein. What each essentially states, albeit in different ways and with different emphases, is this: Dasein is concerned about being, where being is an issue for it and that this concern is constitutive to, or innate in, Dasein. It is Dasein—and only Dasein—that is capable of inquiring into these concerns over/about being.

Dasein is the term Heidegger uses in lieu of "human being," "person," or "subject" (Slaby 2021, 554), and it is that which is concerned with itself, that is, with its own being or existence. Dasein is concerned with itself because it *is*, which is to say that Dasein exists and exists in the world. Dasein, thus, is immensely and inherently social, a point that sociologists influenced by Heidegger are quick to note because, for them, it points to the fact that much of Heidegger's concerns are sociological and thus relevant to sociological inquiry (see Dreyfus and Rabinow 1993, 38; Aspers and Kohl 2013, 490; Nielsen and Skotnicki 2018). As such, it is neither possible nor appropriate to think of Dasein as existing in a vacuum: Dasein already presupposes a world in which it exists. It is, thus, always concerned with itself, which Heidegger puts as Dasein's concern with the care of itself.

Given that Dasein is concerned with itself, it is in a position to understand being or, to put it differently, it is an understanding of being (Haugeland 2013, 222). Here, Heidegger's preparatory and methodological framework (noted above) is brought to light where Dasein is the entity that is capable of revealing being pure and unadulterated. This is because, given that it is concerned with itself, Dasein can understand being because something is or can be an issue for Dasein only if Dasein has a sense for what it is concerned with or concerned about (see Slaby 2021, 555). Dasein is therefore capable of probing its existence and the meaning of being. Partly—and importantly—this also means that Dasein is concerned with its future, that is, what it can be, its potentialities (see Nichols 2014, 39).

Dasein, then, is a way of being—being-in-the-world—that has as its concern its very existence. This means that Dasein is in the habit of probing the meaning of existence, what it means to be, or what Heidegger calls the being of beings.

For Heidegger, then, an inquiry into fundamental ontology requires an inquiry into Dasein because it is Dasein that aids in approaching the question about the meaning of existence, given that it is Dasein that is interested in such a question. This, however, and crucially, does not mean that ontical questions are irrelevant. This is far from the case. "The two are," Taylor Carman (2013, 92) notes, "always inextricably interwoven." Consequently, "the phenomenological route to the ontological passes through the ontic" (Thomson 2021, 525). Thus, ontical questions are crucial for preparing the way for the more fundamental questions of ontology, though ontical questions and inquiries by themselves will not succeed in resolving ontological ones (Gelven 1989, 25). Charles Champetier (2001, 18) puts the connection this way: "Heidegger's Being is not reducible to beings, any more than it can be isolated from them. The deployment of its truth is always given to the thought in the ontic itself."

Heidegger's explication of the approach to ontology reads thus:

> Therefore *fundamental ontology*, from which alone all other ontologies can take their rise, must be sought in the *existential analytic of Dasein*. Dasein accordingly takes priority over all other entities in several ways. The first priority is an *ontical* one: Dasein is an entity whose Being has the determinate character of existence. The second priority is an *ontological* one: Dasein is in itself "ontological," because existence is thus determinative for it. But with equal primordiality Dasein also possesses—as constitutive for its understanding of existence—an understanding of the Being of all entities of a character other than its own. Dasein has therefore a third priority as providing the ontico-ontological condition for the possibility of any ontologies. Thus Dasein has turned out to be, more than any other entity, the one which must first be interrogated ontologically. (BT, 34; emphasis in original; see also Slaby 2021, 555)

If Dasein is crucial to making sense of ontology—of undertaking an ontological inquiry—and if Dasein is both ontical and ontological, then, it makes sense that an ontical inquiry will prepare the way for a (in fact, *the*) more fundamental inquiry. This is Heidegger's approach. What he cautions against—in terms of the philosophical tradition and approach that preceded him—is either terminating the inquiry with an ontical question or confounding an ontical inquiry for an ontological one. Interestingly, this is a criticism recently levelled by those sociologists who claim, in various ways, that the discipline of sociology confounds the ontic for the ontological and essentially reproduces ontic analyses (see Aspers and Kohl 2013, 495–496; see also Swedberg 2011). As this argument has it, sociology, despite its pretentions, fails to deliver on its promises of ontological inquiries and claims, let alone ontological truths and realities. This relates in part to the supposed preoccupation of the sciences with studying objects and its reluctance to look to the abstract, a point that Heidegger noted in his critique of the sciences in "What Is Metaphysics?" (see also Swedberg 2011; cf. Barad 2012, 2017).

For Heidegger, an ontical inquiry is important to set the stage for what is to come. As Gelven (1989, 29) says, in an ontological inquiry, "[w]e are not studying an object, but a process"—a process that is designed to permit an ontological inquiry. This is the purpose of an ontical inquiry. "Because phenomena, as understood phenomenologically," Heidegger writes, "are never anything but what goes to make up Being, while Being is in every case the Being of some entity, we must first bring forward the entities themselves if it is our aim that Being should be laid bare; and we must do this in the right way" (*BT*, 61). Gelven's (1989, 34; emphasis omitted) explication helps put this into context:

> Everydayness as the source of the data of the question of Being is not contested; in fact, it is determined. What must be transcended is the everyday perspective. But to go beyond the everyday perspective to a perspective of ontological insight, we must first thoroughly examine the range of the everyday perspective, lest in ascending to the broader perspective we emphasize what is inessential or peculiar. In addition, the ontological inquiry will place everydayness in itself in a new light.

That is, drawing upon Gelven again, "[w]hat is asked about is Being. What is interrogated is a particular being or entity, the human being. And what is gained is the *meaning* of Being" (27; emphasis in original). Echoing this, Carman (2013, 93) notes that "ontological horizons of intelligibility are what they are depending on what particular ontic phenomena they embrace, just as the ontic phenomena are what they are thanks to the ontological horizons within which they manifest themselves." This is Heidegger's focus and Dasein permits him the means to disclose the being of beings: "[I]t is only in the ways in which a human being exists that one can discover what it means to be" (Gelven 1989, 139). In other words, and to slightly modify this presentation: in the way that humans are—that is, exist and behave—is the only possibility to explore and examine what it means to exist. The meaning of existence, then, is what humans do and why they so do.

The foregoing attests to the important and inextricable relationship between fundamental ontology and Dasein. This relationship, as will become apparent shortly, especially as developed in the next chapter, also points to the importance of time and temporality to the essence of being. Temporality is the name Heidegger gives to describe "Dasein's 'ekstatic-horizontal unity'" (Haugeland 2013, 221). In other words, it is temporality that makes humans human, that brings meaning to the existence of beings. Simply put, beings are temporal creatures, but what really separates beings from other entities is that they are forward-looking or future-oriented, which is to say, in Heideggerian terms, that beings have the capacity—though not always realized—to think about the possibilities available to them.

Thus, Heidegger writes:

> [W]henever Dasein tactically understands and interprets something like Being, it does so with *time* as its standpoint. Time must be brought to light—and genuinely conceived—as the horizon for all understanding of Being and for any way of interpreting it. In order for us to discern this, *time* needs to be explicated *primordially as the horizon for the understanding of Being, and in terms of temporality as the Being of Dasein, which understands Being*. (BT, 39; emphasis in original)

This crucial passage points to an important interconnection among being, Dasein, time, and temporality. In other words, *being* (the focus of *Being and Time* and generally of Heidegger's larger body of work), *Dasein* (what concerns itself with being), and *time* (specifically, linear time, or the time of the clock) [Gelven 1989, 112; Rae 2021, 263; Nichols 2014, 81] all "come as a package—no one of them makes any sense without the other two" (Haugeland 2013, 221). As such, and based upon the "package" of being, Dasein, and time, temporality is (or can be thought of as) the connection between being (understood in/through Dasein) and time. In other words, "[t]emporality is the manner in which being in general, or Dasein's being in particular, is *conditioned* by time" (Blattner 2021b, 727; emphasis added). This means, then, that the condition of being according to time (which is to say that beings live according to the time of the clock and relate to it and make sense of it, and there is no escaping this fact) is referred to as temporality or, another way to put this is that temporality is the way being is determined by time. This determination, as will become apparent, speaks to the future and the possibilities that await beings. This also means, then, that time and temporality are not to be confounded nor conflated, something that Heidegger severely cautions against (see Blattner 2021c, 760; Gelven 1989, 112).

Inquiring into Dasein vis-à-vis temporality, Heidegger says, is the starting point of any ontological investigation. This is why Heidegger claims that *"the central problematic of all ontology is rooted in the phenomenon of time"* and that "the fundamental ontological task of Interpreting Being as such includes working out the *Temporality of Being"* (*BT*, 40; emphasis in original). For present purposes, what is important to underline is that an ontological inquiry is an inquiry into Dasein and Dasein can only be conceived temporally: that is, Dasein conceives of being temporally. This, as discussed next, is what Heidegger seeks to explicate. To do so, Heidegger relies upon what he refers to as fundamental attunements.

Dasein and Fundamental Attunements: Disclosing the Human Way of Being

Dasein—as a way of being-in-the-world that has as its primary concern its very being, that is, its existence—needs to be revealed. To do so, Heidegger draws upon what he refers to as moods to shed light upon the essence of Dasein and tap into Dasein's revelatory potential. As noted above, Dasein is simultaneously ontological and ontical, and the being of beings needs to be approached via a preparatory analysis of ontical entities. Thus, Heidegger writes, "[w]hat we indicate *ontologically* by the 'state of mind' is *ontically* the most familiar and everyday sort of thing; our mood, our Being-attuned" (*BT*, 172; emphasis in original). Ontologically, Dasein is manifested in a "state-of-mind [which] is a basic existential way in which Dasein is its 'there'. It not only characterizes Dasein ontologically, but [...also] discloses" itself (178). This state of mind, as already noted, cannot be immediately accessed but must be approached gradually, as a process, recalling that it is the process that is key, not the object.

This means that what needs to be grappled with first is the way beings relate to entities and the world (Gelven 1989, 139), what Heidegger calls being-in-the-world. An ontical analysis paves the way for such an inquiry and for Heidegger this is the only method that is appropriate for such a task. The equivalent of a state of mind, in the everyday being-in-the-world, is a mood.

It is important to note that, for Heidegger, moods (what he also calls *attunements*) "are not a mere emotional event or a state" (*FCM*, 65). This is not to claim that they are not these, but that to relegate them strictly to emotions is to limit the analysis to an ontical level, and Heidegger insists that the analysis must move beyond this. Thus Heidegger looks at moods as much more than mere feelings. The primary reason for this, as Gelven (1989, 80) suggests, is that for Heidegger, "Dasein is always in a mood." Indeed, Heidegger writes that "we are never free of moods" (*BT*, 175). This means that "the reader must not take 'moods' as those occasional attitudes of mind that belong to the study of psychology" (Gelven 1989, 80). Heidegger is explicit about this, stating that "[h]aving a mood is not related to the psychical in the first instance, and is not itself an inner condition which then reaches forth in an enigmatical way and puts its mark on Things or persons" (*BT*, 176).

What is important about moods (or attunements) is that they have the potential to reveal being and do so by disclosing Dasein *as* Dasein. In other words, moods reveal much more than the feelings of humans; they reveal what it means to be in the world *as* a human. As Heidegger puts it differently in his later work on boredom (discussed in the next chapter), "an attunement is a fundamental manner, the fundamental way in which Dasein is as Dasein," and it is moods "which give Dasein *subsistence and possibility* in its very foundations" (*FCM*, 67; emphasis in original). Moods, then, disclose and reveal. The importance of disclosure is significant. Heidegger uses the word repeatedly to speak of the role of moods vis-à-vis Dasein, namely, that they disclose Dasein (e.g., *BT*, 178, 225), and what is significant here is Heidegger's underscoring that it is only Dasein that can disclose itself to itself as itself, purely and unadulteratedly. That is, "ontologically[,] mood is a primordial kind of Being for Dasein, in which Dasein is disclosed to itself *prior to* all cognition and volition, and *beyond* their range of disclosure..." (*BT*, 175; emphasis in original). Moods, then, are what permit Dasein to *see* Dasein as Dasein: "A mood makes manifest 'how one is' and how one is fairing. In this 'how one is,' having a mood brings Being to its 'there,'" and given this, "Dasein becomes satiated with itself" (*BT*, 173).

There are some moods that are much more important than others, and these are capable of revealing Dasein to/as Dasein. These moods Heidegger refers to as fundamental attunements. A good example of the difference between moods and fundamental attunements is what Heidegger calls "bad moods" (*BT*, 175; emphasis omitted)—in contrast to "bare moods" (177)—where "Dasein becomes blind to itself, [and] the environment with which it is concerned veils itself, [and thus] the circumspection of concern gets led astray" (175). Fear, as will become apparent in the next section, is a good example of a mood that is incapable of revealing Dasein to/as Dasein (reveal, that is, pure and unadulterated). Conversely, a fundamental attunement can properly reveal Dasein as Dasein to Dasein. In *Being and Time*, this fundamental attunement is anxiety, which Heidegger refers to as "a basic state of mind of Dasein" (179) and "one of the most far-reaching and most primordial possibilities of disclosure" because "Dasein becomes accessible as simplified in a certain manner" (226; see also Käufer 2021, 74). A few years later, in *The Fundamental Concepts of Metaphysics*, it is profound boredom, as will become apparent in the next chapter, that is taken up as the fundamental attunement said to be able to reveal Dasein as Dasein, where it is seen "as the basic disposition of our epoch" (Emad 1995, 65; see also Freeman 2021). Both attunements, anxiety and profound boredom, as will become apparent, reveal the temporality that grounds life. What this leads to, then, is that for Heidegger, it is Dasein that reveals the being of beings, that is, the meaning of existence, and for this to unfold, Heidegger relies upon fundamental attunements because they permit a disclosing of Dasein as Dasein. As alluded to earlier, *Being and Time* draws upon anxiety, which is juxtaposed to fear, to reveal the being of beings. The next section turns to Heidegger's discussion of these moods, which are reread as an explication of the being of beings as nothingness.

On the Without-Nature of Fear: Preparing the Way for Anxiety's Disclosure

According to Heidegger,

> If the existential analytic of Dasein is to retain clarity in principle as to its function in fundamental ontology, then in order to master its provisional task of exhibiting Dasein's Being, it must seek for one of the *most far-reaching* and *most primordial* possibilities of disclosure—one that lies in Dasein itself. The way of disclosure in which Dasein brings itself before itself must be such that in it Dasein becomes accessible as *simplified* in a certain manner. With what is thus disclosed, the structural totality of the Being we seek must then come to light in an elemental way. (*BT*, 226; emphasis in original)

At least when Heidegger penned these thoughts in *Being and Time*, the "most far-reaching" and "most primordial" attunement was anxiety because anxiety, unlike other attunements, was said to reveal Dasein in a "simplified" and straightforward manner. In other words, anxiety reveals Dasein *as* Dasein, undisguised and unadulterated. A few years later, as will become apparent in the next chapter, profound boredom is invoked by Heidegger as another fundamental attunement that reveals Dasein as Dasein. Thus, it is important to underline, as Gelven (1989, 118) notes, that it is not only anxiety that has revelatory capacities, but rather, that this is what Heidegger chooses in this instance to make his case. To do so, however, Heidegger must prepare the way for such an existential analytic, and to do this he first discusses the mood of fear which is described as "the kindred phenomenon of" anxiety (*BT*, 227).

To situate the relevance and import of fear, Heidegger claims that "Dasein's Being reveals itself in *care*" (*BT*, 227; emphasis in original). Care can be thought of as the being of Dasein (see Blattner 2021a, 137; Haugeland 2013, 227, 230). To say that the being of Dasein is care is to say that Dasein is concerned with the care of itself, its very being. This means that Dasein is necessarily future-oriented. In other words, the temporality of Dasein is one that privileges the future, pertaining to, as noted above, the possibilities available to Dasein.

"Like every ontological analysis," Heidegger writes, "the ontological Interpretation of Dasein as care, with whatever we may gain from such an Interpretation, lies far from what is accessible to the pre-ontological understanding of Being or even to our ontical acquaintance with entities" (*BT*, 227). In other words, Heidegger is claiming, as alluded to before, that much preparatory work needs to be undertaken to fully reveal Dasein in its purity. "Accordingly," Heidegger writes, "our existential Interpretation of Dasein as care requires pre-ontological confirmation. This lies in demonstrating that no sooner has Dasein expressed anything about itself to itself, than it has already interpreted itself as care, even though it has done so only pre-ontologically" (227; emphasis omitted). This pre-ontological confirmation is undertaken by examining the mood of fear and its relation to care: it is through fear that Heidegger can illustrate that beings care—specifically, that they care about their existence. However, as noted before, fear can only illuminate this up to a certain point, and it is through anxiety that Heidegger is able to fully bring this point to its rightful conclusion.

Heidegger claims there are three related "points of view" through which fear must be examined: "that in the face of which" one fears, "fearing," and "that about which" one fears (*BT*, 179). Concerning the first, Heidegger notes that "that in the face of which we fear, the 'fearsome', is in every case something which we encounter within-the-world" (179; emphasis omitted). This fearing, Heidegger says, "can be characterized as threatening" (179). To say that fear emanates from "within-the-world" is to say that it does not emerge from within the individual, but from without. This is important because it is from the without-nature of fear that the potentiality for its threatening character is found. To say that something is threatening, Heidegger explains, is to claim that this something "has detrimentality as its kind of involvement" (179), that is, this something is detrimental to being. This detrimentality, Heidegger writes, "is itself *made definite*, and *comes from a definite region*," but "is not yet within striking distance...but it is coming close" (179–180; emphasis added). The threatening character, in other words, emanates from being at a striking distance, which is to say that it is either nearby or perceived to be so. Here, the without-nature of fear is illuminated, for the steps from which something moves from being innocuous to being a concern is situated in a specific object with a specific locus and time frame that originate from the outside: as "that which is detrimental draws close and is close by...[w]e [can] say," Heidegger writes, that "'[i]t is fearsome'" (180).[2]

Two important points emerge from this. First, it is possible to see not only the process by which an object gets turned into something to be feared, but also that this is always something that emanates from without, never from within. This, as will become clear, is an important distinction between fear and anxiety underlined by Heidegger.[3] Secondly, and related, the locus and source of fear is *definite*. That is, there is nothing indefinite nor indeterminate about fear. A subject can precisely say what is causing fear in him/her, as in, "I am afraid of the impending snowstorm." Here it is something specific, a snowstorm, emanating from without, at some point in time, that is the source of fear. This, too, as will become apparent, separates anxiety from fear, for it is indefiniteness and indeterminacy that characterize (that which leads to) anxiousness (as in the case of profound boredom as well, discussed in the next chapter).

Given the foregoing, it is possible to see that in the process of fearing—the second vantage point from which Heidegger examines fear—something needs to transpire to turn the object in question into a concern about a threat, one that is detrimental to being, and as such, the relation between care and its future-oriented nature becomes evident. As Heidegger says, "[i]n fearing as such, what we have thus characterized as threatening is freed and allowed to matter to us" (*BT*, 180; emphasis omitted), and the fact that it matters precipitates the threat being turned into something to fear. The step of coming to fear something, the fearing—the move from point one to point two—is possible because Dasein is always concerned with its being, its existence (Dasein cares for/about itself), and this concern constitutes Dasein. It is, to put it differently, something that is within Dasein, and this within-nature means that Dasein is always on the lookout for things that are detrimental to its being. Thus, Heidegger writes that "[c]ircumspection"—Dasein's urge to be cautious about itself and everything surrounding it—"sees the fearsome because it has fear as its state of mind" (180). This latter point leads to the final

Anxiety and the Revelation of Nothingness 15

vantage point from which to make sense of fear, that is, that about which one fears. This last point, essentially the shift from points one and two to point three, is only possible because Dasein, as noted above, is itself fearful, that is, that it has fear as one of its moods: "That which fear fears about is that very entity which is afraid—Dasein. Only an entity for which in its Being this very Being is an issue, can be afraid. Fearing discloses this entity as endangered and abandoned to itself" (180).

In the Heideggerian perspective, fear should not merely be looked at as a negative, as is common in some sociological—and especially criminological—analyses of the way people relate to external stimuli and sources, perhaps best evinced in the hypotheses laid down in the "broken windows" theory (Wilson and Kelling 1982; Ranasinghe 2012) or even in the scores of self-help manuals that tout a do-it-yourself attitude. Rather, fear has important positive aspects in relation to both the constitution of being and the very cognizance and understanding of it. As Heidegger says, "[f]ear always reveals Dasein in the Being of its 'there', even if it does in varying degrees of explicitness" (*BT*, 180). This statement hints at a particular and important problem: while fear reveals, it appears to do so with limitations; or, to put this differently, while fear reveals it does not do so fully, that is, purely: "Fear discloses Dasein *predominantly in a privative way. It bewilders us and makes us 'lose our heads'.* Fear closes off our endangered Being-in, and yet at the same time lets us see it, so that *when the fear subsided, Dasein must first find its way about again*" (181; emphasis added). That said, fear is that first, and preparatory, step in Dasein recognizing its limits—its mortality (discussed in a later section)—and this has important implications for how beings come to terms with being: "Dasein is in every case concernful Being-alongside. Proximally and for the most part, Dasein *is* in terms of *what* it is concerned with. When this is endangered, Being alongside is threatened" (180–181; emphasis in original).

Fear, as a state of mind of Dasein, reveals, though as already noted, it does not and cannot reveal Dasein as Dasein in a pure manner. As such, Dasein, which is concerned with the care of itself, is unable to take the necessary steps to adequately and properly care for its well-being. This is why Heidegger writes that fear "bewilders us and makes us 'lose our heads'" (181), essentially highlighting that as much as fear discloses, it simultaneously occludes and conceals because of the very nature of fear itself, that is, its inability to be fully transparent owing to its emanation from the without. In expanding upon this, Jonathan McKenzie (2008, 575; emphasis omitted) notes that for Heidegger, "[f]ear is inauthentic because it backs away from itself and it does not take hold of any definite possibility." Here, inauthenticity—as discussed in the introduction—concerns the fact that beings are separated and distanced from their essence because they fail to come to terms with what it means to exist: namely, that beings are social creatures to whom the world matters, but also that this world inhibits them and their progress (see Käufer 2021), which is to say that the very possibilities open to beings in relation to breaking free from the strictures of the world are foreclosed to them (see also Nichols 2014, 39–58). Anxiety, on the other hand, as will become apparent in the next sections, reveals in a clearer manner, and does so by forcing beings to question and examine their very selves without any pretensions.

Preparing the Way for an Existential Analytic: Understanding and Possibilities

As noted before, while fear has the capacity to reveal, it is also limited in this capacity. Specifically, fear is unable to reveal the being of beings: that being can be thought of as nothingness, and that nothingness is revealed in the ontological homelessness of beings. The disclosing of the world to beings Heidegger refers to as "understanding" and writes that it is "one possible kind of cognizing among others" (*BT*, 182; emphasis omitted). Heidegger explains understanding as "the existential Being of Dasein's own potentiality-for-Being; and it is so in such a way that this Being discloses in itself what its Being is capable of" (184; emphasis omitted). Put simply, understanding refers to the capacity of, and how, beings—via the conscience of Dasein—come to see and realize the state and status of their existence. This means that understanding can be thought of as Dasein's *vision*, its ability to see the state of its being. Heidegger refers to this as "Dasein's '*sight*'" (186; emphasis in original). Understanding, then, reveals to beings by letting them see themselves vis-à-vis the world.

Being-in-the-world, Heidegger claims, means that beings will have immersed themselves—Heidegger calls it falling or fallenness—into what he calls the they-self, essentially embracing what the world has to offer. This leads to "a mode of *groundless floating*" (221; emphasis added), which already hints at the way beings go through their lives with little to no consideration of/about it. Mugerauer (2008, 28) writes that this "everydayness substantially focuses on comfort and ease, on the lack of distress, and thus amounts to dwelling in the familiar, convenient and reliable." As such, there is little questioning of oneself vis-à-vis the world (because the need to so question is rendered null), which all but eviscerates the possibility of probing and appreciating the meaning of existence. In the state of groundless floating, it is as if Dasein is "tranquilized" and, as a result, "drifts along towards alienation in which its ownmost potentiality-for-Being is hidden from it" (*BT*, 222). That is, in such a state, "alienation closes off from Dasein its authenticity and possibility" (222; emphasis omitted) and, as a result, Dasein is unable to realize its "full potential" (Mugerauer 2008, 34).

By "alienation," Heidegger refers to the emptiness, perhaps meaninglessness, of life, despite an apparent fullness of/about the world. This means that the full potential of beings cannot be realized because they are focused, even fixated, upon the now. The now is whatever it is that grounds and constitutes beings as they are in the world, be it technology (certainly a significant issue facing beings presently, especially if one thinks in terms of addiction) or, for present purposes, property and housing (and home). The time and focus spent on the "now," especially given that such a focus is read as contentment, even joy, of/with life, means that it is not possible to look forward in terms of potentialities (Nielsen and Skotnicki 2019, 121) because the need to so look and search is not evident. As a result, the potential to realize one's true self, one's essence, is all but lost. As Kelly Nielsen and Tad Skotnicki (2019, 113) put it, alienation has to do with an absent or deficient relationship with oneself and one's world, which necessarily means that one is unable to fully maximize and realize one's potential. Such inauthenticity, however, speaks not merely to the fact that beings fail to progress but that their current status is one that is constituted by unfreedom, precisely the point made about the perils of inauthenticity (see also Nichols 2014).

Despite the foregoing, it should be underlined that Heidegger is uninterested in imputing a value—such as good or bad—to such lives or even to the ways they unfold. Rather, he is highlighting that beings are uninterested in—and thus unaware of—the meaning of existence. It is this lack of awareness of/about the meaning of life and the absence of any interest in probing it that Heidegger refers to as alienation. It is alienation that gives rise to inauthenticity. In other words, an inauthentic life, for Heidegger, is a life that fails to come to terms with *its* meaning (see also Mugerauer 2008, 37).

It is from this very place of alienation that the possibility of understanding the meaning of existence also emanates, and this is precisely why, as alluded to above, Heidegger wishes not to impute value on it. As he puts it, "this alienation cannot mean that Dasein gets factically torn away from itself. On the contrary, this alienation drives it into a kind of Being which borders on the most exaggerated 'self-dissection', tempting itself with all the possibilities of explanation" (*BT*, 222). This is because, as noted before, what transpires in and through alienation is a revelation—understanding as Heidegger puts it—that beings are, in fact, blind to the being of beings. In this revelation, there is another important and related matter, and this concerns what Heidegger refers to as "possibilities." Specifically, Heidegger speaks of what he calls "projections" and refers to the fact that Dasein projects itself into the future and sees what lies ahead; it is its way of concerning itself with the care of itself. Understanding, Heidegger claims, "has in itself the existential structure of what we call '*projection*'" (184–185; emphasis in original), and projection allows understanding, which, recall, is Dasein's sight (or vision) "to press itself forward into possibilities" (184). For Heidegger, "any Dasein has, as Dasein, already projected itself; and as long as it is, it is projecting. As long as it is, Dasein always has understood itself and always will understand itself in terms of possibilities" (185). By "possibilities," Heidegger means precisely what is meant by the term in the ordinary sense, that is, what is possible, and he speaks of the possibilities open to Dasein as it looks into the future: essentially, authenticity or inauthenticity. It is in projecting, then, that Dasein is able to see the possibilities that lie ahead of itself: "Projection always pertains to the full disclosedness of Being-in-the-world; as potentiality-for-Being, understanding has itself possibilities" (186).

It is when Dasein looks into the future that it understands its possibilities, and an important one for Heidegger is its own mortality. This, Heidegger claims, Dasein can reveal to itself, so that Dasein can see Dasein as Dasein via the state-of-mind of anxiety, and this reveals the temporality of Dasein. To put the foregoing into perspective, recall that in the preceding discussion of fear, Heidegger is clear that fear is unable to truly and fully reveal the possibilities that lie ahead of Dasein: in fear, Dasein is unable to understand its mortality and thus understand that its being is temporal. Instead, in fear Dasein is left bewildered. Anxiety, as the next section argues, is capable of revealing Dasein as Dasein.

The Revelatory Nature of the Paradoxes of Anxiety

Echoing Sigmund Freud (1916–1917/1974, 441), that "there is no question that the problem of anxiety is a nodal point at which the most various and important questions converge, a riddle whose solution would be bound to throw a flood of light on our whole mental existence," Heidegger goes beyond the psychological and claims that "[a]s one of Dasein's possibilities of Being, *anxiety…provides the phenomenal basis for explicitly grasping Dasein's primordial totality of Being*" (*BT*, 227; emphasis added). In other words, and as Dreyfus (1991, 176, 177) explains, Heidegger "needs to find a special method for revealing Dasein's total structure"—that is, Dasein *as* Dasein—and, therefore, "[t]o reveal Dasein simple and whole Heidegger chooses anxiety." For Heidegger, "the basic state-of-mind of anxiety [i]s a *distinctive way* in which Dasein is disclosed," and this is because "in anxiety Dasein gets brought before itself through its own Being…" (*BT*, 228; emphasis added). There is, in other words, as already alluded to, something authentic about anxiety, which is not true, for example, of fear (cf. McKenzie 2008, 575). As Heidegger puts it, "*Fear is* anxiety, fallen into the 'world', *inauthentic*, and, as such, *hidden* from itself" (*BT*, 234; emphasis added). It requires underlining, then, that something profoundly different constitutes fear and anxiety despite being, as noted before, kindred phenomena.[4] Anxiety is closer to the constitution of being than fear and thus provides a portal through which the meaning of existence can be examined.

A lengthy passage introduces the distinction Heidegger carves between (the origins of) fear and anxiety:

> What is the difference phenomenally between that in the face of which anxiety is anxious and that in the face of which fear is afraid? *That in the face of which one has anxiety is not an entity within-the-world.* Thus it is essentially incapable of having an involvement. This threatening does not have the character of *a definite detrimentality* which reaches what is threatened, and which reaches it *with definite regard... That in the face of which one is anxious is completely indefinite.* Not only does this indefiniteness leave factually undecided which entity within-the-world is threatening us, but it also tells us that *entities within-the-world are not 'relevant' at all...[T]he world has the character of completely lacking significance.* In anxiety one does not encounter this thing or that thing which, as something threatening, must have involvement. (*BT*, 231; emphasis added)

This passage highlights several matters of import. First, and to repeat, fear originates from without, anxiety from within. Heidegger is unequivocal about this. The implication of this premise is even more significant: with anxiety, unlike fear, the issue is not about the way *something* gets turned into a threat because of its detrimental nature to being; rather, in anxiety, concern over being reigns supreme—certainly more than with fear—because the threat to being is *already* extant, that is, *ex ante*, to life (cf. Freud 1916–1917/1974, 443; see also Giddens 1984, 44–45).

The most important premise from the above passage, however, needs further elucidation, and this is undertaken in two steps. First, Heidegger is clear that what beings are anxious about is "completely indefinite." Given this, two significant issues arise. First, if something is indefinite, it means that it is not definite, which means that it is, in many (or some) ways, intangible or indeterminate, and this would render it difficult (even impossible) for the subject to clearly articulate, even get a hold or grip of (that is, to get a lucid sense of what the *it* is) (see also Ranasinghe 2020a; 2020b). Second, to claim that definiteness is inexistent is to claim the absence of certainty, precision, and the fixed-nature of something, this something being not only the source of anxiety, but anxiety itself. That is, the uncertainty, imprecision and, most importantly for present purposes, lack of clarity mean that there are no conditions or characteristics that can be extrapolated for the subject to meaningfully make sense of anxiety. To claim, then, that anxiety is indefinite—and, to underline, Heidegger states that this indefiniteness is complete or completely so—is to say that the source of anxiety and, most importantly, anxiety itself, are unclear to the subject and thus are not (easily) subject to clarity and clarification. Unlike fear—which has a clear and definite external source and can be pinpointed and located—anxiety has no such source or locus, and what might look like such is itself murky and confounding. Thus, if Heidegger's premises are followed to their rightful conclusion, it is not just the sources or origins of anxiety that are unclear, but anxiety itself. This is perhaps what leads Matthew Ratcliffe (2013, 172) to claim that "the referent of the term 'anxiety' starts to look a little unclear."

The indefiniteness of anxiety leads to the second part and, with it, the most significant conclusion to draw, namely, that given the lack of clarity about (and surrounding) anxiety, it is, unlike fear, not easily amenable to explication, something that the subject must bear and come to terms with. Indeed, if the argument is followed logically through to the end, what must be concluded is not just that anxiety is not easily explicable but that it is (largely) inexplicable. Heidegger writes that "when something threatening brings itself close, anxiety does not 'see' any definite 'here' or 'yonder' from which it comes. That in the face of which one has anxiety is characterized by the fact that what threatens is *nowhere*" (*BT*, 231; emphasis in original).

Here, the import of *sight*— recall in relation to Dasein's vision and how understanding plays a part in this—and *site* require attention. It is not simply that in anxiety beings are unable to see the source of anxiety, but that this inability to see is a product of the fact that there is *nothing* (read also in terms of *no-thing*, as noted in the introduction) to see (the import of nothing/no-thing will be brought to light shortly). This conclusion is drawn from the fact that a locus of (and for) anxiety does not exist. Anxiety, unlike fear, cannot be properly sited. It can be claimed, for example, that anxiety emanates from the unconscious, that is, the within, as Freud (1916–1917/1974, 459) claims (see also Giddens 1984, 44–45). Yet, this site is not simply vast, but also ambiguous. It exists, but in a paradoxical way, in that it exists—and certainly takes hold of beings—but is simultaneously "nowhere." Crucially, if anxiety is nowhere and yet constitutes being, then, it must be so while also *not-being* and, as well, being nowhere while also concomitantly being somewhere (perhaps, everywhere). Heidegger alludes to this: "Anxiety 'does not know' what that in the face of which it is anxious is…Therefore that which threatens cannot bring itself close from a definite direction within what is close by; it is already 'there', and yet nowhere; it is so close that it is oppressive and stifles one's breath, and yet it is nowhere" (*BT*, 231). If this reasoning is plausible, then, the inexplicable nature of anxiety for the subject must be acknowledged. Anxiety exists but its existence cannot be meaningfully made sense of. It consumes and swallows as a whole, but again, an explanation for it cannot be provided. Anxiety is *the* inexplicable mood that constitutes being. Gelven (1989), who prefers the term *dread* to *anxiety*, though he means the same thing (see 115), describes this inexplicability thus:

> But what is it that I dread? I cannot put my finger on one single object. I cannot say what it is that bothers me in the case of dread. In fact, if one were to ask me what bothers me, I would probably say, 'Nothing'. In saying that I do not mean that I am not bothered at all, but that there is no *thing* that bothers me. What bothers me is my *existence*. (116; emphasis in original)

Before unpacking the significance of the foregoing—the indefiniteness and inexplicability of anxiety—another important point of consideration needs introduction. Another way to conceptualize the nowhere/somewhere paradox of anxiety is through what Heidegger refers to as *the uncanny*. "In anxiety," Heidegger writes, "one feels 'uncanny'" (*BT*, 233). By uncanny, Freud (1919/1997), who popularized its meaning, refers to "something which is secretly familiar, which has undergone repression and then returned from it" (222) so that "the uncanny is the class of the frightening which leads us back to what is known of old and long familiar" (195). The uncanny, to put simply, is the familiarity with something frightening.[5] Drawing on this, Heidegger expands the notion of the uncanny to speak of its intangible nature, which is also implicit in Freud's formulation. With the uncanny, Heidegger says, "the peculiar *indefiniteness* of that which Dasein finds itself alongside in anxiety, comes proximally to expression: the 'nothing and nowhere'. But here 'uncanniness' also means 'not-being-at-home'" (*BT*, 233; emphasis added; see also Mugerauer 2008, 23). One reason that anxiety leaves beings in an indefinite state constituted by the absence of clarity is because it is nowhere, and in this nowhere from which it emerges (itself a paradox), anxiety, which is something, is also nothing (yet another paradox). Thus, to the nowhere/somewhere paradox, it is necessary to also add the nothing/something paradox that constitutes anxiety: anxiety emanates from nowhere and is yet somewhere and is simultaneously something while being nothing (read: no-thing).

All of this points to two important and related features of the state-of-mind of anxiety: the first concerning its indefinite or indeterminate character, the second concerning the difficulties of explicating it and its origins. From this, two important points, yet to be given full consideration, can now be brought to the forefront by rereading Heidegger's analysis of anxiety. These concern how anxiety shines light on the nothingness of being and, second and related, how this nothingness illuminates the ontological homelessness of beings. What follows explicates each, commencing with nothingness and being.

Anxiety and Its Revelation of Being as Nothingness

As explicated above, "the 'nothing'...exhibits itself as that in the face of which one has anxiety" (*BT*, 232). In what follows, Heidegger's reading of anxiety vis-à-vis being is reread as the nothingness of being. As noted in the introduction, nothingness, for Heidegger, refers to the absence of a something, though exactly what that something is, is difficult or impossible to explicate. The term *nothingness* rather than *nothing* (but still related to *no-thing*) is used here—and

Heidegger uses the term *nothingness* as well—because the absence is not nothing in the tangible and precise sense, as in "there is no snow on the ground," but rather *nothing-like*; yet, as already noted, what this something is, is not amenable to full and proper explication. In other words, there is an absence, a something that is missing, though this is uncertain and unclear. There is, then, an indeterminacy—premised upon an indefiniteness—that constitutes nothingness. This comes perfectly to light in anxiety as shown in the preceding section. As noted, anxiety emanates from nowhere but is—and needs to be—somewhere, but exactly where this is, is impossible to say (or locate). Anxiety, then, cannot be sited. Equally, and relatedly, anxiety is a something, but what this something is—this *it*—is difficult, even impossible, to speak of. Here, anxiety cannot be sighted. This means, as noted in the previous section, anxiety is constituted by an indeterminacy based upon its indefiniteness—the paradoxes of something/nothing and somewhere/nowhere and this characterizes and illuminates its nothingness.

To put this into perspective, it is worth focusing on Gelven's (1989, 116–117) lucid explanation of nothingness:

> The existential meaning of "nothingness" is really a rather simple matter. A human being, through the reflection of his own possibilities, becomes aware of his finitude—i.e., he knows he is going to die, to cease to be. The strangeness of this feeling cannot be compared to any other form of human experience, since all other forms of experience are structured in a continuum of time in which the continuation of existence plays an essential role. But in death, or in the awareness of the meaninglessness of existence, one is aware of something quite unlike any experience. To call this "nothingness" might seem an outrage to language—but any term used to designate that which in principle is incapable of being experienced will be an outrage to language. The term "nothingness" is really quite apt; for what is meant is something that is indeed existentially significant, but is incapable of being the object of experience.[6]

Gelven focuses upon the inability of an object to be experienced as the criterion of nothingness, which is certainly in keeping with what

Heidegger claims:

> [T]he state-of-mind which can hold open the utter and constant threat to itself arising from Dasein's ownmost individualized Being, is anxiety. In this state of mind, Dasein finds itself face to face with the "nothing" of the possible impossibility of its existence [read: death]. Anxiety is anxious about the potentiality-for-Being of the entity so destined, and in this way it discloses the uttermost possibility. (*BT*, 310; emphasis omitted)[7]

As such, it is possible to appreciate the fate that befalls beings vis-à-vis their inability to explicate the nothingness that constitutes their being. As Heidegger puts it, "[a]nxiety is anxious in the face of the 'nothing' of the world" and "our concernful awaiting finds nothing in terms of which it might be able to understand itself; it clutches at the 'nothing' of the world" (*BT*, 393). Thus, the inability to articulate the paradoxes that constitute anxiety can be thought of as a product of the nothingness of being. It is in this way that Heidegger's discussion of being can be reread to disclose the being of beings as nothingness.

It is possible to now ask: how is it that nothingness comes to constitute being? To fully bring this to light, focus is cast on an essay penned by Heidegger a few years after the publication of *Being and Time*, titled "What is Metaphysics?" Heidegger writes that "[a]nxiety reveals the nothing" (WIM, 101), that is, *no*-thing. This is because, even though a feeling of unease exists or persists because of anxiety, it is difficult, if not impossible, to explicate why such a feeling envelops, permeates, consumes, and swallows one. "We can," Heidegger says, "get no hold on things" and thus "[i]n the slipping away of beings only this 'no hold on things' comes over us and remains" (101). This means, Heidegger says, that "anxiety leaves us hanging" (101) and rather unsettled, that is, without firm footing or ground(ing) to know and understand being. "In this altogether unsettling experience," he writes, "there is nothing [again read: no-thing] to hold on to" (101), even though one is still "hanging" or at least has a profound sense or need to hang (onto something). In other words, and most crucially, one is hanging onto nothing (no-thing). What remains is an emptiness that is, however, or at the same time, not empty. It is this indeterminacy that is here read as nothingness: "We must say that that in the face of which and for which we were anxious was 'properly'—nothing. Indeed: the nothing itself—as such was there" (101). The very attempt to explicate anxiety—itself something yet nothing, itself somewhere but nowhere—only leaves beings bewildered (just as fear does), because there is a constant grasping onto something that needs immediate and grave explication but one that cannot be (easily) provided. Dreyfus (1991, 180) explains this as follows:

> Anxiety is thus the disclosure accompanying a Dasein's preontological sense that it is not the source of the meanings it uses to understand itself; that the public world makes no intrinsic sense for it and would go on whether that particular Dasein existed or not. In anxiety Dasein discovers that it has no meaning or content of its own; nothing individualizes it but its empty thrownness.

Thus, it is possible to see that anxiety reveals a something that certainly emanates from somewhere or something but in the same breath leaves beings "hanging." It leaves beings in such a predicament because beings seek desperately to make sense of what this something is and where it originates from, even though it originates from nowhere and thus, this something becomes a missing-something that cannot be explicated. This is the nothingness of being, which it is claimed here, anxiety shines light upon. To put this differently, anxiety shines light upon a fullness that is, in fact, empty, and an emptiness that is equally full: the nothingness of being.

None of this is nor should it be read as problematic. The opposite is precisely the case. Heidegger, as mentioned repeatedly, is solely interested in shining light upon the being of beings. In so doing, what is claimed here is that his reading of being can be read as nothingness, from which it is possible to understand the possible inauthenticity of human existence. This is because nothingness casts light upon the ontological homelessness that constitutes beings. The final section of this chapter seeks to bring this aspect to the forefront.

Anxiety, Nothingness, and Ontological Homelessness

Uncanniness, Heidegger states, "pursues Dasein constantly" (*BT*, 234). As such, Heidegger alludes to the fact that, constitutionally, Dasein is homeless, that is, not at home, and it is this that Dasein seeks to reveal to itself. As already explicated, anxiety permits Heidegger to reveal how beings are hanging, but hanging onto nothing (no-thing) despite the sense that they are hanging onto something (and the profound sense that they need to hang onto something, anything). This signifies that beings are hanging onto an emptiness, one which is, however, veiled as the fullness of everyday world. Thus, Heidegger explains that "Being-in," that is, being-in-the-world, "enters into the existential 'mode' of the '*not-at-home*'" (233; emphasis in original), and it is this homelessness that Heidegger is interested in unveiling and bringing to the fore. To be, then, for Heidegger, is to be homeless, and this homelessness, as the preceding section shows, is that of nothingness, an indefinite sense of being where one's authenticity is premised and grounded upon the very foundation that one is inauthentic, though one is cognizant of and has fully come to terms with this fate, what is essentially the paradox of human existence.

All this unfolds as follows. Being-in-the-world entails a falling into the they-self, essentially imbibing everything (or almost everything) the world offers, and often, such offerings appear to provide the freedom of choice, when, in fact, the opposite is precisely the case (one can think of Heidegger's cautionary note in "The Question Concerning Technology," to get a sense of this, and while that caution might appear to be abstract theorization, two examples of the virtual inability to live without a credit card or a cellphone and the applications (apps) that come with them, put into perspective how much and how far the ethos of society consumes and constitutes beings). In such falling, "we flee *into* the 'at home' of publicness" (*BT*, 234; emphasis in original). In other words, in embracing the world and what it has to offer, beings feel at home and believe that this is the fulfillment of life. In this instance, as noted before, Dasein is trapped in an inauthentic state of "groundless floating" (221). Thus, in this feeling, as noted above, beings, Heidegger claims, "flee *in the face of* the 'not-at-home'; that is, we flee in the face of uncanniness which lies in

Dasein—in Dasein as thrown Being-in-the-world, which has been delivered over to itself in its Being" (234; emphasis in original).

For Heidegger, then, the more beings embrace the world (and, as noted above, there is no choice in this matter given the impossibility of extricating oneself from the world) the more beings are, ontologically, homeless, because they are driven further and further away from their very essence, and this is the inauthenticity of beings that is a product of failing to recognize the very homelessness that grounds life. This is why Heidegger claims that beings are unable to see that they are, in fact, homeless and living inauthentic lives. Inauthenticity, as noted in the introduction, refers to the inability (or refusal) to see and appreciate the homelessness that constitutes the being of beings (or, to put this another way, to see that the being of beings *is* homelessness) and to understand that being-in-the-world is, and largely can only be, homeless (this would mean, unsurprisingly, that authenticity refers to the capacity to come to terms with the homelessness of life, which, as will be developed in chapters three and four, is the very condition and basis for coming and being at home). This is also why Heidegger claims that "from an existential-ontological point of view, the 'not-at-home' must be conceived as the more primordial phenomenon" (*BT*, 234; emphasis omitted), suggesting that the essence of beings is homelessness (and, as will be revealed in later chapters, this homelessness is *the* ground upon which a homecoming can be conceptualized and realized). As such, the failure or, inability or, refusal to see, appreciate, and come to terms with the homelessness of beings is the very condition of inauthenticity.

As alluded to before, this is precisely what concerns Heidegger: to reveal the homelessness of beings and the inauthenticity of a life that fails to come to terms with its homelessness. "With regard to Dasein," Heidegger notes, "'that *nothing* ensues' signifies something *positive*" (*BT*, 324; emphasis in original). What is positive is that the being of beings—the meaning of existence—is (or can be) clearly revealed to beings: that their being is one of homelessness. Or, to put this another way, what is revealed is that what beings are hanging onto is, in fact, nothing, and the nothing—what is referred to as nothingness to capture the sense of a something that is not there—is representative of their homelessness. This is the redemptive aspect of anxiety, a redemption of (and about) being *as* being in its true self, brought to the fore and illuminated brightly. To a large extent, this is because of a particular quality about anxiety that is capable of revealing the being of beings—to be precise, this is applicable only to what Heidegger calls "'real' anxiety," which he says is "rare" (BT, 234). This is the fact that anxiety individualizes and brings each being in front of him/herself, so to speak:

> *[I]n anxiety there lies the possibility of a disclosure which is quite distinctive*; for anxiety individualizes. This individualization brings Dasein back from its falling [the failure to see it in its truest sense], and makes manifest to it that authenticity and *inauthenticity* are possibilities of its Being. These basic possibilities of Dasein...show themselves in anxiety. (235; emphasis added)

Gelven (1989, 118; emphasis omitted) says this in another way:

> We dread our being able to be ourselves. Since dread puts us before ourselves, naked, as it were, we are now aware of the possibilities: either to be genuinely ourselves, or to lose ourselves once more in the comforting chatter of the "they." It is in tranquility and everydayness that one can avoid one's self, though one can turn away from it. That's what dread is. It is the uncanny awareness of the self as free to be either authentic or inauthentic.[8]

The disclosing that Heidegger (or the awareness that Gelven) speaks of comes from Dasein via its conscience and the call it makes to itself. That is, "The caller is Dasein in its uncanniness: primordial, thrown Being-in-the-world as the 'not-at-home'—the bare 'that-it-is' in the 'nothing' of the world" (BT, 321). The call, Heidegger says, "is what makes it possible first and foremost for Dasein to project itself upon its ownmost potentiality-for-Being" (322). Thus, "[u]ncanniness [read: homelessness] reveals itself authentically in the basic state-of-mind of anxiety; and, as the most elemental way in which thrown Dasein is disclosed, it puts Dasein's Being-in-the-world face to face with the 'nothing' of the world; in the face of this 'nothing', Dasein is anxious with anxiety about its ownmost potentiality-for-Being" (321).

What anxiety does, then, that fear does not is reveal the essence of being: essentially the paradoxes of life, but more precisely, that life lived in the world renders beings ontologically homeless. Even more acutely, what anxiety reveals is that there is simply no way around the homelessness of beings: homelessness constitutes the essence of being. As repeatedly noted, ontological homelessness ought not to be viewed pejoratively. Such a value judgment is not intended here nor does Heidegger intend such a pejoration. Rather, ontological homelessness highlights a basic but nonetheless significant point about the constitution of beings: beings are homeless and the essence of being is homelessness. This state of homelessness is reread here as (and from) the nothingness of beings, which speaks to the indeterminacy of the meaning of existence: that beings are "home" in the world (and in some ways have no choice but to make themselves at home in the world), even though this being home is a status of not being (at) home. Thus, ontological homelessness captures the status of beings. It is the failure to come to terms with the essence of being that is read as inauthenticity, which is developed further in later chapters. This means—and necessarily entails—that beings engage in myriad things of and about the world to seek to offset such homelessness, which, however, are far from able to ensure that beings are home (see Gelven 1989, 74–75). In the same vein, via anxiety, Dasein is prodded to reveal to itself not simply this inauthenticity, but also that authenticity is a possibility to itself. With the latter, Heidegger claims, beings can understand that they are homeless and prepare their way to return home, which essentially amounts to embracing the meaning of existence: that is, not merely the homelessness of beings, but that the very status of being (at) home is to be in this very homelessness.

2

Profound Boredom

THE PREVIOUS CHAPTER examined Heidegger's invocation of the moods of fear and anxiety, which he uses to help shed light on the being of beings, that is, the meaning of existence. Fear, which emanates from without, is unable to disclose being purely; anxiety, conversely, discloses being fully and truthfully because it emanates from within. As such, anxiety reveals what Heidegger calls the "utter insignificance" of life (*BT*, 231; see also Käufer 2005, 487). In rereading Heidegger's discussion of anxiety (and fear), chapter one claimed that the indeterminacy of anxiety, pertaining to both its origins and constitution (revealed in the two paradoxes of nowhere/somewhere and nothing/something), helps situate and make sense of the nothingness that constitutes the lives of beings. Chapter one was largely devoted to substantiating the claim that it is possible, indeed fruitful, to reread Heidegger's exposition of being as one of nothingness: that being is—or, at least can be read as—nothingness, an indeterminacy that holds beings in flux, pertaining to their inherent homelessness, even while they simultaneously perceive themselves to be at "home."

In *Being and Time*, anxiety was upheld as capable of revealing the being of beings. A few years after *Being and Time*, another state of mind, profound boredom, is introduced by Heidegger in *The Fundamental Concepts of Metaphysics* (in fact, the attunement of boredom was first mentioned in *The Concept of Time*, though only in passing). With this work, it becomes clear that there exist several attunements, anxiety and profound boredom being two, that are capable of revealing the being of beings. Neither anxiety nor profound boredom is privileged over the other, and perhaps more importantly, the discussion of the latter and the conclusion Heidegger reaches through it "builds upon the insight developed in *Being and Time*" (Goodstein 2005, 305; cf. Svendsen 2005, 132), though, as will become evident in this chapter, there are important points of departure. Partly, the turn to boredom must be contextually understood: Heidegger saw boredom not merely as a "potent disposition" but "as the basic disposition of our epoch" (Emad 1985, 64) or the "'fundamental mood' of modernity" (Goodstein 2005, 297). Thus, boredom served as the eminent means to disclose the being of beings in that period.

As such, it could be claimed that these moods are, and operate as, historical categories. Such a claim would be fair to the extent that it is understood that Dasein is social, which is to say, as explicated in the previous chapter, that Dasein cannot be understood apart from nor extricated from the world it finds itself in. This would mean that boredom—any mood for that matter—is social and thus historical. Yet moods—or, ontologically, states of mind—cannot be *reduced* to historical categories because Heidegger is interested in utilizing them to reveal a truth about being, one reread here as nothingness, which is not necessarily unique to a historical epoch.

Additionally, that boredom is a significant topic of conversation today, even so almost one hundred years after Heidegger's discussion of it, appears to suggest that it cannot necessarily be reduced to a historical moment (it can certainly be read as such, but not reduced to it), especially when considering its origins and etymology (cf. Kuhn 1976; Spacks 1995; Goodstein 2005; see also Ranasinghe [2020b] for the [dis]connections and [dis]continuities between forms of malaise that culminate in boredom). Perhaps more importantly, however, relegating boredom to a historical phenomenon tends to tie it largely or strictly to an emotion and this would negate the Heideggerian endeavour because it would examine the subject solely at the ontical level and fail to examine the profound ontological implications.

This chapter examines Heidegger's discussion of boredom, pertaining to both superficial boredom and profound boredom (also referred to as deep boredom). Unlike anxiety (which, recall, reveals the *insignificance* of life), profound boredom, Heidegger claims, leaves beings completely *indifferent* to things or beings, "a comprehensive and all encompassing indifference" (Emad 1985, 74). In indifference, it is possible to appreciate the indeterminacy that frames the lives of beings, and that is drawn upon in this chapter to make a case for being as nothingness.

As already alluded to, the discussion of boredom continues the work commenced in *Being and Time*, and most importantly, expands upon it. In anxiety, the insignificance that comes to frame life is constituted by temporality, one pertaining to the future-looking nature of beings: that beings are mortal (recall, however, that by death Heidegger does not mean dying in the orthodox sense, as in perishing). *The Fundamental Concepts of Metaphysics* expands upon the import of temporality (and time) to the being of beings, but in a more relatable manner because the focus is upon an everyday and ubiquitous phenomenon that can only—and easily—be experienced in the present: that of how time is passed, spent, even managed. What the discussion of boredom shows is the way time profoundly matters to and shapes beings. Drawing upon Heidegger's detailed exposition of boredom—superficial and two forms of profound boredom, one being the profoundest, each of which is given significant attention—this chapter examines the relation between the fundamental attunement of profound boredom and temporality, and as such, rereads Heidegger's exposition of profound boredom as evidencing the being of beings as nothingness.

Fundamental Attunements

As explicated in the previous chapter, Heidegger's ontological inquiry does not permit a direct engagement with being and thus requires preparatory work in the way of an ontical inquiry. For this, Heidegger relies upon moods or attunements to reveal Dasein as Dasein. An attunement, as noted in the previous chapter, "has to do with the innermost essence of man's being, with his Dasein" (*FCM*, 63; emphasis omitted). To put this differently, "[a]ttunements are the '*how*' according to which one is in such and such a way" (67; emphasis in original). Boredom is one such attunement and *The Fundamental Concepts of Metaphysics* explores the way the fundamental attunement of profound boredom (in juxtaposition to the attunement of superficial boredom) provides a portal to access Dasein as Dasein, and thus being itself.

For boredom to be able to reveal Dasein, and through it being, Heidegger is clear that "[w]e must awaken a fundamental attunement" (*FCM*, 69) and to do so "is a manner and means of grasping Da-sein with respect to the specific 'way' in which it is, of grasping Da-sein as Da-sein, or better: of letting Da-sein be as it is, or can be, as Da-sein" (68). What Heidegger means by awakening an attunement in practice "does not mean making it awake in the first place, but *letting it be awake, guarding against it falling asleep*" (79; emphasis in original). In other words, profound boredom is already extant, already awake, and the task is to ensure that it remains so. Letting profound boredom remain or stay awake is paramount for Heidegger because "he believes that we are…'asleep' in our everyday pastimes in our actual life" (Svendsen 2005, 116) of the "they." In other words, humans have fallen far away from—and are quite uninterested in, and essentially have no way to return to—the essence that constitutes them, the very essence of humanity (partly because beings are uninterested in returning to their essence since the very need to return is not evident to them because they are asleep, so to speak). Heidegger finds this a "destructive sleep," destructive to humanity, to the authenticity of life, "because it conceals the true possibilities" open to humanity (Svendsen 2005, 116; see also Ranasinghe 2020a). Thus, letting profound boredom be or remain awake is the primary focus of *The Fundamental Concepts of Metaphysics*.

Boredom, Structural Moments, and Time and Temporality

As already noted, *The Fundamental Concepts of Metaphysics* is an exhortation to let profound boredom remain awake, that is, not be muzzled and restrained. (Beyond abstract theorization, and as an aside, this is relevant to and evident in what transpires today with the scores of complaints from people, especially students, about how bored they are, and the myriad activities undertaken to combat or overcome boredom.) Heidegger engages this task by examining the essence of boredom, starting first with superficial boredom and culminating with the profoundest boredom. Prior to so doing, however, Heidegger explicates two *structural moments* of boredom that are common to every form of boredom, though the way these structures exist and unfold are significantly different. These moments are "being held in limbo" and "being empty in time."

Even the most cursory look at these structures immediately reveals their relation to time: they are, before anything else, "moments," which already evokes duration. According to Heidegger, "Boredom, *Langeweile*—whatever its ultimate essence may be—shows, particularly in our German word, an almost obvious relation to time, a way in which we stand with respect to time, a feeling of time. Boredom and the question of boredom thus lead us to *the problem of time*" (*FCM*, 80; emphasis added). Time, in other words, is heavily implicated and involved in any understanding of boredom. According to the translators of *The Fundamental Concepts of Metaphysics*, "The German *Langeweile* literally means 'long while' and Heidegger, taking this up, will argue that the various forms of boredom are ultimately nothing other than various ways in which *time temporalizes*" (McNeill and Walker 1995, xx–xxi; emphasis added). It is possible to see that the words *long* and *while* already point to time: both point to a duration, which, in this context, can only be made sense of and measured in time. The word *boredom* in English, however, (and unfortunately), does not fully disclose and reveal boredom's relation to time. *The Oxford English Dictionary*, for example, defines boredom as "the state of being bored," and the term bored as "feeling tired and impatient because one is doing something dull or one has nothing to do." These ways of explicating boredom do not reference time or temporality and, as such, what Heidegger has in mind about the essence of the term is possibly lost on the English-language reader and for good reason given that there is no mention of any semblance of time to such a way of feeling (in contrast to the above quoted passage on *Langeweile*, where the word time appears four times). As such, the term boredom in English "is unable to convey the temporal sense which Heidegger makes central to his phenomenological analysis" (McNeill and Walker 1995, xx). For Heidegger, boredom and time, specifically temporality, go together, and it is in this relation that the essence of boredom can be gleaned: "[B]oredom is only possible at all because each thing, as we say, has *its* time. If each thing did not have *its* time, then there would be no boredom" (*FCM*, 105; emphasis in original).

As noted in chapter one, time refers to linear time (the time of the clock) while temporality refers to the relation of beings to linear time. That is, temporality concerns the way being is conditioned by time, which can be thought of as how time moves and drives beings in specific ways and in specific directions. In *The Fundamental Concepts of Metaphysics*, Heidegger notes that in "boredom...we find, as we ourselves say, that time becomes drawn out, becomes long" (*FCM*, 78). Elsewhere in the text he says this differently: "We pass the time in order to master it, because time becomes long in boredom. Time becomes long for us" (80). What is at issue here, then, is the length of time, which, in boredom, is or appears to be stretched. Heidegger's detailed explication of passing the time puts this into perspective:

> What is at issue in boredom is a while, tarrying a while, a peculiar remaining, enduring. And thus time, after all. And as opposed to that, passing the time. In such passing the time we see the peculiar comportment of continually pulling out our watch, the watch by which we measure time. Thus what is decisive in passing, and indeed in *what* it shakes off, namely boredom, is, after all, time. Passing the time is therefore a shortening of time that drives time on, namely the time that seeks to become long. It is thus an intervention into time as a *confrontation with time*. We must therefore begin here and ask what is happening to time in this context, how we relate to time, and so on. (96; emphasis in original)

At the very outset, what Heidegger means by the term *Langeweile* is plainly evident not simply in the explicit reference to time but also given that the concept of time is temporalized, as when, for example, it is referred to as "long," and this long-ness is birthed in the "drawn-out" feeling that envelopes beings, a feeling they are forced—or feel forced—to grapple with. The drawn-out nature of the relation between this feeling and time, which is long, means that beings are found "making an effort, whether consciously or unconsciously, to pass time" (78).

After situating the import of temporality to boredom, Heidegger asks: "Yet what does it mean to say that we *drive away* and *shake off* boredom?" (*FCM*, 79; emphasis in original). He adds:

> We constantly cause it to *fall asleep*. For evidently we cannot annihilate it by passing the time, however intensively. We "know"—in a strange kind of knowing—that boredom can return at any time. Thus it is already there. We shake it off. We succeed in making it fall asleep. We wish to know nothing about it. This does not at all mean that we do not wish to be conscious of it, but rather that we do not wish to let it be awake. (79; emphasis in original)

What Heidegger is alluding to is that the desire to pass time—because of a desire to drive away and shake off boredom—results in a situation where the possibilities for/of understanding existence become impossible because the ability of Dasein to speak is silenced when boredom is put to sleep. Heidegger refers to boredom as an "*insidious creature* that maintains its *monstrous* essence in our Dasein" (79; emphasis added) (it is important to note that in this context he is speaking specifically about superficial boredom). This way of phrasing the matter is intentional and significant: boredom, like a creature, is something with immense power to move; boredom also has effects that are immensely harmful, hence the term monstrous; however, these effects move subtly and gradually, so that beings are unable to fully see and realize what is transpiring. What beings fail to see, as will be developed throughout the chapter, is that it is not boredom that is the problem; the problem is the silencing of boredom. This is why beings are eager to put boredom to sleep and why Heidegger is adamant that it needs to be kept awake.

It is worth underlining, even if digressing somewhat, that Heidegger's concerns are far from philosophical musings. Boredom is seen by many individuals as an ill or an evil that ought to be eradicated lest the quality of their lives be threatened. This, for example, is evident in the complaints of those in the workforce (Roy [1959] is perhaps the classic study; see also Fisher [1993]), and boredom is said to be responsible for myriad deviancies, especially in law enforcement (see Ratcliffe et al. 2011, 807; Phillips 2016, 581–582; Steinmetz, Schaefer, and Green 2017, 352). Similarly, among the population that is materially homeless, numerous efforts are undertaken to attend to boredom (see Desjarlais 1997, 87–94, 123–128; Liebow 1993, 26–32; Snow and Anderson 1993, 127). In juxtaposition to this, there is voluminous literature, largely in philosophy, that has underlined the import of boredom to the essence of life and cultivating its quality (see Barthes 1973/1975, 25–26; Beckett 1931, 16; Bauman 2000, 1; Phillips 1993, 78). Perhaps the two well known examples are Gaston Bachelard's (1958/1994, 16–17) imperative that boredom creates the potentiality and space for freedom, a concept of immense import for what is discussed here, as well as Walter Benjamin's (1936/1970, 91) equation of boredom as the apogee of mental relaxation (as sleep is to physical relaxation). Heidegger's endeavour can be fitted within the latter line of inquiry, one designed to bring beings face-to-face with the essence of their very being, which would function as a direct critique of and antidote to the efforts to counteract boredom especially when it is viewed as inimical to the well-being of life.

As alluded to, Heidegger's focus is to temporalize boredom, which already connotes its inextricability from time. Thus, the symptoms of boredom—"wearisome, tedious; it does not stimulate and excite, it does not give anything, has nothing to say to us, does not concern us in any way" (*FCM*, 84)—can only be meaningfully understood if boredom is situated in time and understood as a temporal aspect of being. Thus, boredom might leave the subject weary and it might leave a feeling that nothing is happening; however, these feelings emerge only because beings are in relation with/to time that cannot be severed. Thus, it is the temporality of beings that grounds boredom and any understanding or appreciation of it.

To put this into perspective, Heidegger locates boredom—or, properly, what he will call boringness—not simply in the object but also in the subject. Thus, immediately after the above-quoted passage on the wearisome, tedious, and unexciting nature of boredom, Heidegger notes:

> [I]f we explain whatever is boring in this way, we have indeed unexpectedly proceeded to interpret the initially objective character of the book's boringness as something which *concerns us in such and such a way* and therefore stands in such and such a relation to us as subjects, to our subjectivity, influences us in such and such a way, determines our attunement. Then boringness is not some exclusive objective property of the book after all, such as its bad cover, for instance. The characteristic of "boring" thus *belongs to the object* [e.g., a book] and is at the same time *related to the subject* [the reader]. (*FCM*, 84; emphasis in original)

Boringness, then, is located (or found) in the subject–object relation. This is because "even those properties of things which are apparently most objective are related to the subject" (84). This means that "[c]haracteristics such as 'boring'...*belong to the object and yet are taken from the subject*" (85–86; emphasis in original). As an example, whether a book is or is not boring depends not simply on the book but on the reader, and this relation or connection is mediated in the way that time is experienced by the subject in relation to that object. The implication of this is that "boredom—and thus ultimately every attunement—is a hybrid, partly objective, partly subjective" (88). The significance of this will become apparent as the chapter unfolds: namely, that boringness, especially when it is profound, is ex ante to beings (in a similar way that anxiety is).

These insights lead Heidegger to note that "[w]e are not really starting from boredom, but from *boringness*...boringness is what makes something *boring* what it is whenever it is *boring* us" (*FCM*, 82; emphasis in original). To say that the inquiry concerns boringness rather than boredom is Heidegger's attempt to underline that the essence of boredom is what needs exploration and explication. "Perhaps we do not understand *this* [profound] boredom," Heidegger says, "because we do not at all understand boredom *in its essence*. Perhaps we do not understand its essence because it *has never yet become essential* for us" (81; emphasis in original).

It is through the temporality of boredom, then, that Heidegger seeks to situate the universality of boredom, what has thus far been spoken of as its essence. To do this, Heidegger refers to two structural moments found in all forms of boredom: being held in limbo and being left empty. Heidegger argues that these moments are "tailored to one another, structurally interlinked" (*FCM*, 107) in a way that aids in disclosing the essence of boredom. This, however, which is related to the hybridity of boredom noted above, needs further unpacking.

Returning to the example of the boringness of the book, Heidegger claims that the book is deemed boring because, at the very outset, "we do not at all understand 'boring' as though it were synonymous with inducing boredom" (*FMC*, 86). That is, "[w]e straightaway take 'boring' as meaning *wearisome, tedious*" (86; emphasis in original). Wearisome and tedious, however, for Heidegger, do not imply and should not be read as *indifference*. That is, beings are not wearisome and tedious, and thus claim to be bored, because they are indifferent to a thing. Rather, the opposite is the case: beings are partial to a thing and expect something from or out of it, and it is this that leads to a feeling such as weariness. That is, "if something is wearisome and tedious, then this entails that it has not left us completely indifferent, but on the contrary: we are present while reading, given over to it, but not taken by it" (86). Thus, Heidegger underlines that "[w]earisome means: it does not rivet us; we are given over to it, yet not taken by it, but *merely held in limbo by it*" (86–87; emphasis in original). Here, the first structural moment of boredom is revealed: what makes something or someone boring is that a thing or being holds beings in limbo. To hold in limbo means to be held in uncertainty. "Holding in limbo" already evokes and references time: an expectation of/about a thing or being (that it will rivet, for example) that fails to come to fruition within a desired or expected time. It is the breakdown of the expectation—of wanting to be riveted—that holds beings in uncertainty, and this holding, again in relation to a unit of time, precipitates beings to describe such a feeling of/about a thing or being as boring. Thus, it is incontrovertibly the case that an expectation about something or someone in relation to a framework of time is responsible for feelings commonly described as and associated with boredom.

Heidegger continues the discussion of tediousness to explicate the second structural moment of boredom, stating that "[t]edious means: it does not engross us, *we are left empty*" (*FCM*, 87; emphasis in original). Here, because a thing or being does not hold us or engross us, as he says, beings are overwhelmed by a sense that things are long and slow moving. This feeling—again based upon an expectation that does not come to fruition—leaves beings empty, which is to say that something appears to be missing. This missingness (or missing-like feeling) further precipitates that thing or person to be constructed as boring (as this chapter unfolds, this missing-ness will be theorized as an indeterminacy which will then be tied to nothingness). Hence, Heidegger concludes, "that which bores, which is boring, is *that which holds us in limbo and yet leaves us empty*" (87; emphasis in original). In this way, Heidegger can paint a universal picture of boredom. This, however, as Heidegger is at pains to illustrate, is only possible when the temporality of beings is accounted for. That is, being held in limbo and being empty—experiences that emerge in relation to time—are also what force beings to pass time, to seek to drive away and shake off boredom. This is what gives rise to boringness, the essence of boredom. Thus, Heidegger claims that "it is precisely in *passing the time* that we first gain the correct *orientation* in which we can *encounter* boredom *undisguised*. Consequently, we may not make boredom into an object of contemplation as some state that arises on its own, but must consider it in the way that we move within it, i.e., in the way that we seek to drive it away" (91; emphasis in original).

Heidegger's foray into boredom thus far provides, as he says, an "initial gain" or a movement "in the proximity of a proper interpretation" (*FCM*, 87; emphasis omitted). This proper interpretation paves the way toward the essence of boredom (recall that Heidegger must first prepare the way for an ontological inquiry). The essence of boredom, as the foregoing attests, must be obtained from the structural moments of boredom. However, while each form of boredom shares the same structural moments, these moments themselves are fundamentally different in each form. It is important, therefore, to appreciate each moment vis-à-vis different forms of boredom. To do so, Heidegger examines each form in detail, beginning first with superficial boredom and culminating with the profoundest boredom. The discussion of each that follows in this chapter, which should be read as building upon the other, provides a path toward understanding the essence of profound boredom and how it might be reread to theorize being as nothingness.

Becoming Bored By...: Superficial Boredom

As an example of superficial boredom, Heidegger provides the case of passing time in an insipid train station while awaiting the next train, which is not expected for a few hours. Heidegger explains that in such a situation, what happens is that beings, who now must occupy themselves until departure, seek to, unsurprisingly, pass time. After posing roughly the same question as he had posed before—"what does it mean to pass time?" (*FCM*, 93)—Heidegger explains that "[w]e cannot, after all, shake time off. To pass here means to make it pass by, to propel it, drive it on so that it passes. Our passing the time...is really a passing of boredom, where passing now means: driving away, shaking off. Passing the time is *a driving away of boredom that drives time on*" (93; emphasis in original). It is clear, as discussed in the previous section, that boredom can only be understood in relation to time, specifically, the temporality of beings: where boringness, itself in relation to time, sets in, the negation and offsetting of it is attempted by attending to time by focusing on the future, and this involves attempting to drive time or propel it forward toward some end. This act, for Heidegger, is indicative of an attempt to pass time. It is purposeful and forward-looking action (it is worthwhile pondering how time would have been passed some one hundred years ago in the situation that Heidegger speaks of versus how it is passed today. In both periods, boredom is an issue; what has changed is how time is passed, for example, by pacing versus by looking at one's phone. Thus, the historicity of boredom, as noted early in this chapter, appears to speak to the passage of time, not to the fact that boredom is necessarily "new").

Heidegger notes the meaningfulness of such action—meaningful because it is purposeful, and purposeful because it is future-oriented—by explaining that passing the time, which is really passing or driving away boredom, ought to be differentiated from waiting, though waiting forms an important element of/in boredom. Waiting is an important aspect because the subject who must pass time has no choice but to wait: in Heidegger's example, he has to wait until the next train arrives. In this sense, Heidegger claims that "it is waiting itself that is boring and bores us," but is also quick to point out that "*boredom is not itself waiting*" (*FCM*, 94; emphasis added). In other words, the need to wait—and do so without agency (one has to wait because one has no choice but to wait)—brings about boredom, but the essence of boredom cannot and should not be understood as or reduced to a waiting, even though this waiting is meaningful only because of temporality.[1] It is not simply that one has to wait that makes something boring; rather, and as briefly noted in the previous section and fully explicated in this section and the sections to follow, it is the expectation surrounding an event and its relation to time that brings about boringness. That expectation, as noted above, concerns the ways that beings are held in limbo and left empty because of and in boredom.

What is key for Heidegger with respect to superficial boredom is that in the desire to pass time, what transpires is a "confrontation with time" (*FCM*, 96; emphasis omitted), which he also describes as "*wanting to overcome the vacillation of time*" (98; emphasis in original). It is, however, not simply that beings are brought into a confrontation with time that is important. Heidegger writes that "[b]ecoming bored is a *peculiar being affected in a paralyzing way by time as it drags and by time in general*, a being affected which oppresses us in its own way" (98; emphasis in original). This means that the need to confront time, and more specifically, the effect of confronting time, are paralyzing: paralyzing because beings do not (fully) understand the consequences of propelling time forward and letting boredom sleep. This, as mentioned before, is because time drags, and with it comes the need and desire to confront and combat time, that is, pass it. For Heidegger, there appears to be an important difference between the feelings of "dragging," which already implies slowness, and "slow," which need not be about dragging. In other words, it is not that time is slow, or made slow, or made to slow down, that is deemed a problem but that it drags, and it is this dragging that brings beings into a confrontation with time and the desire to pass it. This is why Heidegger equates the dragging of time with oppression, and claims that it oppresses beings (99; again, it is not the dragging of time that is oppressive; rather, it is the resultant need to pass it and thus to let boredom sleep that is the

Profound Boredom 45

concern). Thus, Heidegger notes that "*[b]ecoming bored* and *boredom* in general are...entirely *rooted in this enigmatic essence of time*" (98; emphasis in original), by which he is seeking to capture the fact that beings have not fully comprehended their relation to temporality and, as well, the oppressive effects that accrue in seeking to propel time forward in a specific manner. This becomes clearer when Heidegger examines the two structural moments of boredom—namely, being held in limbo and being left empty—in relation to superficial boredom.

Superficial Boredom, Being Left Empty, and Being Held in Limbo
Heidegger writes that "becoming bored is a *being held in limbo by time as it drags over an interval of time*" (FCM, 100; emphasis in original). Additionally, there is also a "*being left empty* that is emerging in boredom" (101; emphasis in original). Both of these—being held in limbo and being left empty—form the structural moments of the essence of boredom. Heidegger is clear, however, that these two moments are not one and the same and should not be conflated. It is by working with them individually that it is possible to come to terms with the essence of boredom.

Taking the example of the train station, Heidegger once again asks, "*What does it mean to leave empty, to come to be left empty?*", and responds, "*Being left empty* and *being satisfied* are associated with our *dealings* with things" (FCM, 101; emphasis in original). His response suggests that beings expect certain things from certain entities, which, when they materialize, provide satisfaction, and when they do not, result in emptiness. With the example of the train station, a train that arrives on time provides satisfaction (or at least has the potential to do so) whereas a train that is late leads to emptiness. Based upon this reasoning, Heidegger underlines an important aspect about emptiness and, by extension, boredom: "To leave empty means to be something at hand that *offers nothing*. Being left empty means to be offered nothing by what is at hand" (103; emphasis in original). This suggests that the resulting emptiness is a product of the failure—not necessarily inability, though perhaps that too—of an entity to bring to fruition what it is supposed to do, that is, what is expected from it. When that expectation is not fulfilled, emptiness results. Thus, for Heidegger, emptiness is a product of an absence which he calls nothing (at this point, the connection between emptiness and nothingness is only intimated, and will be developed as the chapter progresses). Here, the referent *nothing* is as specific as it is precise: there is a specific expectation or outcome that is not met, namely, a train that is supposed to be on time is late. Thus, it is not nothingness in the sense of an inability to fully articulate an absence. That is, here, the absence is easily articulated: the train does not arrive at the scheduled time and thus there is nothing on the train tracks at that time, and thus there is nothing to get into to commence or resume one's journey. This is why Heidegger says that in boredom, things "abandon us to ourselves," and they do so because "they have nothing to offer" and thus "leave us empty" (103; emphasis omitted).

The phenomenon of superficial boredom provides Heidegger a means to elucidate the place of emptiness to boredom, as one structural moment, and the way emptiness is "*co-determined* by *a particular time*" (*FCM*, 105; emphasis in original). In other words, Heidegger is underlining the place of temporality in boredom. Regarding the other structural moment, namely, being left in limbo, Heidegger writes that "[t]hings can leave us empty only along with that being held in limbo that proceeds from time" (105). That is, "*holding in limbo itself determines and sustains leaving empty*" (106; emphasis in original). This is why, for Heidegger, these two moments are structurally linked and speak to the essence of boredom, that is, boringness.

As will become clear(er) momentarily, in boringness, unmet expectations result in emptiness precisely because uncertainty takes hold concerning whether the expectation will or will not be met. Recall that there is nothing indeterminate about the expectation or emptiness because the nothing that presides is specific and precise. With respect to being held in limbo, however, while it is true that it is the same expectation that is unmet, there is uncertainty about the entire matter, and this uncertainty is not easily determinable. Returning to the example of the late train, the emptiness that emerges is directly tied to an unmet expectation about time and place: the train is not on the tracks when it is supposed to be. In the state of limbo, however, the uncertainty that prevails is indeterminate. This is because while the train is not on the tracks at a specific moment, it is still not clear whether the train will arrive at some point or not, and if it is to arrive, it is uncertain at what time it will arrive (this uncertainty will only be resolved if/when the train arrives). Thus, the train's arrival is situated in the future, and this means that the subject is always in an uncertain and indeterminate state. The contention here is that in this state of uncertainty, it is not nothing but nothingness that captures what beings are subjected to, because while nothing speaks to a specific and determinate absence, nothingness pertains to an indeterminate state. What is claimed in this chapter is that nothingness captures the being of beings that is articulated through profound boredom. This is not fully brought to light in superficial boredom, though the foundation for such an inquiry is present. This is brought to light fully and clearly in the examples of profound boredom.

Being Bored With…: Profound Boredom

To further illustrate the structural moments of boredom and their temporal grounding, Heidegger casts attention upon "the *depth* of boredom" (*FCM*, 107; emphasis in original). By this Heidegger means a boredom that is profound, that is, not only deeper substantively but in its effects as well. As will become apparent, what the depth of boredom allows Heidegger to demonstrate is that a certain type of boredom, namely, that which is profound, does not emanate from outside entities, as with superficial boredom, but from the very core of Dasein itself. This is why, at the outset, he states that profound boredom is "more deadly and grasps more at the root of our Dasein" (107). Superficial boredom, too, behaves in a similar fashion—recall that Heidegger described it as an insidious creature with monstrous essence (79). That said, what Heidegger seeks to highlight is that there is a form of boredom that is far more insidious, with even more monstrousness in its core—the very boredom, interestingly, that he desires to let stay awake and not put to sleep.

To illustrate this, Heidegger takes as an example an evening spent at a dinner party, where one comes to realize that one was bored during its entirety—despite what otherwise looked like a pleasurable time—*only* after arriving home and casting attention to the work that was suspended to attend the party. Heidegger begins by probing whether, in such a situation, passing time—crucial to the first form of boredom—is present, because, he claims, when one looks back upon the evening, it does not appear that there was any desire to pass time, let alone an attempt to pass it. It is this, supposed, absence, he claims, that lends itself to a belief that the subject was not bored during the evening; that is, when the subject looks back at the evening, s/he not only has to confront the fact that s/he did not engage in activities that would constitute passing the time—e.g., tapping fingers on a table, yawning, etc.—but that there appears to have been little need to do so because s/he was enjoying the evening.

Upon further probing, however, Heidegger says that it is not that passing time is absent, but that it is "repressed" (*FCM*, 111). This repression, he claims, is a product of the desire and need to follow the rules of civility, rules that necessitate that one comports oneself in a particular manner while in public.[2] This would mean, then, that the daily routines of passing time when alone—e.g., tapping fingers on a table—cannot be practised when one is in the company of others. This is why Heidegger claims that it is "admittedly hard to find" (112) evidence of passing the time even though it is clearly present. To make his point, he describes the rolling and then smoking of a cigar during the dinner party which, when looked back upon, strikes the subject as evidence of passing time (111–112). This leads Heidegger to an important conclusion about the nature of profound boredom and its relation to passing time: "[T]he *inconspicuousness* of passing the time as such—not inconspicuousness merely or in the first instance for others, but insofar as passing the time does not specifically occupy us ourselves as such passing the time" (116; emphasis in original). That is, coming to terms with the passage of time in profound boredom first requires coming to the realization that this passage of time is largely inconspicuous. Crucially, however, this inconspicuousness is one that "blinds" the subject who is trying to make sense of whether s/he was bored, and if so, how and why. In other words, the subject may not have yawned or tapped his/her fingers and refrained from such actions to appear polite; despite not engaging in these acts, the subject nevertheless engaged in other activities, which, when examined closely, easily point to not merely the fact that s/he passed time, but that s/he was bored.

The inconspicuous nature of passing the time that constitutes profound boredom permits Heidegger to dig deeper into what is unfolding. From so digging, he concludes that it is not so much that passing the time is "hidden or repressed," as he previously stated, "but...*transformed* in a particular way" (*FCM*, 111; emphasis in original). The issue, then, is in what way(s) is passing the time transformed in profound boredom, because it is this transformation that sheds light not simply upon profound boredom, but upon its relation to nothingness and, by extension, being.

Prior to examining this, however, an important point needs underlining. Even though in profound boredom the passage of time is different from its other forms (e.g., superficial boredom), it is still a fact that in it—in all forms of boredom, in fact—passing time is present. Heidegger notes that "[t]he evening is that with which we are bored, and *simultaneously, what* we are bored *with* here is *passing the time*. In this boring situation, *boredom and passing the time become intertwined* in a peculiar way. Passing the time creeps into our becoming bored" and, therefore, "[w]e find nothing boring, and yet passing the time takes on such proportions that it lays claim to the whole situation itself" (*FCM*, 113; emphasis in original). Thus, if there was no need to pass time, then boredom would not exist. Passing the time is a necessary condition of boredom. This is an important factor because it grounds the temporality of boredom and, with it, being (this premise is taken up in detail in the final section of this chapter). This means that even in the example of the dinner party, passing the time is present, though it is "hard to find" (112), and this is because the manner that this passing unfolds has been transformed and is, thus, largely inconspicuous.

What differentiates profound boredom from its superficial counterpart is that in the former "we are *not* able to say *what* is boring us. Accordingly...it is not that there is nothing boring at all, rather what is boring us has this character of '*I know not what*'" (*FCM*, 114; emphasis in original). In the example of superficial boredom—passing time in the train station—while the emptiness that emerges can be precisely determined, the state of uncertainty cannot, at least in terms of the future, and given this, it can be said that both nothing (the specificity of what is absent or missing) and nothingness (the uncertainty and ambiguity of what the absence will bring) constitute its structural moments. In profound boredom, however, it is possible to see, at the very outset, that nothingness appears to form its essence (the structural moments will be discussed shortly to elucidate this). There is no doubt that boredom constitutes the experience of the subject during the dinner even though the subject is not able to say what is boring him/her. In fact, part of what leaves the subject unable to understand what is boring him/her is that, first, it is not fully clear to the subject that s/he was bored to begin with, and second and related, that when s/he is pressed to look back, s/he cannot clearly (or easily) think of passing time during the evening, even though this is what s/he engaged in. Thus, from the outset, there is a lack of clarity surrounding the make-up of profound boredom, and this contributes to clouding its explicability (this lack of clarity, as will become apparent, is a product of its indeterminacy, another one of its important features).

Heidegger refers to an "indeterminate unknown" (*FCM*, 116) or "indeterminate unfamiliarity" (117) to describe this characteristic of profound boredom. In explicating the difference between the two forms—as I have already pointed to above—Heidegger notes that in "the first form [superficial boredom] we have *a determinate boring thing*" (114; emphasis in original), that is, a train station, "whereas in the second form we have *something indeterminate that bores us*" (114; emphasis in original). Here, the indeterminacy, pertaining to what is boring, thereby leading to boringness, makes it difficult for the subject to come to terms with what is unfolding and thus leads to the "I know not what" state. That is, in a comment such as "it is boring"—as often found in myriad declarations such as "it is snowing" or "it is raining"—it is the "*It* [...that] bores us" (115; emphasis in original). Yet exactly, or even vaguely, what this "it" is, "we know not what" of/about (115). Profound boredom, then, is not simply constituted by ambiguity, in relation to its inconspicuousness that renders subjects just about unable to decipher that they are, in fact, passing time, but it also leaves its subjects in indeterminacy. This is because they are unable to clearly articulate what makes them feel this way and why so (precisely the same fate, recall, that befalls the subject who is overcome by rare anxiety, as detailed in the previous chapter). This indeterminacy is reread here as nothingness, an amorphous sense or feeling of a missing-something (that something is missing) which does not fully make sense and cannot be explicated.

The indeterminacy of profound boredom—the subject's inability to articulate the "it" that bores—is a product of its emanation, and this source flummoxes beings. In superficial boredom there is a specific and clear entity that brings about boringness (the train station). As such, it is easy to pinpoint what is boring to the subject, even when that thing leads to nothing, an emptiness. In profound boredom, this is all but impossible. This is because the profounder the boredom, "the more and more concentrated on us, on our situation as such" (*FCM*, 113) it is, and thus it is "that *with* which we *ourselves* are bored" (113; emphasis in original). In the example of the dinner party, it is, technically, not the dinner party that is boring and brings about boredom, but, and rather strangely, the subject him/herself. In other words, in profound boredom, it is not a something or someone else that is responsible for boredom, but oneself, to be specific, one's Dasein. This, however, is not easy for beings to grasp and come to terms with: it is they, themselves, and not something or someone else, who are responsible for their own boredom, and that this emerges from within, (with)in themselves.

If there is any doubt about this, let the scores upon scores of university students who lay the blame about their poor scholarship upon the feet of their "boring" professors be a testament to their inability to see that what is boring (to) them is, simply put, themselves. More pointedly or even poignantly, this aspect of within-ness is important because it nicely illuminates Heidegger's reading of boredom vis-à-vis the explications of boredom in sociology, which tend to, for the most part, locate boredom in the experience of the subject, where something without (that is, outside the subject) is responsible for that experience. For example, this is evident in the way that labour is viewed as boring (Roy 1959). While Heidegger, too, views boredom as emanating from without—in superficial boredom—he clearly underlines its hybridity, its object–subject relation, and this is a testament to the imperative that the within–without must be accounted for when considering boredom. This means that Heidegger is able to demonstrate how the examination of boredom can be drawn on to reflect upon broader and deeper questions, namely, the meaning of existence, in a way that sociology and other social sciences might not be able to or are uninterested in doing (see Roy 1959; Corrigan 1979; Darden and Marks 1999).

The foregoing has articulated that profound boredom is constituted by nothingness given the indeterminacy surrounding boringness, one that emanates from within. To put this into perspective and further explicate this point, focus now turns to the structural moments of profound boredom: being left empty and being held in limbo.

Profound Boredom, Being Left Empty, and Being Held in Limbo

As one of two structural moments of boredom, the notion of emptiness is vital to understanding the essence of boredom, and Heidegger occupies himself with explicating the metamorphosis that unfolds in emptiness vis-à-vis profound boredom. In superficial boredom, recall, emptiness arises when a particular expectation about entities remains unfulfilled or unsatisfied, what Heidegger refers to as "the absence of fullness" (*FCM*, 117). That is, there is an extant void produced by the failure of something not materializing or not materializing as expected. This emptiness, as noted before, is determinate and easily pinpointed. In profound boredom, by contrast, emptiness "*grows from the depths*, because its own precondition, namely, seeking to be satisfied by beings, is already obstructed in such casualness" (117; emphasis in original). According to Heidegger, emptiness pervades in profound boredom, though because of the convoluted and murky nature of it, beings are unable to properly see and appreciate it. This is because of a false sense of fullness—even a modicum of satisfaction that is simultaneously ephemeral—that pervades and envelops beings. This fullness emerges from entities (in the case of the dinner party, from the guests), but does so in a rather casual manner (i.e., the subject's conversations and interactions with the guests are casual if not superficial). For Heidegger, the casual manner by which fullness is sought evidences emptiness. In other words, and for the sake of the argument, if there is any fullness, it is only of a casual ilk and thus not only ephemeral but also superficial. Accordingly, Heidegger notes that "our being satisfied, in being there and part of things, manifests itself, if only faintly and indeterminately, as an illusion (a peculiar dissatisfaction!)—as a passing the time which does not so much drive off boredom as precisely *attest* to it and let it *be-there* [da-sein]" (117–118; emphasis and brackets in original). Thus, the satisfaction that beings believe they are deriving from such a casual interaction is, simply put, an illusion. This is because they are unaware that not only are they empty to begin with, but that their actions merely reproduce and exacerbate their emptiness and do so in a concealed manner. This means that—and building upon what was developed in the previous chapter—the very nature of being is an emptiness. Emptiness, here, is in reference to a perceived fullness that is, however, not only not full (or half full) but empty, and empty because beings cannot see and appreciate the illusion of fullness (or the emptiness of fullness). This, again, is another aspect of the indeterminacy that constitutes life—full yet empty—that is theorized as the nothingness of being.

What is particularly concerning to beings, and crucial to underline here, is that this emptiness is a product of an extant void from within rather than something that emanates from, and because of that which is, without. Heidegger writes that in "*being bored with. We are bored with....* This indicates that the boredom in this being there alongside beings as part of a situation comes *from us*" (*FCM*, 118; emphasis in original). In other words, and as Heidegger explains in more detail, "what is boring can bore us without directly coming toward us from particular boring things. What is boring is that which thwarts us and spreads this peculiar casualness...In such casualness there arises a *slipping away, away from ourselves* towards whatever is happening" (118; emphasis in original).

These two passages, taken in tandem, highlight two important matters about profound boredom and emptiness. First, as noted earlier, what distinguishes profound boredom from superficial boredom is that in profound boredom, boringness cannot be located in an exterior entity, whether a being or thing, but is found in the being him/herself, specifically in his/her Dasein. Thus, the essence of profound boredom is to be located in and understood from within. This is precisely why profound boredom is inconspicuous and leaves the subject with the "I know not what" conundrum. Second, and perhaps even more crucially for Heidegger, in profound boredom, there is a failure, in fact an inability, to fully see and appreciate what is transpiring, specifically, in the first instance, that one is, indeed, bored, in the second instance, that one is passing time, and in the third instance, that one is doing so in an extremely superficial and casual manner that only creates the illusion of fullness and results in the reproduction of emptiness. This means that beings are distancing themselves from their very being, their very essence. This is what Heidegger means when he claims that there is a slipping away from our very selves. The significance of this can be pictured as follows: if it is imagined that one is situated at a particular point, and this point is one's fullness, one's authenticity, then, what Heidegger is claiming is that in trying to pass time in a rather superficial manner to overcome both the boredom that beings do not realize is boredom, nor realize that they are passing time, and in a way that will not provide fullness, beings are merely distancing themselves from this point, from their very selves. The further they distance themselves from this point, the further away from their very essence do they slip (recall, as developed in the introduction and chapter one, that the authenticity of beings refers to the recognition of and coming to terms with the inauthenticity that is the essence of beings as they are in the world. As such, counteracting boredom under the guise of counteracting emptiness is inauthenticity epitomized because it shields and occludes beings from recognizing that emptiness, as one aspect of indeterminacy, constitutes life, and second that attempts to counteract emptiness without realizing what is transpiring reproduces not only inauthenticity but also unfreedom. To put this differently, it is an unfree subject that is consumed with counteracting boredom, though the subject is oblivious to his/her unfreedom).

    Thus, profound boredom helps illuminate the inauthenticity of life. It is crucial to note that profound boredom itself is not responsible for inauthenticity; it is the ways that beings think about their relation to time (and their temporal relation with themselves) that does this. This is why Heidegger strives to ensure that profound boredom remains awake and is not put to sleep. He writes:

> In this casualness of *leaving ourselves behind in abandoning ourselves* to whatever there is going on, *an emptiness can form.* Becoming bored or being bored is determined by this emptiness forming itself in our apparently satisfied going along with whatever is going on...[I]n this form of boredom, we find a being left empty, and indeed an essentially *more profound* form thereof in contrast to the previous case [superficial boredom]. There, the being left empty consisted merely in the absence of fullness. It consisted in the fact that particular things with which we were seeking to entertain and occupy ourselves refused themselves to us. Here, however, there is not simply an emptiness that remains unfulfilled, rather an emptiness precisely first *forms* itself. (*FCM*, 119–120; emphasis in original)

This passage simultaneously accomplishes two things: it situates the emptiness of two forms of boredom by underlining how each takes shape and, most importantly for present purposes, it outlines the emanation of each. In this emanation, as raised earlier, a significant point is revealed. In profound boredom, the emptiness is not determinate upon something else: it is already present, already there, already lying dormant, so to speak, in Dasein, belonging to Dasein ex ante. This is why Heidegger says it forms from within and is formed by itself. This is also why, to underline again, Heidegger is keen to let it remain awake, given the naturalness of profound boredom to the core of being.

After explicating the transformation of emptiness vis-à-vis profound boredom, Heidegger discusses the second structural moment of boredom, being held in limbo. He begins with a straightforward question about this moment: "*What is happening to time here?*" (*FCM*, 121; emphasis in original), and responds that "time does not bind us to itself" (122). Unlike superficial boredom, where time grips and takes hold of beings, thereby enveloping them with a sense of uncertainty, in profound boredom, time "*abandons us entirely to ourselves*, i.e., it leaves us free and lets us be entirely there, alongside and part of things" (121; emphasis in original). Thus, it appears that in profound boredom beings have access to at least some semblance of agency. Heidegger is, however, quick to note that as much as time releases beings, or at least appears to do so, it also takes hold of them, so that beings are not entirely released from the grip of time. This means that in profound boredom beings are held in limbo. Heidegger thus says that

> [i]n this having time for...there lies the possibility that the time we take for things [such as going to the dinner party] will be filled; and precisely here there arises this being bored. In boredom, therefore, nothing happens through the fact that we have taken time, rather it is ultimately the very fact that we have taken time that gives time the possibility of *holding us in limbo* and indeed *in a more profound way*. (121; emphasis and ellipses in original)

It is possible to appreciate the way (the apparent) agency turns (or is turned) into unfreedom: beings freely choose to do something. In this case, they accept an invitation to and then attend a dinner party; yet in accepting the invitation and attending the party, where beings seek to be filled, the possibility of uncertainty, and with it unfreedom, emerge precisely because the casualness of the dinner does not—and most importantly, cannot—fulfill, even fill, beings. As a result, time continues to grip and hold beings in limbo. On the one hand, this means that boredom leads to unfreedom given that time grips beings. On the other hand, however, letting boredom remain awake is tantamount to freedom (or produces freedom) because beings can see and appreciate their essence: that being-in-the-world is inauthenticity and the very realization of this is itself authenticity. As such, the very basis of freedom lies in unfreedom.

Thus, the appearance of agency—time releases beings in the sense that they are free to choose to attend or not attend the dinner and they only do so because time is available to them—notwithstanding, the grip of time looms present. However, and this is the important point, the grip of time is inconspicuous, and because of this, beings believe that they are in control of utilizing time as they see fit. Heidegger's point, however, is that it is time that is holding onto and grasping beings and the choices they make in relation to it (in fact, the choices made are contingent upon it). What this means is that time continues to grip and hold beings, not simply keeping them in limbo, but doing so in a more profound way: "this *standing of time is a more originary holding in limbo*, which is to say, *oppressing*" (*FCM*, 122; emphasis in original). This unfolds as such because, unlike in superficial boredom, time does not drag in profound boredom; rather, time whiles or endures, and this whiling holds beings in limbo in a profound manner. Given that this unfolds inconspicuously, Heidegger says, much of it is "ungraspable" to beings (128).

The ungraspable nature of the uncertainty of time, what Heidegger refers to as a "strange ungraspability" (*FCM*, 128), unfolds as follows. Given that time whiles and endures rather than drags, it stands still. In this standing, something strange takes place, where our "own having-been," that is, the past, and our "own future," that is, what lies ahead, "become modified in a peculiar manner of becoming enchained with the mere present...The time during which we are present thereby comes precisely to stand" (124, 125). In other words, the future (the unknown) and the past (the known) become dissolved into the present so that they stand, but stand in a peculiar way: that is, not only is time stuck—to be precise, appears to be so—but this sense of being stuck is stretched (where the past and future fold into one) so that the grip that time has over beings, as it stands, expands because of its stretching or elongation. The stretching of the present, "this stretched 'now,'" as Heidegger puts it, "stands into our Dasein" (*FCM*, 125). The temporality of being, then, is modified and transformed in a peculiar manner: time grips and holds beings and does so in an uncertain way because of how the present is elongated, but *it is elongated in such a way that the uncertainty of the future itself remains uncertain*. Heidegger's lengthy description puts this into perspective:

> The standing "now," the "during" of the evening in which the invitation endures, can manifest to us as such precisely this being held in limbo, being bound to our time. This *not being released* from our time, from our time which impresses itself upon us from the direction of the standing "now," is our *being held in limbo to time in its standing*, and is thus the sought-after structural moment of being bored with....Not only does time in its standing not release us, it precisely summons us, it sets us in place. When, letting ourselves go

along with being there and part of things, we are thus set in place by standing "now" that is our own, albeit relinquished and empty self, then, we are bored. (126; emphasis and ellipsis in original)

For Heidegger, it is "[t]*his standing 'now' which...sets us in place*" (126; emphasis in original), that brings about boredom.

For present purposes, the point to underline about the boringness of profound boredom is that the "standing now" of time is both indeterminate and unfamiliar. These two characteristics shed light upon the way profound boredom can be read to reveal the nothingness of being. Heidegger writes that "[t]he *standing 'now'*...is something *unfamiliar*, and it is simultaneously *indeterminate*," and qualifies this indeterminacy by stating that it is "indeterminate in an emphatic sense" (*FCM*, 126; emphasis in original). The standing of time is unfamiliar to beings because, unsurprisingly, "[i]t is time that flows that is familiar to us" (126), and to speak, thus, of being held in limbo because time is stretched and then remains immobile (that is, still) is foreign and difficult to grasp (the strange ungraspability Heidegger points to). The standing of time is indeterminate as well because it is thrown into an unfamiliar present, where the past and future are folded into a present state that is, as noted above, static and held in abeyance. This means that beings face an ambiguous and amorphous sense of being in relation to time. This is why they are in limbo, in an uncertain state, because the uncertainty of the future (that it is unknown) is itself now made uncertain (that is, it is unclear when the present will commence its move toward the future). For these reasons, Heidegger writes that "because what is boring is here diffused throughout the particular situation as a whole, *it is far more oppressive*—despite its *ungraspability. It oppresses precisely in and during the inconspicuous way in which we are held at a distance in our passing the time*" (128; emphasis in original). As a result, this indeterminacy and unfamiliarity, leave beings empty.

What is contended here is that profound boredom reveals the nothingness of being, an ambiguous and amorphous state in the way beings are temporal (that is, relate to time, specifically in terms of what lies ahead). As noted above, in profound boredom the past and future fold into one, and the present is thus held in abeyance. Beings are, therefore, indeterminate—stuck in indeterminacy or stuck indeterminately—as they look toward the unknown, that is, the future. That being is here read as nothingness comes precisely from the fact that profound boredom is a product not of something or someone—that is, an outside entity—but of Dasein itself: "*Boredom springs from the temporality of Dasein*" (FCM, 127; emphasis in original). Thus, if profound boredom is a product of something within beings (Dasein), then, it is something that is natural or innate to beings. This truth, however, is unfamiliar and ungraspable, and strangely so to beings, and this leaves them empty. This is a "self-forming emptiness" (127), which means, again, that it emanates from within. It is for these reasons that it is possible to claim that being—the meaning of existence—can be read as nothingness, because not only are beings in an unfamiliar state that they cannot fully recognize given its inconspicuousness, but they are also in a profoundly indeterminate state. This nothingness is, as the next two chapters seek to demonstrate, the homelessness of beings, and the homelessness of beings is the very essence of being human, which is also, and perhaps ironically, the very condition or basis upon which being (at) home and authenticity are grounded and formed.

For Heidegger, profound boredom is vitally important to reveal the meaning of existence and how far beings are and have strayed from their essence. In profound boredom, Heidegger says, "we are held *more towards ourselves*, somehow enticed back into the specific gravity of Dasein, even though, indeed precisely because in so doing we leave our own proper self standing and unfamiliar" (FCM, 128; emphasis in original). In other words, in profound boredom, it is as if beings are standing naked, permitting their essence to be revealed (FCM, 143)—the same, recall, that unfolds with anxiety (cf. Gelven 1989, 118). Thus, while in profound boredom beings are in an unfamiliar standing, Heidegger lauds this very state because it is from here that Dasein can be revealed to Dasein as Dasein. This will become clearer through a third form of boredom, which Heidegger sees as the most profound.

The Profoundest Boredom: "It" Is Boring for One

The final iteration of boredom examined by Heidegger is the profoundest of all forms. Heidegger claims that he is unable (perhaps unwilling) to offer an example, though, if pressed, he would settle on walking the streets of a large city on a Sunday afternoon (*FCM*, 135). As such, what Heidegger develops is not merely abstract, but also cryptic, and abstruse, certainly more so than what he articulated with the preceding two forms of boredom.

Before proceeding, it is worth noting that similar examples are found in Georg Simmel's (1903/1950) treatment of mental life (or perhaps mental health) and city life during the dawn of the twentieth century. Simmel speaks of a "blasé attitude" that encompasses life, something quite akin to the indifference produced by boredom that Heidegger wishes to develop. Simmel's treatment, however, does (tend to) reduce such a feeling to a "psychic phenomenon" (413). It should be noted as well, even if at the risk of oversimplification, that this appears to be a staple in numerous sociological analyses of boredom, which largely tie boredom to an emotional disposition (see Darden and Marks 1999; Spacks 1995, 13; Fisher 1993, 396; Gardiner 2012, 41; Barbalet 1999, 33). Another example of boredom and indifference is Walter Benjamin's (1938/2006) exploration of the *flâneur* via the poet Charles Baudelaire. Benjamin examines how the arcades of Paris provided strollers, smokers, and others "an unfailing remedy for the kind of boredom that easily arises under the baleful eye of a sated reactionary regime" (68). Here, Benjamin tends to tie boredom to an exteriority. Heidegger, as ought to be clear by now, examines boredom to explore and explicate being rather than merely capitalist production and social relations, what Benjamin is largely interested in (interestingly, it has been conjectured that Heidegger's neglect of capitalism vis-à-vis the constitution of life is perhaps one reason that many (or at least some) sociologists have dismissed his work; see Neilsen and Skotnicki 2019, 114). In that sense, and as raised earlier in this chapter, the key is not necessarily to tie boredom to a historical moment—though Heidegger himself admits that in the time in which he writes boredom aptly helps bring to light his endeavours—but to probe the essence of being itself. Thus, while Simmel's and Benjamin's analyses can be read as pinpointing a specific history, it is not entirely certain or clear that Heidegger's insights ought to be read in that manner (see Gardiner 2017; Gardiner and Haladyn 2017, for historical readings of boredom). The final form of boredom that Heidegger develops, the profoundest boredom, confirms this (if such a confirmation is, in fact, necessary, given what has been explicated thus far).[3]

The profoundest form of boredom enables Heidegger to awaken a fundamental attunement (to be precise, as noted earlier, to let it remain awake and not be put to sleep). This would permit Dasein to see Dasein as Dasein, truly and undisguised. To do this, Heidegger briefly outlines what the profoundest form of boredom entails (which he, perhaps for the sake of simplicity, also refers to as profound boredom).[4] Heidegger writes that "profound boredom bores whenever we say, or better, whenever we silently know, that *it is boring for one*" (*FCM*, 134; emphasis in original). The key to understanding the essence of this boredom is its "it is boring for one" character or quality. However, this quality, crucially, is one that one knows—in fact, can only know— "silently." This qualification means that the "it" in the "it is boring for one" can only be known from within, and this evidences Heidegger's stipulation that profound boredom (in both iterations) emanates from within and not without. Yet it is not merely that the source of this knowledge is from within, but that it is difficult to explicate, perhaps even comprehend (in that sense, this knowledge is not knowledge proper, at least in the sense of what would be considered valid in the sciences—on which the social sciences are, at least loosely, modelled, as formulated in the works of Emile Durkheim and Max Weber—which is to say that such knowledge is not [or might not be] subject to empirical documentation). This would be akin to saying that "one knows when or because one knows," a statement that at its heart is tautological. However, it is precisely this sort of circuitous path that Heidegger wants to underline about coming to the essence of the profoundest boredom.

This is seen by probing what Heidegger means by the phrase "it is boring for one." "*It is boring for one. What is this 'it'?*" (*FCM*, 134; emphasis in original), Heidegger queries and writes that, "[t]he 'it' that we mean whenever we say that it is thundering and lightening, that it is raining. *It*—this is the title for whatever is *indeterminate*, *unfamiliar*" (134; emphasis added). As discussed in the previous section, it is possible to see that the "it" in "it is boring" can only be indeterminate and unfamiliar; it cannot be anything else. This is because when one is forced to articulate the "it," one can never be precise, but, rather, one can only explicate it in a round-about, even convoluted, fashion. Already, then, it is possible to see that even in language there is room made for indeterminacy. As this and the previous chapter have argued, indeterminism is the basis of being. As such, Heidegger claims that "*the more profound the boredom, the more silent, the less public, the quieter, the more inconspicuous and wide-ranging it is*" (134; emphasis in original). These qualities point to the indeterminacy of "it" and its being.

If the profoundest boredom, as a fundamental attunement, reveals the being of beings, this means that being is, itself, indeterminate, an indeterminacy that has been here described as nothingness (perhaps this is why Taylor Carman [2013, 84] claims that Heidegger's being of beings can be read in myriad ways, especially post *Being and Time*, where Heidegger appears to have grown uncomfortable with reducing its meaning to a singular and monolithic definition). Conceptualizing the profoundest boredom as giving rise to a sense of, and revealing being as, nothingness is meant to capture Heidegger's thinking because it speaks to the ambiguity and amorphousness in the way that one knows (and can know) the essence of the profoundest boredom (and profound boredom as well).

At the risk of redundancy and labouring the point, it does need underlining that none of this means that the profoundest boredom is not revelatory. The profoundest boredom reveals powerfully:

> In this "it is boring for one" lies the fact that this boredom wishes to tell us something, and indeed not something arbitrary or contingent. This attunement to which we give expression in "it is boring for one" has already *transformed Dasein* in such a way that in our being transformed we also understand not only would it be hopeless to want to struggle against this attunement with some form of passing the time, but that it would almost be something presumptuous to close ourselves off from what this attunement wishes to tell us. (*FCM*, 135–136; emphasis in original)

Specifically, the profoundest boredom "brings us ourselves into the possibility of an *exceptional understanding*" (136; emphasis in original). That is, the profoundest boredom, the "it is boring for one," might only reveal silently and do so because it is unfamiliar and inconspicuous. Yet it is "exceptional" in its ability to disclose, and it can disclose Dasein to Dasein purely and truthfully. This means that beings are able to see and understand the nature of authenticity: authenticity is the very recognition of, coming to terms with, and embracing of the very inauthenticity that constitutes beings as subjects in the world (see Freeman 2021, 129). To be, in other words, is to be inauthentic and it is from this inauthenticity that authenticity is possible, just as the very basis of freedom, as noted before, is grounded upon the unfreedom (inauthenticity) of beings. To put this into perspective, it is necessary to locate the profoundest boredom vis-à-vis time and its passage.

Given the inconspicuousness of the profoundest boredom, Heidegger claims that it is difficult to locate the place of passing time in it, if, in fact, passing time takes place (*FCM*, 134) (the same issue, recall, that befell the subject in profound boredom). Indeed, Heidegger concludes that in the profoundest boredom, "[p]assing the time *is missing*" (135; emphasis in original) and says that it is not simply that passing the time is absent, but that its absence is a product of something specific unfolding, and this happens because it "*is no longer permitted* by us *at all*" (136; emphasis in original). This is significant because "[t]o no longer permit any passing the time means to let this boredom be overpowering. This entails already understanding this boredom in its *overpowering nature*" (136; emphasis in original). Recall that in the earlier forms of boredom—both superficial and lesser profound—passing the time related to the dragging of time (superficial boredom) and the whiling of time (lesser profound boredom), and these left beings empty and held them in limbo, though in very different ways and for very different reasons. In the profoundest boredom, passing the time ceases to exist. This emerges precisely because to pass the time is no longer seen as necessary, because the problems associated with time, that is, dragging or whiling, are not constructed as problems. This is because beings come to *see* the profoundness of boredom—its overpowering quality—and its importance to their being. This is why, as noted before, Heidegger claims that the profoundest boredom, as a fundamental attunement of being, provides beings with an exceptional understanding of being and authenticity. This requires coming to terms with the essence of boredom, that is, of boringness. To aid in this, focus turns to the two structural moments of boredom, being empty and being held in limbo.

The Profoundest Boredom, Being Left Empty, and Being Held in Limbo

According to Heidegger, "in this 'it is boring for one'...*emptiness and being left empty* are quite unambiguous and straightforward" (*FCM*, 137; emphasis in original). This suggests that in the profoundest boredom, in comparison to the lesser profound boredom, it is easier to understand and make sense of the place of emptiness. In this form of boredom, the extant emptiness has nothing to do with seeking fulfillment or fullness (as it did in superficial boredom). "It is an emptiness," Heidegger writes, "precisely where, as this person in each case, *we want nothing from the particular beings* in the contingent situation as these very beings" (137; emphasis added). In fact, and as Heidegger clarifies, "the fact that precisely here we want nothing is already due to boredom" (137).

Here, nothing is not nothingness, and should be neither confounded nor conflated with it. However, it reveals something important about what is unfolding. In the profoundest form, beings want nothing from other beings or things. This nothing is specific and determined (nothing from beings and things) while simultaneously broad (everyone/thing and anyone/thing that encompasses the nothing). The sweeping nature here should, however, not be read as indeterminacy. What is peculiar and interesting is that there is something about/in the profoundest boredom that leads beings to want and wish for nothing from other entities. Thus, the profoundest boredom leaves beings indifferent, and as will become apparent, it is this indifference that is responsible for the emptiness that overcomes beings. "This boredom," Heidegger says, "takes us precisely back to the point where we do not in the first place seek out this or that being for ourselves in this particular situation; it *takes us back to the point* where all and everything appears indifferent to us" (137; emphasis in original). To say that something is *indifferent* means that regardless of the value or form or any other aspect of/about an entity, being, or thing, it does not (spawn) interest. That is, there is no concern or care—or any emotion, for that matter—about it. As Parvis Emad (1985, 73) puts it, "[i]n this form of boredom the self which has a history, a social standing, an age, a name, a profession and a destiny—the self bound to an I—is left behind to such an extent as to become identical to an 'indifferent nobody.'" It is, however, and importantly, not just that beings are indifferent to other entities, but that "[w]e become indifferent to ourselves" (74). It is, then, the very fact that, in the profoundest boredom, *a being is indifferent to his/her very self* that leads him/her to be indifferent to everything else. Here, it is possible to see that the profoundest boredom functions by penetrating the being of the subject (its within) and it is as such that the subject may reflect upon the without (his/her relation to the world, and why time matters to him/her and the way that time matters as such) and come to an indifference about the way his/her life is constituted in the world.

To be precise, Heidegger claims that it is not anything—something—specific about a particular entity, be it beings or things, that brings about this feeling of indifference, but that it simply emerges from nowhere, in a rather sudden fashion. This is where the indeterminacy of the profoundest boredom can be appreciated because it is difficult, even impossible, to explicate the origins of such a feeling of indifference, especially when it is claimed that its origin is nowhere to be located (the same plight, recall, that beings face when overcome by rare anxiety, as detailed in the previous chapter). Thus, Heidegger notes that "[t]his *indifference of things and of ourselves with them* is not the result of a sum total of evaluations" (*FCM*, 138; emphasis in original). This suggests that there is nothing necessarily calculative or rationally laden about feeling indifferent. Beings, it appears, are not in a pondering state when they come to the point where entities do not interest them. Rather, Heidegger claims, "each and every thing at once becomes indifferent, each and every thing moves together at one and the same time into an indifference. This indifference does not first leap from one thing over onto another…;

rather all of a sudden everything is enveloped and embraced by this indifference" (138). In other words, from nowhere and, more importantly, as if without warning, this feeling emanates and holds beings. It is this that leaves beings empty. As Heidegger says, "The *emptiness* accordingly here consists in the *indifference* enveloping beings *as a whole*" (138; emphasis in original).

Yet, it is incorrect to claim that this feeling emerges from nowhere: it emerges precisely and specifically from, and only from, within. That said, what is important to note is that beings are still not (fully or even partially) able to explicate why such a feeling, suddenly and from what appears to be nowhere, comes to be, and comes to be from within, that is, from themselves. This is the indeterminacy of the profoundest boredom that constitutes being as nothingness, that amorphous state. Heidegger writes that "we abandon ourselves to this boredom as something that becomes overpowering in us and which we understand in a certain way in this overpowering, without being able to explain it while we are bored or even wanting to explain it" (*FCM*, 138). This is significant because what Heidegger is conveying is not simply that beings are unable to fully make sense of what is making them indifferent, but that, and crucially, they are in some ways *indifferent about/to this very indifference*. As he writes,

> Being left empty in this third form of boredom is Dasein's being delivered over to beings' telling refusal of themselves as a whole. In this "it is boring for one" we find ourselves—as Dasein—somehow left entirely in the lurch, not only not occupied with this or that being, not only left standing by ourselves in this or that respect, but as a whole. Dasein is now merely suspended among beings and their telling refusal of themselves as a whole. The emptiness is not a hole between things that are filled, but concerns beings as a whole and yet is not the Nothing. (140; emphasis omitted)

It is paramount to underline, then, that it is not that beings are ignorant of the indifference that envelops them: they are certainly cognizant and aware of what is unfolding; they simply are unable to explicate how and why such indifference takes hold of themselves, especially given that it emanates from within. Rather, what is unfolding here is not an ignorance of/about indifference, but an indifference about the very indifference that sweeps over their lives.

Heidegger does not see the foregoing as problematic. The profoundest boredom, he claims, permits Dasein to see Dasein as Dasein when beings "experience a peculiar compulsion in it, a compulsion to listen to what it has to tell us" (*FCM*, 139). Heidegger sees this as important and necessary:

> [T]his "it is boring for one"—from whatever depths it may arise—does not have the character of despair. This being left empty as being delivered over to beings' telling refusal as a whole does not singularly dominate Dasein, it alone does not constitute boredom, but in itself it is *associated with* something else, as we know formally: with a *being held in limbo*, together with which it first constitutes boredom. Without an essential transformation of itself, in which it leaps over into another attunement, this profound boredom never leads to despair. (140; emphasis in original)

The declarative and emphatic statement, that the profoundest boredom does not lead to despair, is refreshing because in and through it, Heidegger exhorts beings to (find) hope. In other words, rather than holding trepidations about boredom, including the profoundest form, and thereby putting boredom to sleep, Heidegger encourages beings to see that in and through the profoundest boredom it is possible to come to terms with the meaning of existence and the authenticity of life. To fully put this into perspective, the other structural moment, being held in limbo, needs discussion as well.

If the emptiness extant in the profoundest boredom is a product of the indifference that sweeps the consciousness of beings, then being held in limbo is a product of unexploited possibilities. As discussed earlier, one possibility of the trajectory of Dasein is that it can be "left entirely in the lurch" (*FCM*, 140), by which Heidegger means that beings are rendered unsteady. This happens when beings do not experience, but more commonly do not listen to, the compulsion of Dasein, which, as explicated in the previous chapter, Heidegger refers to as the calling (*BT*, 317–348; *FCM*, 143). The calling concerns

Dasein, which calls itself because it sees itself lost in what Heidegger calls the they-self (*BT*, 149–224), that is, in its existence in the world, which Heidegger calls being-in-the-world. As such, Dasein seeks to underline to itself the inauthenticity of its life. It is a call, then, by Dasein to Dasein about Dasein (*BT*, 317–348). Michael Gelven (1989, 163; emphasis in original) writes that "[t]he calling is *about* the self in the sense that conscience awakens an awareness of the mode of existence in which the self finds itself—authentic or inauthentic. The call is *to* the self in that it is an appeal to the self to be authentic." At this point, Dasein can decide to either embrace the call and choose authenticity or continue to live inauthentically by declining the call. What the call does, and why it is important for Heidegger, is that it presents Dasein as Dasein: "[I]n this 'it is boring for one[,]' [the call] first *brings* the *self* in all its nakedness *to itself* as the self that *is there* and has been over the being-there of its Dasein. For what purpose? *To be that Da-sein*" (*FCM*, 143; emphasis in original). By being left in the lurch, that is to render unsteady (beings are unsteady and unstable because of inauthenticity), Heidegger is stating that Dasein either does not answer the call or does not heed the warning of inauthenticity. Where the call is not answered or its warnings are left unconsidered, the possibilities open to Dasein, possibilities of an authentic life, remain unexploited. Thus, the call, and with it the refusal or embracing of the possibilities extant in it, go hand-in-hand: "This telling refusal is in itself…a telling announcement of the unexploited possibilities of Dasein" (142). By being held in limbo, then, Heidegger means this position of uncertainty about whether Dasein will be able to see Dasein as Dasein. In other words, being held in limbo means "*being impelled toward the originary making-possible of Dasein as such*" (144; emphasis in original).

The profoundest form of boredom illuminates what ails beings while simultaneously revealing the possibilities open to them, possibilities which can be mobilized for authentic life. To understand the essence of boredom, Heidegger illustrates the ways that emptiness (caused by a sense of indifference toward outside entities, brought on, however, by a sudden and inexplicable feeling that emanates from within) and being held in limbo (brought on by unexploited possibilities which hold beings in uncertainty) work as structural moments. All this is, however, premised upon the temporality of being, which is, as argued here, constituted by nothingness, an amorphous sense of what it means to be. The discussion of the profoundest boredom has already explicated the indeterminacy of being and why it can be read as nothingness. Here, it suffices to say that an emptiness that is difficult to explicate, as in the lesser form of profound boredom, clearly shows its amorphous nature, as does an uncertainty that characterizes whether possibilities will be explored or not. As such, the being of beings as conceptualized by Heidegger can be reread as nothingness.

Boredom, Temporality, and Nothingness

It is now possible to concretely connect profound boredom, temporality, and nothingness, and to do so in a manner that builds upon but importantly adds to what has been developed in the previous chapter in relation to the being of beings. There is, for Heidegger, "nothing to be found…of time" in profound boredom: "neither a dragging of time nor the spending of a determinate time that we leave ourselves" (*FCM*, 141). In fact, "[o]ne is…almost tempted to say," Heidegger writes, "that in this 'it is boring for one' one feels timeless, one feels removed from the flow of time." Yet the previous section unequivocally shows that time matters profoundly in/to the profoundest form of boredom (all forms of boredom, in fact, as this chapter attests). This means that there is a specificity about the way time matters to/in the profoundest boredom, and the preceding two quotations—that time appears not to matter—must be read in this context. That is, unlike the other forms of boredom, in the profoundest boredom, time does not drag (as in superficial boredom) nor necessarily while (as in profound boredom). Rather, it is the way time brings into its fold the past, present, and future that reveals the temporality of this boredom. Heidegger speaks of a *"unifying horizon of time,"* where "beings are enveloped by the single yet simultaneously threefold horizon of time" (145; emphasis in original). The threefold horizon refers to the present (what Heidegger calls respect), the past (what he calls retrospect) and the future (what he calls prospect).

Given the tenor of this chapter, it is unsurprising, then, "that time ultimately participates in making possible *the manifestness of beings as a whole*" (*FCM*, 145; emphasis added). That is, the ability of Dasein to see Dasein as Dasein—to hear the calling and see the extant possibilities—is present when the relation of beings to their temporality, regarding the threefold horizon, can be appreciated. Accordingly, Heidegger claims that this requires a rupturing of the temporal entrancement, that is, to be able to see the import of temporality to being in a specific manner: that the past, present and future are related but related in a very precise sense. This ability to see the threefold horizon of temporality, Heidegger calls "the moment of vision" (151; emphasis omitted): it "is the look of Dasein in the three perspectival directions...namely present, future and past. The moment of vision is a look of a unique kind" (151).

The importance of this can be gleaned by recalling what Dasein reveals to itself about temporality via rare anxiety. As discussed in the previous chapter, Dasein is temporal, which is to say that it has its future, its care, as its primary concern, even its obligation. It is, to put this differently, future-oriented, and being future-oriented means that it has open to it possibilities and is concerned with these possibilities. In the profoundest boredom, as evident here, the folding of the three modes of time into one means that the futurity of Dasein, as it is revealed to itself in this attunement, is different from what anxiety reveals (in that sense, however, while anxiety and profound boredom serve as two important moods which disclose being, it is quite apparent now why Heidegger focuses at length on both because each shines light on something specific and different about the meaning of existence).

In profound boredom, Dasein whiles (*FCM*, 152). This means that Dasein is temporal in the sense of whiling and tarrying (155). The fact that Dasein whiles and tarries is what makes boredom possible: "*Only because this constant possibility—the 'it is boring for one'—lurks in the ground of Dasein can man be bored or become bored by the things and people around him*. Only because *every* form of boredom comes *to arise out of this depth* of Dasein, although we *initially do not know* this depth and *even less pay attention to it*" (156–157; emphasis in original). This whiling is not simply about chronological or linear time (the time of the clock). It is about the lengthening and shortening of time (152) in relation to the past and the future of the present, the threefold horizon. Heidegger describes this as follows:

> That the while becomes long means that the horizon of whiling—which at first and for the most part shows itself to us, if at all, as that of a present, and even then more as what is now and today—*expands itself into the entire expanse of the temporality of Dasein. This lengthening of the while* manifests the while of Dasein in its indeterminacy that is never absolutely determinable. This indeterminacy takes Dasein captive, yet in such a way that in the whole expansive and expanded expanse it can grasp nothing except the mere fact that it remains *entranced* by and toward this expanse. The lengthening of the while is the *expansion of the temporal horizon*, whose expansion does not bring Dasein liberation or unburden it, but precisely the converse in *oppressing* it with its expanse. (152–153; emphasis in original)

There are several points to underline here. First, Heidegger appears to use the term *horizon* to mean a specific location—colloquially where the sky and earth apparently meet (the relevance of the sky and the earth will be evident in the next two chapters in the discussion of Heidegger's fourfold). The apparent meeting place of the two is important as well because it leads to a second way to make sense of the horizon. This concerns the limitations of mental perception and understanding, precisely the point that John Haugeland (2013, 235) highlights about temporality. Heidegger is unequivocal about this. He is taking the folding-together (or into one) of the threefold nature of time (past, present, and future) and underlining the perception of time being simultaneously lengthened and shortened (a paradox in its own right, yet another, as the previous chapter attests to). As such, Dasein has difficulty processing this, and as a result, an indeterminacy constitutes and frames Dasein and holds it. It is Dasein's inability to fully make sense of what is transpiring, Heidegger says, that oppresses Dasein so that it is stuck in inauthenticity.

None of this means that profound boredom has little or nothing to offer. Profound boredom, as a fundamental attunement of being, deeply reveals the being of beings and it does so by highlighting the uncertainty of the future not just in terms of what will transpire, but more importantly, *when* it will (or might) transpire—that is, when the present will move forward (as articulated in relation to the lesser profound boredom). This also raises the issue of whether the present will, in fact, move (forward). Beings, thus, are (or feel they are) stuck in indeterminacy, the very indeterminacy that is here read as nothingness. This indeterminacy, Heidegger says, is revealed in the moment of vision of Dasein.

The significance here, then, is this: in rare anxiety, the temporal nature of Dasein as future-oriented and oriented to its possibilities is revealed, and anxiety, as already developed in the previous chapter, can be reread to reveal the nothingness of beings via the indeterminacies of its constitutive paradoxes (somewhere/nowhere and something/nothing). Profound boredom reveals the nothingness of being via indeterminacies as well, but does so via a different framework, revealing that the future-oriented nature of beings is, itself, indeterminate because the future is entangled with the past and the present. As such beings are left in limbo and empty. If boredom is a significant part of the social world, both when Heidegger penned his thoughts and as it certainly is today (see Gardiner 2017; Gardiner and Haladyn 2017), then it is possible to see and appreciate that boredom is a constitutive feature of beings. Boredom reveals that beings are constituted by nothingness pertaining to their temporality, and profound boredom brings this to the fore by revealing the way time not only matters but also how it matters.

As such, Heidegger can now finally define boredom, which, he underlines, should be read only "as a more *incisive directive for interpretation*" (*FCM*, 153–154; emphasis in original): "Boredom," he says, "is the entrancement of the temporal horizon, an entrancement which lets the moment of vision belonging to temporality vanish. In thus letting it vanish, boredom impels entranced Dasein into the moment of vision as the properly authentic possibility of its existence, an existence only possible in the midst of being as a whole, and within the horizon of entrancement, their telling refusal of themselves as a whole" (153; emphasis omitted). Boredom, then, is essentially an entering into a temporal horizon where the three moments of time are blurred and folded into one. This folding, as articulated here, reveals the indeterminateness of being, which is here reread as nothingness.

Heidegger's foray into profound boredom is a venture to highlight what a fundamental attunement can reveal about the being of beings. Thus, he claims it is crucial to dispel the "ordinary assessment of boredom," that it is "disturbing, unpleasant, and unbearable," along with the view that "[b]ecoming bored is a sign of shallowness and superficiality" (*FCM*, 158). For Heidegger, it is crucial to move past these ways of looking at boredom (as already noted, Heidegger's call to embrace boredom is certainly not new. Numerous exhortations, many made during the time of Heidegger or shortly prior to it abound, with Benjamin's [1936/1970, 91] declaration of boredom as the apogee of mental relaxation perhaps being the most famous. Heidegger's, of course, is an ontological exploration, which thus does not reduce boredom to an emotion, and in that sense is, at least somewhat, unique). So doing permits the possibility to see and appreciate boredom differently, as an indication not merely of the relation of beings and temporality, but that this relation is—always will be—indeterminate, thereby revealing how beings spend and relate to time or, to be more precise, how time holds beings and holds them indeterminately. In this sense, what Heidegger offers to the critique of boredom is novel and its significance as an exposition of the meaning of existence is not only important but also timely given what is unfolding today, despite being close to a century since he penned his thoughts.

This chapter has argued that Heidegger's discussion of boredom—both superficial and profound—shows that boredom can only be understood as an indeterminacy. This is because when the structural moments of boredom—emptiness and being held in limbo—are accounted for, the essence of boredom reveals itself as such. It is true that each of these moments unfolds differently in different forms of boredom, but what cannot be denied is that there is an immense uncertainty about profound boredom itself—e.g., how and why it emanates, and where from. This means that boredom cannot be fully known to beings, as Heidegger reminds readers: "Because...the origin of boredom and the original relationship between the various forms of boredom remain and must remain completely concealed from our everyday understanding of this attunement, our everyday consciousness is also governed by uncertainty as to what properly bores us, as to what *that which is originarily boring is*" (*FCM*, 157; emphasis in original).

As such, this chapter has read the indeterminacy of boredom as nothingness. Nothingness does not mean nothing in the tangible sense, as in there being no snow on the ground. Rather, it refers to a sense or feeling that something is missing: there is nothing there, but exactly what that nothing (the missing something) is, is inexplicable. What the chapters to follow seek to show is that what is missing is the foundation of beings, being (at) home. In other words, beings are distanced from home, and the absence they feel, which they cannot fully explicate, is the ontological status of homelessness. The nothingness of their being constantly prods them to this, though they are not able to fully make sense of it. Heidegger hints at this very early on in *The Fundamental Concepts of Metaphysics*: "This is where we are driven in our homesickness: to being as a whole. *Our very being is this restlessness*" (5; emphasis in original). Profound boredom, then, highlights the being of beings as nothingness, and nothingness prods beings toward recognizing their homelessness, setting the path toward a possible homecoming. The next two chapters seek to bring to light the homelessness of beings.

3

Ontological Homelessness and Revelation

CHAPTERS ONE AND TWO, which can be read as constituting part one of this book, engaged in detail with Heidegger's discussion of the moods or attunements of anxiety and profound boredom. Heidegger's reliance upon each mood is specific and purposive: each reveals the being of beings, but differently. Anxiety, recall, reveals how time and temporality are inextricably linked to the meaning of existence, that is, how beings come to terms with their mortality (though, also recall that for Heidegger, death does not mean perishing but the revelation of the possibility of no further possibilities and the implications of this). The profoundest boredom also vividly brings to light the place of time and temporality in the being of beings, but because of boredom's slower and more lingering effects, Heidegger can home-in on temporality and being in a way that is not necessarily possible with/in anxiety: "dread [anxiety] grips us instantly, all at once, and keeps us in its hold suddenly[;] boredom has the peculiarity of gradually increasing its depth and only then of holding us in its grip completely. Dread is said to bring us face to face with Nothing 'only for a few moments'…But boredom is considered to be lingering on, to be enduring, slowly overwhelming us" (Emad 1985, 68). As such, recall that profound boredom explicates how the three modes of time—past, present, and future—are folded into one or come together, thus giving rise to the indeterminacy of beings in relation to time where what unfolds transpires slowly and gradually or might even have the appearance of not moving at all. In sum, then, anxiety reveals the insignificance of beings, while the profoundest boredom reveals that beings find entities utterly indifferent and, in the end, find themselves indifferent to their very selves.

Both attunements, as the previous chapters show, shine light upon the nothingness of being via the indeterminacy that takes hold of life. This nothingness is a product of an absence, a missing-something, that is not easily explicable: there is nothing because something is missing, though what that is, is unclear. The indeterminacy of something yet nothing has been referred to as nothingness because of the constant flux that characterizes beings who are always in search (of something). Heidegger's discussion of anxiety and the profoundest boredom can, then, be read to reveal the being of beings as nothingness: "Anxiety and boredom both confront us with the abyss of Being as nothingness. Both anxiety and boredom bring us face to face with the threatening insignificance of the finite self. In anxiety, however, one experiences a profound concern for this terrifying mystery, a concern that may transform into wonder if courageously digested. In boredom, the mystery is avoided by a listless or frenzied turning away" (Thiele 1997, 502; see also Svendsen 2005, 127, 145; Emad 1985, 77).

The nothingness of beings points to their ontological homelessness: beings are, constitutionally, homeless despite apparently being (at) home. This is the indeterminacy of beings: they are (at) home ontically but are ontologically homeless, and yet, the very condition of being home ontologically is to be found in the condition of ontic homelessness. Chapters three and four, which can be read as constituting part two of this book, begin to work through Heidegger's concern with ontological homelessness. As chapters one and two have shown, this concern is clearly at the heart of both *Being and Time* (see Mugerauer 2008, 24–53) and *The Fundamental Concepts of Metaphysics* (where Heidegger refers, very early on, to the restlessness of beings concerning their homesickness). However, it is in Heidegger's middle phase of work that ontological homelessness is given its full and proper due, and is perhaps fully and clearly articulated. This chapter focuses upon one such effort, namely, *Hölderlin's Hymn "The Ister,"* where Heidegger draws upon a specific poem by the German poet Friedrich Hölderlin to theorize the journey homeward, which first requires coming to terms not simply with the fact that beings are not at home, but are, in fact, travelling in the wrong direction, away from and against home—against, that is, their very essence. This theme is carried into chapter four, where Heidegger's essay "Building Dwelling Thinking" is reread exegetically to illustrate the import of Heidegger's concept of dwelling to understanding the homelessness of beings and the path home. The current chapter, then, begins the work of explicating the ontological homelessness of beings. It commences with a shift in form, noted in the introduction, that characterizes Heidegger's work as it transitions from the early to the middle and later phases.

Poetizing, Thinking, and the Path to Authenticity

Being and Time and *The Fundamental Concepts of Metaphysics*, two of Heidegger's early works, have a specific focus and relation vis-à-vis metaphysics, namely, to *ground* metaphysics, that is, to lay a platform or foundation upon which metaphysical inquiry can be formulated and undertaken for the purposes of exploring and discovering the being of beings. In the middle phase of Heidegger's scholarship, to which *Hölderlin's Hymn "The Ister"* belongs, the concern is to *overcome* metaphysics (a concern that continues and is cemented in the later phase of Heidegger's work). As is perhaps most clearly evinced in *On Time and Being*,[1] metaphysical inquiry is, in Heidegger's later phase, seen as a hindrance or limiting factor to the task of probing the meaning of existence. This is why, for example, in "Nietzsche's Word: 'God is Dead,'" Heidegger is sympathetic yet critical of Nietzsche: for while Nietzsche sought to overturn metaphysics, he failed to overcome it, precisely what Heidegger's turn seeks to accomplish. By overcoming metaphysics, Heidegger *does not mean* its *renunciation*, but rather a *transformation*. In particular, he means that the history of metaphysics—a history that, apparently, needlessly conflated being and/with beings—needs to be overcome so that the journey toward the being of beings can be fruitfully undertaken (see LH; OM; see also Mugerauer 2008, 163–181, 74–92). Heidegger claims that

Nietzsche confounds overturning with overcoming. As a result, beings are forever rendered homeless because the failure to overcome metaphysics results in nihilism, and nihilism is a recipe for homelessness (see NW). Specifically, it is the language of metaphysics that Heidegger saw as limiting and leading to nihilism, and it is this limitation that he sought to overcome. This is precisely why Heidegger saw poetry as the solution to the limits of philosophical language. As such, he drew inspiration from poetry and poets. Heidegger saw a freedom in poetic thinking, that poetry was a "source of...creative disclosure and new meaning" (Thomson 2021, 523) geared toward the meaning of existence, what Heidegger would call, after the turn, *ek-sistence* (see LH). This led to Heidegger's "subtly yet profoundly transformative engagement with...Hölderlin" (Thomson 2021, 521), where he found an affinity with the poet, seeing him as not only focused upon homelessness and homecoming but also as providing a path through which to overcome homelessness (see Mugerauer 2008, 93–136). Perhaps this is why Robert Mugerauer (2008, 134) speaks of Heidegger as "a homecoming thinker" and Hölderlin as the "homecoming poet."

Prior to examining Heidegger's reading of one of Hölderlin's poems, attention briefly shifts to locate the place of poetizing in/to Heidegger's middle stage of thinking and how this propels him forward to chart the ontological homelessness of humanity. As noted, ontological homelessness certainly appears as a theme in *Being and Time* and *The Fundamental Concepts of Metaphysics*, though it is not given full consideration until Heidegger fully begins to turn toward and draw inspiration from poetry, while simultaneously seeking to overcome metaphysics.[2]

Very early in *Hölderlin's Hymn "The Ister,"* Heidegger writes that "'To poetize'...means to write down, to fore-tell something to be written down. To tell something that, prior to this, has not yet been told" (*I*, 8). What has been left untold, at least fully and properly, as Heidegger sees it, concerns the homelessness of beings as they are in the world. Specifically, for Heidegger, poetizing brings with it a particular type of thinking that is more profound than other forms of philosophical inquiry, certainly metaphysics. Thus, he writes that "[t]houghtful reflection is meant to awaken our attentiveness. Such attentiveness is distinguished in an essential way from mere curiosity that wants only to 'get to know' something without gaining knowledge of it" (13). For Heidegger, poetizing is a path toward a particular kind of thinking: one that is profound and can situate itself in the roots of being.

The link between thinking and poetizing needs underlining and elaboration, and this is specifically the task Heidegger sets himself in another of his lecture courses. Heidegger is interested in illuminating a type of thinking that, he claims, provides beings the path to understanding the meaning of existence. In *Introduction to Philosophy—Thinking and Poetizing*, the lecture course delivered only a few years after *Hölderlin's Hymn "The Ister"*—Heidegger explicitly links the connection between philosophy and the sort of poetic thinking he envisages as being capable of shining light upon the being of beings. He states pithily that "philosophizing is thinking, and all thinking is already, somehow, philosophizing" (*IP*, 2). More specifically, he says that "[p]hilosophy is the thinking of thinkers. They think that which is. But even in general, humans always think that which is, although usually ineptly and imprecisely and slightly forgetfully. Humans are the ones who think but not always because of this are they also thinkers. The thinking of thinkers we call *thinking*; this word is said strictly for this" (11; emphasis in original). For Heidegger, it is what occupies the thinker that makes thinking, thinking. Thus, Heidegger notes that "[t]he thinker thinks that which is. The thinker thinks beings. The thinker thinks beings in the sole consideration that beings are and what they are. What beings 'are', how they 'are', and the fact that they 'are', is what we call the being of beings" (36).

The being of beings (the meaning of existence) is what guides thinkers and thinking. Specifically, the being of beings, as noted, concerns the nothingness that speaks to the ontological homelessness of beings. Thus, Heidegger states that "a guide is required in order for humans to become more at home and to learn *genuine dwelling* where they always already sojourn, although ineptly and unadvisedly" (*IP*, 11; emphasis added; it is possible to see that the relation between *journeying* and *sojourning* and *home* and *dwelling* are inextricably interwoven, a connection taken up later in this chapter and in the next). Heidegger continues by stating that "[t]he guide to thinking strives for it to become brighter around us, and for us to become more circumspect of the brightness" (11; emphasis omitted). Here, Heidegger is claiming that thinking—the specific and precise sort articulated above—will shine light upon the homelessness of beings so that they can become "more at home" and learn to dwell genuinely. As Heidegger says, "The thinking of a thinker is true if it guards the advent of being" (15). Thinking, put simply, and despite the danger of reduction, concerns the meaning of existence.

The specific sort of thinking that Heidegger focuses on is, then, what allows beings to truly understand their plight: that of ontological homelessness. Thus, Heidegger claims that "[t]he introduction to philosophy is the guiding of initially inept thinking to the careful thinking of that which is" (53). Here, the "that which is," is the alienation of beings: "Having become God-less and world-less, the modern human is home-less. Indeed, in the absence of God and the ruin of the world, *homelessness* is especially expected of the modern historical human. Therefore, modern humans do not feel at home, and this is even and especially the case when they flee to that which makes them forget the failed home and what should replace it" (24; emphasis in original; see also NW). In a world where meaning is fleeting and without footing—emanating, amongst others, from the secularization of the world and the rabid "technologization" of life (see BDT, LH), especially so in contemporary times—beings who seek meaning in the they-self are only further cementing their ontological homelessness. As Heidegger puts it, "[p]ursuing what is easiest, human beings avoid what is most difficult" (*I*, 130). This is what Heidegger seeks to shine light upon, and as will become apparent, the "guiding" that he alludes to is to be shepherded by the poet via poetizing.

Hölderlin's Hymn "The Ister" focuses on a poem by Hölderlin about the river Ister and its flow (*Ister* being the ancient name given to the second-largest river in Europe, the Danube, which flows east from Germany into Austria and Romania and then into the Black Sea). Heidegger reads the water's journeying (e.g., *I*, 68, 69) or sojourning (*IP*, 3) in the poem as evidence of its quest for homecoming. This chapter rereads the river as a metaphor for being, specifically, the ontological homelessness of beings. Heidegger claims that Hölderlin's work can be thought of as "a meditation on what it is that is essentially to be poetized" (*1*, 124) and "[w]hat is worthy of poetizing...is nothing other than *becoming homely in being unhomely*" (121; emphasis added), which, at this juncture, can be read as being home in homelessness (this theme is expanded upon throughout the chapter). What follows explicates how Heidegger's reading of *Hölderlin's Hymn "The Ister"* is aimed at providing those interested in thinking in this profound sense, the path toward (thinking about) being. While this entails working closely with Heidegger's exposition, it eschews any desire for a schematic and systematic summary.

The Ister: The Locale and the Journey Home

As Heidegger reads it, the flow of the Ister is an enigma (*1*, 33–39; this could presumably be said of any river). With regard to this enigma, Heidegger warns that "[w]e should not wish to 'solve it'. Yet we must try to bring the enigma *as* enigma to us" (35; emphasis added). According to Heidegger, the enigmatic nature of the Ister concerns the counsel of the river (the significance of which will become apparent later). Upon deeper reading, however, it becomes clear that what the enigma speaks to is an apparent duality—or, if one prefers, paradox—between what is static and elastic, between what is fixed and ambulant, between what is here and there, all of which must be situated and explicated via time-space: "To this end, we choose the distinctly unpoetic assertion: The river is the locality of journeying. The river is the journeying of locality" (35).

The enigma of the river unfolds as follows. For Heidegger, the river is, without a doubt, located in a particular locale. This would amount to what is referred to as place, that is, that the river, as a site or locale, has a place, and to be in one place means not to be in another or, to put it differently, if one is here, then, one cannot be there (see De Certeau 1980/1984, 117). This is what Heidegger refers to as the locality (derived from the locale) of the river. At the same time, however, the river is not fixed, static nor stationary: it flows. This flow does not necessarily disrupt its locale. Rather, the flow is representative of its journey, the journeying of the river:

> The river is the locality of journeying because it determines the "over there" and the "there" at which our becoming homely arrives,

yet from which, as a coming to be at home, it also takes its departure. The river does not merely grant the locale, in the sense of the mere place, that is occupied by humans in their dwelling. The locale is intrinsic to the river itself. *The river itself dwells.* (*I*, 35; emphasis added)

What this passage highlights, then, is a simultaneous arrival and departure. That is, at the moment the river arrives (and therefore is), it also, at that very moment, departs, so that it is neither here nor there. In other words, while still being here, the river is also there (a fact that echoes the aphorism of Heraclitus, that no man steps into the same river twice): this speaks to the constant journeying of the river, despite being, as noted above, having a place, that is, a locale. In other words, if the river leaves at the moment it arrives, it is not here, but now there, even though it is still here. What this illuminates, then, is the difficulty of siting the river. Despite ambiguity in locality and despite its movement (essential traits or else it would not be a river, but simply a pool of water), Heidegger is unequivocal that the river dwells. The phenomenon of dwelling is detailed in the next chapter, though for now it suffices to read dwelling as meaning to be or live. That the river dwells means that the river *is*. Heidegger is clear that there is, at a minimum, a circularity that cannot be effaced in such a statement, but Heidegger's scholarship is not allergic to circularity, tautology, or other so-called limitations especially as found in the positive and social sciences: "Insofar as the river itself dwells in the locale of human dwelling, it, in its dwelling, guards this locale in its essence, it *is* its locality. Yet the river is equally essentially the journeying of locality. The essence of the locale, in which becoming homely finds its point of departure and its point of entry, is such that it journeys. The essence of this journeying is the river" (*I*, 35; emphasis in original). For present purposes, what is important to highlight is that Heidegger's quest to explicate the ontological homelessness of beings leads him to read the duality of the river as enigmatic. Heidegger relies upon this duality to explicate the essence of the being of beings, which is read here as nothingness. To further explicate this, the relation between locality and journeying needs exploration.

The duality of the river represents its constant (and incessant) journey; and, at least on the face of it, a journeying (toward) home. The qualifier "constant" is crucial because it signifies the incessant quest of beings for fulfillment. What Heidegger wishes to draw attention to is that this desire leads beings in the wrong direction, not toward authenticity but further into inauthenticity. What follows here, thus, rereads the river—in particular, its journeying—as a metaphor for the life of beings: that is, beings are, like the river, consistently journeying, a journey that is, however, misdirected. As Heidegger puts it: "Insofar as we are attentive to Hölderlin's poetizing of the rivers, we may ponder both the fact that, and the way in which, the spirit of the river bears a relation to becoming homely in one's own" (*1*, 49). Often, however, beings are not fully aware of what their lives are constituted by and the path of their journey. Yet this is not the main problem. Rather, what is a pressing matter is that humans seek to counteract their very journey—as with the case of profound boredom, for example—and it is this that drives beings toward inauthenticity. Thus, Heidegger notes, "that which is their own often remains foreign to human beings for a long time" (21). By this, he seeks to underline that the essence of humanity, their very homelessness, is foreign to them. As such, beings are unaware that their lives are inauthentic. Equally important, this passage reveals the temporality of inauthentic existence, that is, "a long time," which underscores that this state plagues and holds humans as they journey through life. The reason for this—both the inauthenticity that holds humans and for the length of time it does—is simply "because they [beings] abandon what is their own because it is what most threatens to overwhelm them" (21). Thus, it is possible to see and appreciate that inauthenticity continues to hold beings because they have become quite comfortable in such a state (partially because they cannot recognize their own inauthenticity).

The river, then, gives rise to the relation between locality and journeying. The latter, as noted, concerns the journey (toward) home, while the former refers to a specific site that is fixed, that is, where the river is sited. In the locality, spatiality is evoked, a spatiality that is not static but elastic and in flux. In the journey, temporality is evoked. As Heidegger writes, "locality and journeying also carry with them a relation to space and time, the attempt to think locality and journeying in their essence must always do so with a thought to the metaphysical essence of space and time. For it could be that the essential origin of space and time lies concealed in what we are attempting to think in a unitary manner in the names locality and journeying" (*1*, 47–48). As alluded to above, locality and journeying, in reference to time-space, speak to home, a homecoming of sorts. For Heidegger, then, "human beings come…to be at home via journeying and locality" (49), and the river, as poetized by Hölderlin, represents this journey home. Thus, it is already possible to see—especially in portending what Heidegger would pen later in his essay on dwelling, discussed in the next chapter—that home is not simply a site but *a state of being*. According to Mugerauer (2008, 99), "Hölderlin has told us a great deal about the nature of home. Home is much more than a purely human fabrication since…what we do is only a part of what is required." That is, it is not merely a structure or product of materiality, but a process that unfolds and reveals something, in this case that beings are bereft of authenticity. In further explicating this, Heidegger writes, "Locality and journeying…relate to becoming homely in what is one's own. And this is so in the distinctive sense that one's own, finding one's own, and appropriating what one has found as one's own, is not that which is most self-evident or easiest but remains what is most difficult" (*1*, 48–49). Being at home, then, is a process, an incredibly difficult and enigmatic one that beings must learn to embrace. Only then is it possible to see authentically and to see authenticity: "This *coming to be* at home in one's own in itself entails that human beings are initially, and for a long time, and sometimes forever, not at home. And this in turn entails that human beings fail to recognize, that they deny, and perhaps even have to deny and flee what belongs to the home. Coming to be at home is thus a passage through the foreign" (49; emphasis in original).

To focus on this, it is necessary to return to the enigma of the river, specifically, the duality of its flow. After acknowledging and explicating the enigmas of locale and journey, Heidegger gives colour to this matter by focusing upon the flow of the river (its journeying):

The locale is both there and here, not according to some contingency, but under the concealed law of a journey. The locale is not something that is first there and then here, in a mere succession or arbitrary arrangement of places that are occupied and then relinquished. The previous locale remains preserved in the subsequent one. And the subsequent locale has already determined the previous one. This is why the "there" and the "here," indeed the transition between the two locales, are everywhere named by rivers. (*I*, 35–36)

The simultaneity of "here" and "there" partly explains the enigma. In fact, it is simultaneity that confounds the flow of the river and its direction. Heidegger explicates this more substantively as follows:

"Here" at the Ister, "there" from the Indus; and this "from there to here" passes via the Alpheus. The river determines the journey, and the relation grounded therein, the relation of those locales that have been brought about in journeying and thus themselves journey. The journey proceeds from the Indus, thus from the East, via Greece, here to the upper Donau toward the West. In actuality, however, the Donau flows precisely in the opposite direction. If, therefore, the river itself were the journeying from the land of morning to the land of evening, and were able to be this, then the Ister would have to run counter to the actual direction of its own flow. Yet the actual course of the Donau from West to East has been ascertained with such certainty that nothing needs to be said about it. (*I*, 36)

The crux of this passage gives rise to two significant points, both fundamental to what is developed here. First, and as already explicated, the river is, it appears, simultaneously multi-sited: it is both here and there (in other words, here and not here) at the same time. This, as noted before, is partially connected to the enigma of the river, in particular its flow. Related, and secondly, the flow, that is, the direction of the river, is confounded and muddled. This is so, it should be underlined, even though the direction is clear and well settled upon in terms of what is visible to the eye. What confounds and muddles the view of the flow and its direction is the apparent, where it appears as if the direction of the destination is clear. This means, then, and this is the important point to underline—in what is perhaps the most creative and penetrating moment in *Hölderlin's Hymn "The Ister"*—it could be said that, and reread as if, the river, which is flowing in a particular direction and, thus, with it, moving or flowing forward, is, in reality, flowing backwards. It is misdirected. To be clear: the claim here is not that the direction has been erroneously mapped or that once the flow has been inverted or reversed, the problem will either cease to exist or can be corrected. Rather, the issue is this: the direction has been, all the while and all along, correctly formulated, but *the destination* has been erroneously mapped. That is, the river is flowing and flowing to some point; it is, however, flowing backward, not forward, which is to say that it is not progressing. In other words, the river is flowing, but it is not flowing (toward) home; it is flowing away from and against home, which is to say that the river's direction is toward homelessness. Heidegger thus writes, "It looks almost as though the river were going in the opposite direction, although in actuality this is 'naturally' a mere illusion. Rather, thought poetically, this line is saying: The river in truth goes backwards. Such is its provenance" (*I*, 36).

In its natural state, a river flowing forward is a river that is journeying (toward) home. This is the "end point" it searches for, and Heidegger reads this point as home. Thus, if one stands upon a bank of a river and watches as the water gushes or flows downstream, then, one naturally—and rightfully—concludes that the water flows forward (the argument could even be made that the water does not—cannot—*naturally* flow backwards). This is the only sensible way to make sense of the river and the flow of its water. Yet, such a picturing is limited and limiting, Heidegger claims, and his appeal—and attraction—to Hölderlin is premised upon what poetizing provides, what it opens up: the possibilities of imagining, seeing, and appreciating what is often occluded. In other words, poetizing reveals what other formats (only) hide. This is the clearing that Heidegger is in search of (the phrase itself can be found in *Being and Time* at a time when the poetic imaginary had yet not necessarily engrossed Heidegger; or, it could be said, when he did not necessarily see the need for poetizing as he had not yet fully encountered the limits of metaphysical language). Thus, here, Heidegger, via Hölderlin, is claiming that one can read the flow of the river differently, so that the direction of the flow is read in opposite terms: the river is not flowing forward; rather the "river...goes backwards" (*1*, 36).

If reading the flow of the river as such is meaningful, then, this also gives rise to an important point: the river is not flowing home; it is fleeing from home toward perpetual homelessness. Thus, the river and its flow can be read to exemplify (the pursuit of) homelessness. This is why the direction of the river, as noted above, is not misconstrued; it is the destination that has been confounded. In other words, when one watches the flow of a river, what one has failed to appreciate is that the river flows naturally toward homelessness. Like the river, Heidegger sees the destination of beings as homelessness because the path they traverse is not directed homeward. This is the provenance of beings (*1*, 36). In fact, it is not merely that the provenance of beings is homelessness; homelessness is also their essence, their fate. The flow of the river, then, for Heidegger, helps illuminate the ontological homelessness of beings.

Facially, this is not only sobering but alarming as well. However, for Heidegger, it is precisely such a plight that is first necessary to awaken beings from their slumber (his efforts, as noted in chapter two, to let the profoundest boredom remain awake, are designed to permit beings to see and appreciate their homelessness). This is the first step, in other words, in ensuring that a homecoming can even be fathomed. As such, there is no need to fear a state of perpetual homelessness; it needs to be cherished and embraced because this is the natural state of beings. As Mugerauer (2008, 56, 57) writes, "Heidegger...makes clear that as human beings we face in two directions simultaneously" because "[t]o be human is to move toward both the homely and the not at home; it is to move along the right way and the wrong way too" (as can be appreciated, these directions constitute additional indeterminacies relating to what it means to be human). The problem, as noted above, emerges when beings seek to circumvent homelessness and proceed to impute to it the condition of being (at) home:

> [F]ear does not necessarily have to be that habitual fear or fearfulness that readily degenerates into the avoidance and trembling of cowardice. The fear that the δεινόν [fearsome; marvelous] awakens can also be that fear pertaining to reverence and awe. The δεινόν, as the fearful, is then not that which is frightening, but rather that which commands and calls for reverence: that which is worthy of honor. The fear in such reverence is not avoidance or flight, but rather a turning towards something in heed and respect, the awe pertaining to admiration, a standing firm in honouring that which awakens such fear. (*I*, 63)

As will become apparent in the next section, Heidegger uses the term *uncanny* (borrowed from the Greek and later Freud, as noted in chapter one) to refer to the state of not being at home, that is, homelessness. This state of homelessness, Heidegger states in the above quoted passage, calls for reverence, not fear; it is worthy of honor. In other words, homelessness—and the recognition of it—is a necessary precondition for/of the possibility of homecoming. It certainly is a prerequisite for authenticity because authenticity requires that "[w]e…move from numbing comfort to enlivening eeriness" (Mugerauer 2008, 41). The reason for this is simple: beings are naturally and constitutively homeless; this is their provenance: "to be human is to be homeless" (Mugerauer 2008, 71). This is why homelessness needs to be revered and honoured rather than feared and shunned. The flow of the river, as noted above, can be read to reveal the homelessness of beings and the simultaneous directions they traverse.

The Homely, the Un-homely, and Authenticity

In the second part of *Hölderlin's Hymn "The Ister,"* Heidegger explicates Hölderlin's translation and reading of Sophocles' tragedy *Antigone* to further ground the import of homelessness to the being of beings. A key term that repeatedly emerges in Hölderlin's reading of *Antigone* is *the uncanny*, which Heidegger uses to mean "that which is not 'at home', not homely within whatever is homely" (*I*, 74).[3] That is, the uncanny references a state of homelessness where beings are not "at home" (the "at home" in quotation marks is important to note, a point that will be taken up later). This homelessness, as repeatedly noted, and as will be explicated further, is ontological. At least for Heidegger, ontological homelessness is *the* pressing issue facing humanity: "The most powerful of 'catastrophes' we can think of in nature and in the cosmos are nothing in terms of their uncanniness compared to that uncanniness that the human essence in itself is, insofar as human beings, placed among beings as such and set in place for beings, *forget being*. In this way, the homely becomes an empty and errant wandering for them, one that they fill out with their activities" (77; emphasis added). For Heidegger, the significance and seriousness of ontological homelessness certainly appears to outweigh the material condition of being without a home (or some other form of shelter or lodging). This is because in ontological homelessness, the very meaning of being, of existence, is itself without home.[4] That is, "the human essence," as Heidegger puts it, is in and of itself lost: it wanders to and from with little to no purpose, and as such, humans are inherently unfree. It is as if humans are separated and distanced from their very essence. This is what Heidegger seeks to capture when he writes that beings forget being, noting that beings are uninterested in the meaning of existence. This is what concerns Heidegger, and this is why he underlines the import of ontological homelessness to the being of beings.

For Heidegger, it is "the human being alone [who] can be called by the name 'the uncanny'" (*I*, 69). That is, it is not simply that beings are uncanny, but it is a condition or state that only beings experience (as detailed in the previous section, what is unique to beings is that every person, whether cognizant or not, is, by essence and constitution, homeless). Thus, understanding the being of beings would mean understanding and making sense of the homelessness that is (in) beings. As well, it is not merely that beings are homeless (and that only beings can be homeless) but that, and importantly, their homelessness is all encompassing. This means that homelessness cannot be spoken of in terms of degree—that is, one is more homeless than another—but that all are, in essence, homeless. The homelessness, in other words, is penetrating, overwhelming, and profound. This is why Heidegger writes that the uncanny is "the fundamental kind of essence belonging to human beings" (72–73). To underline this, Heidegger notes that "the human being is the most uncanny" and that "[u]ncanniness does not first arise as a consequence of human kind; rather, *humankind emerges from uncanniness and remains within it*—looms out of it and stirs within it. *The uncanny itself is what looms forth in the essence of human beings*" (72; emphasis added). As such, humanity is not just linked and connected to homelessness. Rather, the very essence of humanity emerges from the condition of homelessness and remains as such. Humanity and homelessness, then, as noted before, are inextricably linked, but this linking is not just that humans are, by essence, homeless, but that it is from this very condition of homelessness that the notion of humanity arises and can arise. As such, at least for Heidegger, there is no more important an issue than ontological homelessness because ontological homelessness is the foundation of making sense of what it means to be (human). As will become apparent, if humans are not ontologically homeless, it would be impossible to speak of humans and humanity.

One aspect of ontological homelessness needs further elaboration. As noted, Heidegger states that "[w]e mean the uncanny in the sense of that which is not at home—not homely in that which is homely" (*1*, 71). This quote is now self-explanatory given the preceding discussion. Given the attention drawn earlier to the phrase "at home," which Heidegger puts within quotation marks, it needs underlining that in the quoted sentence above, the words "at home" are not in quotation marks. Immediately following this sentence, however, Heidegger writes: "It is only for this reason that the un-homely can, as a consequence, also be 'uncanny' in the sense of something that has an alienating or 'frightening' effect that gives rise to anxiety" (71). Two issues arise that deserve attention, one focusing upon the meaninglessness of life (and whether beings are privy to this meaninglessness); the other, what apparently looks like circular logic regarding the homelessness of the homeless. Specifically, there is a paradox around the homelessness of the homed, so to speak, that deserves attention.

It is important to recognize that Heidegger appears to make a distinction between the *non-homely* and the *un-homely*. Before explicating this, it is necessary to explicate the "un-" that precedes and qualifies the homely (or the canny, as in uncanny). Heidegger claims that

> [w]hatever belongs to the "un-" in the uncanny [or un-homely] is of an essence other than that which we could ever grasp with the aid of negations that slide back and forth. We approach whatever belongs to the "un-" more closely in recognizing it as that which belongs to evil, provided we do not conceive of evil in the sense of something morally bad, that is, as characteristic of human activity, but rather as an essential trait of being itself, within whose realm humans journey along their path. (*I*, 78)

Heidegger is uninterested in imputing value—especially negative value—to anything that is qualified with an "un-," such that, for him, the "un-homely" or "un-canny" need not be negative. Each is merely meant to describe an "is" and nothing else—in this case, beings *are* homeless. Returning, then, to the distinction Heidegger carves between "un-" and "non-," it is possible to see that "[t]hat which is un-homely is not merely the non-homely, but rather that homely that seeks yet does not find itself, because it seeks itself by way of *a distancing and alienation from itself*" (84; emphasis added).

In this statement, it is clear that the un-homely refers to a negation, that is, the non-homely. In other words, and to labour a simple point, the un-homely is not the same as the non-homely. There is, however, much more to what Heidegger is conveying. That is, the unhomely refers to, rather strangely, the homely, though here the homely ought to be thought of ontically. In other words, what Heidegger is saying is that the condition of being at home—home in being-in-the-world—makes beings homeless ontologically. To appreciate this, it is important to note that beings are un-homely because, as stated, they are homely in the they-self; but in the they-self they are also seeking home in the ontological sense (this is, as explicated in chapters one and two, Dasein's calling). However, and this is what makes the homely un-homely, beings seek improperly because they are unable to fully see and appreciate their plight, and this means that their very being is homeless. In other words, beings are, as Heidegger says, distancing themselves from their very selves. It is, as he puts it, an alienation of the self from the self. As noted in the previous chapter, if one thinks of a point (a literal point on a piece of paper, for example), and this point is the essence (the core) of being, then, what Heidegger is claiming is that beings are (unwittingly) distancing themselves from this point, their very being. They are doing so not necessarily because they are not seeking this point, although that very well might be the case. Rather, they are distancing themselves because they are looking in the wrong places and in erroneous ways. Meaninglessness, then, prevails and takes hold of beings. This is the only possible outcome because beings understand that they are searching but cannot understand or make sense of why they are unable to find what they are so in need of (any critique that the foregoing is merely abstract theorization—which to some extent it is—can be offset by thinking historically in terms of why and how beings have aligned themselves with a deity or deities, or reflecting on the current predicament of soaring rates of anxiety, depression, and other mental ailments, not to mention boredom, especially after the pandemic, which clearly point to a missing-ness [theorized here as nothingness] and meaninglessness of/about life). Thus, it is not just their lives but their journey toward finding the essence of their lives that begins to look meaningless to beings, and it all looks meaningless to them because *it is* meaningless, though they are unable to see this. This is the clearing that Heidegger was in search of even as early as *Being and Time*.

There is, then, an important relation between the homely and unhomely in shining light upon the ontological homelessness of beings. This is why Heidegger writes that "[i]n those beings they come to, and in which they think themselves at home, *they come to nothing*. Thinking they are homely, human beings are those who are unhomely" (*1*, 76; emphasis added). He expands:

> In human beings reaching everywhere, however, and in each case coming to "something," they still come to nothing, because they remain stuck with particular beings in each case, and fail to grasp their being or essence in such beings. The "nothing" to which they come is that which, turning counter to being, directly excludes human beings altogether from being...Driven to busy themselves

with all beings in every way, human beings are simultaneously (as though) driven out from being. (76)

Heidegger's point is simple but sobering: beings who search for home are searching in the wrong places, and thus will not experience a homecoming (this, of course, does not account for those who are uninterested in searching). As elucidated in the previous chapter, in the same ways that beings search for fulfillment in other beings and yet are still left empty because of the superficial nature of these relations (as the example of the dinner party shows), beings who search for home in the materiality of the world—where they busy themselves with beings in all ways—are alienated from their essence because their focus is upon beings, not being. Their experiences, thus, always amount to nothing, a point that Heidegger repeatedly makes. In this nothing, alienation sets in. While equivocal, this passage also homes-in upon the nothingness of being, one of ontological homelessness, which is addressed later in the chapter. Next, however, a study of Antigone, the heroine in Sophocles' tragedy— and she certainly is a heroine in Heidegger's reading of Hölderlin's reading of the tragedy—gives colour to the homelessness of the homely.

The Hearth and Being

As a foray into the being of beings, Heidegger examines the dialogue between Antigone and her sister Ismene. The dialogue concerns Antigone's steadfastness to disobey the wishes of her uncle, Creon, who forbids her from burying her brother, Polyneices. Antigone is indefatigable in defending her position.

The controversy surrounding the burial in *Antigone* concerns entry into the afterlife in Greek mythology: entering into the afterlife, and thus being (at) home, requires a proper burial. Creon's refusal to change his mind about not permitting Polyneices to be buried would mean that the possibility of entering into the afterlife would be foreclosed for Polyneices, who would thus be forever homeless. Antigone's refusal to obey Creon, thus, is reflective not merely of her loyalty to her brother (and her family more broadly), nor merely of her loyalty to justice and rightness, but more precisely for present purposes, also of her understanding and defence of home: her understanding that her brother was homeless while in his body, and he would need to be buried for his soul to be (at) home. The fight for this, then, is her attempt to safeguard her brother's homecoming. Home and homelessness, thus, are at the heart of the tragedy, and this is what appears to draw Heidegger to the poetry of Hölderlin.

Drawing on this dialogue, Heidegger concludes that Antigone is "the most uncanny being in terms of its essence," that is, "the supreme uncanny" (*I*, 104). This uncanniness Heidegger reads as evidence of Antigone being "*utterly* unhomely" (103; emphasis added). In referring to and describing Antigone's homelessness as "utterly," "supreme," or "most," Heidegger is speaking of a qualitative difference: that is, "there are...various ways of being unhomely" (108). This also means, and Heidegger is explicit about this, focus should not be cast upon a quantitative difference, but rather on the intensity (or intensification) of the qualitative difference (104).[5] Heidegger relies upon the descriptors *most* and *supreme* that qualify the state of being unhomely to underline that the condition of the unhomely is intrinsic to being (104). By this Heidegger means that the unhomely belongs to being ex ante: "the unhomely is nothing that human beings themselves make but rather the converse: something that makes them into what they are and who they can be" (103). As noted, homelessness is the requisite foundation upon which the notion of humanity can even be fathomed. Without this foundation, it is impossible to meaningfully speak of/about existence. As such, humans are, as noted, homeless: if they are not, then, they are not human.

The next step for Heidegger is to explicate what makes Antigone the "most" unhomely. To understand this, it is necessary to grapple with an apparent paradox that concerns what Heidegger calls the "ambiguity of being unhomely" (*I*, 115). There are, as already noted, two sorts of unhomeliness, the first referring to a stage of becoming homely, the second to a stage that does not permit a passing to the homely. The latter, it has been suggested here, is best thought of as the non-homely (a term Heidegger sometimes uses in what appears to be his effort to make this distinction). As Heidegger reads it, Antigone's unhomeliness—which is, in fact, supreme, or of which she has the most—is her quest *for* being (emanating from her defiance against a specific order from her uncle). In this way, this unhomeliness—what is here referred to as *unhomely* to distinguish it from *non-homely*—can be thought of as a way of countering being-in-the-world, and with it, usher in authenticity.

To bring this to light, Heidegger turns to the hearth as it is relayed in the tragedy and what it suggests about being—a fireplace was essential in history for not just the provision of light but also heat, and, thus, signified and represented life. Heidegger probes whether the hearth is being and concludes that "[t]he hearth is the site of being-homely," that is, "the site of all sites" (*I*, 105). "What is essential to the hearth," Heidegger writes, "is the fire in the manifoldness of its essence, which essentially prevails as lighting, illuminating, warming, nourishing, purifying, refining, glowing" (105). The hearth represents home—the hearth symbolizes home because it produces the warmth and light so needed, even desired, in the house (especially in historical times). This is what Heidegger is seeking to convey via the tragedy. However, the warmth also has to do with something else. If it can be said that the fire provides light and thereby illuminates, then Heidegger relies upon this to claim that this illumination refers to knowledge about being (107–108, 117). That is, he claims that if the hearth is being (108–113) such that "[b]eing is the hearth" (112), then this is because the hearth represents vision and illumination via the light it shines upon the home and what it means to be (at) home (it represents the "clearing" he sought in his earlier works).

This can be homed-in upon by returning to the ambiguity of the unhomely, which is brought to light in Heidegger's reading of the dialogue between Antigone and her uncle, Creon. On the one hand, the unhomely can be thought of as an expulsion to the unhomely itself, that is, to remaining within the world. As Heidegger puts it:

> The unhomely one shall not be someone homely, so long as they stick merely and solely to their being unhomely and thus let themselves be driven about amid beings without any consistency. The

closing words [in *Antigone*] reject whoever is unhomely in this way, and at the same time call in the direction of a knowledge of the proper essence of the unhomely one. (*I*, 117)

The first sentence of this passage describes the first form of unhomeliness; the last sentence portends what follows, namely, the second aspect of the unhomely. That is, toward the end of the play, the first form of unhomeliness—remaining in the world merely as beings—is rejected and, instead, a different form of unhomeliness (one that prepares the way toward being) is embraced. "The closing words," Heidegger writes, "conceal within them a pointer toward that risk that has yet to be unfolded and accomplished but that is accomplished in the tragedy as a whole, the risk of distinguishing and deciding between that being unhomely proper to human beings and a being unhomely that is inappropriate" (117). In other words, the countering mentioned above, what Heidegger also calls the "counterplay," reads the *Antigone* tragedy such that "[t]he counterplay is played out between being unhomely in the sense of being driven about amid beings without any way out, and being unhomely as becoming homely from out of a belonging to being" (118). For Heidegger, Antigone is the most uncanny or is utterly unhomely because she represents the desire to search for and belong to being. That is, she is not satisfied merely being among beings.

The foregoing, then, clearly shines light upon the specific (directional) relation between the un-homely and the homely: for Heidegger, the latter is impossible without the former because—if not for any other reason—there is no reason to yearn for being if one is not unhomely. As Heidegger puts it, "*being homely is a becoming homely in being unhomely*" (*I*, 125; emphasis added). What the *Antigone* tragedy reveals, Heidegger says, is that where Antigone is "*becoming homely within being, she is the most unhomely one amid beings*" (120; emphasis added). That is, she is now distancing herself from beings (think in relation to the point on a piece of paper, discussed earlier). This is the ambiguity of the unhomely, an ambiguity that reveals the being of beings, the "being of human beings, their being un-homely–homely in the midst of beings" (121). One needs to be homeless and come to terms with one's homelessness, then, to be able to appreciate what it means to be (at) home. The final section of the chapter seeks to tie the foregoing together by connecting the being of beings to nothingness.

Being, Nothingness, and Ontological Homelessness

The discussion of the flow of the river Ister and the tragedy of Antigone have an appearance of disunity, and to some extent this is so despite the theme of ontological homelessness that unites them. In both, an indeterminacy constitutes beings: they are, at once and simultaneously, homeless even though/while they are (at) home.

The flow of the river vividly illuminates this: its flow, which is said to be flowing toward home, is read as flowing away from home (in fact, fleeing home). Thus, while beings are journeying, and thus on the move, it is the destination that befuddles them. The more they journey, the further away from home they are. The tragedy of Antigone articulates this same point, though in a different narrative. Antigone is certainly homeless, but she appears to be cognizant of her homelessness. Thus, her renunciation of her uncle's wishes represents her desire to break free from the world, and this helps set the stage for a journey back home (in fact, it could even be said that the very recognition of her homelessness itself constitutes her homecoming).

Heidegger's point in both narratives is simple and straightforward: to be able to come home, one must understand not only that one is homeless, but that homelessness is one's constitution. To be home, then, is in many ways not merely to embrace one's homelessness but to live with/in it. This is what leads to authenticity. The moral of the story, of course, is not merely that beings do not recognize and understand their homelessness, but that they do not see it as constitutive to/of their essence. Thus, all the efforts to circumvent it—by putting boredom to sleep, for example—mean that beings will never be home, even though they dogmatically believe that they already are. In fact, every effort to circumvent homelessness means that beings are alienating themselves from their very essence. This means that inauthenticity, and with it unfreedom, holds beings. In other words— as noted in the introduction—inauthenticity is unfreedom, and beings who are unwilling to embrace their homelessness, a homelessness that belongs to them ex ante, are constitutionally unfree.

What this points to—in the same ways that the discussion of the fundamental attunements of anxiety and boredom do—is the nothingness of being. In other words, the being of beings is nothingness in the sense that beings are forever caught in and constituted by an indeterminacy about their status. The ever present (and growing) quest for that missing something already points to the fact that there is something absent, yet beings are flummoxed by what exactly that missing something is. Still, the emptiness that is nothing is, in fact, far from nothing. The void is merely the inability to articulate it precisely (even vaguely). Both anxiety and the profoundest boredom put this in perspective. What *Hölderlin's Hymn "The Ister"* points to is that the status of home (and being at home) that beings are forever in search of and think that they are working toward is, in fact, a status of homelessness. Beings, then, are caught in this state of nothingness. To exacerbate matters, however, and ironically, is this sobering point: rather than seeing homelessness as the essence of beings, and thus to be celebrated and championed, the very quest to overcome it by believing that one is then coming home only further entrenches beings in their homelessness. Rather than seeking to create home with/in homelessness, Heidegger argues that beings should *dwell* in homelessness. This is the focus of the next chapter.

4

Dwelling in Ontological Homelessness

THE PRECEDING CHAPTER examined *Hölderlin's Hymn "The Ister,"* focusing on the flow of the river Ister and Sophocles' tragedy *Antigone* to underline the ontological homelessness of beings. As the chapter argued, it is not merely that beings are ontologically homeless but that being-in-the-world already renders them so. That is, homelessness is the very condition of being human. This is the fate that befalls all beings. For Heidegger, a sobering aspect of Hölderlin's poetry is that beings are oblivious to this fate. More sobering but equally refreshing is that the state of ontological homelessness is to be embraced and cherished rather than shunned. Only the recognition and embrace of ontological homelessness permits a homecoming, as it was for Antigone (who, recall, is lauded because she wholeheartedly embraces her homelessness and faces it head-on). For Heidegger, homecoming *is* the realization and acceptance of the homelessness of beings in all of its manifestations and with all of its implications (or at least the recognition that homelessness paves the way home). What the previous chapter's reading of the flow of the river shows is that beings are, in fact, fleeing from home and are unaware of the path they traverse. Authentic life, thus, is an impossibility. Heidegger's lesson, as the end of the previous chapter briefly noted, is that beings should—

must, in fact—dwell *in* ontological homelessness. This chapter focuses on the concept of dwelling and undertakes its inquiry via Heidegger's essay "Building Dwelling Thinking" (notice that the traditional separation of concepts or ideas with commas or semi-colons is missing from this title, an absence that Heidegger utilizes to speak of the three as one—or perhaps three *in* one). The exegetical rereading of this essay serves two related purposes. First, as noted—and building upon what has been laid in the preceding chapter—it situates the import of dwelling to/in ontological homelessness. Second, it highlights that Heidegger wishes to move past the (rather orthodox) view that dwelling necessarily entails or requires material structures.[1] Thus, the argument is that material sites and structures such as houses are not constitutive of, nor are they *preconditions* for, home or being (at) home. As will become clear at the outset of the next section, these material structures and sites are, in fact, *insufficient* conditions *for* home (indeed the [more] polemical position, that material structures are *irrelevant*, even unnecessary, for home, can be sustained through this line of inquiry and argument, though not pushed to its logical end here). Thus, one can be housed and be in a home, and nevertheless be homeless, that is, not at home. Heidegger states this unequivocally in "Being Dwelling Thinking." While material structures shield and protect beings from many things (inclement weather being one example) and, as such, are vital to/for survival, they will not and cannot shield and protect beings from the condition of ontological homelessness that makes humans, human. Heidegger's essay, as this chapter shows, helps shed light upon the fate of beings by explicating the relations among dwelling, material sites or structures (such as houses), and authentic being.

Dwelling and Building (Act and Deed)
The title "Building Dwelling Thinking" is meant to highlight an inextricable connection between the three concepts it contains. At the outset of the essay, Heidegger notes that "we shall try to think about dwelling and building" (BDT, 347) but warns that his interests are not of a conventional sort. Rather, he claims that a broad and deep question about the *meaning* of building animates his focus. "This thinking about building," he notes, "does not promise to

discover architectural ideas, let alone to give rise to rules for building. This venture in thought does not view building as an art or as a technique of construction; rather, it traces building back into that domain to which everything that *is* belongs" (347; emphasis in original). Beyond outlining the parameters of the essay, this statement also reveals (if only subtly) that the concept of "building" as a noun (e.g., a hospital) and verb (e.g., to erect a building, that is, the act of building), need to be separated and examined individually.[2] This separation is crucial for Heidegger to make sense of the essence of building, the essence of dwelling, and the essence of their relation. Thus, Heidegger poses two related and, facially, simple questions to commence his endeavour: "What is it to dwell?" and "How does building belong to dwelling?" (347).

Heidegger begins by examining the relation between building and dwelling as commonly thought, namely, that building is a precondition for dwelling (recall, for example, how dwelling and dwell are defined in the *Oxford English Dictionary*, as outlined in the first note of this chapter). According to this view, dwelling is an impossibility if it is not tied to and founded upon a building.[3] "We attain to dwelling, so it seems," Heidegger writes in capturing such a limited and limiting view, "only by means of building. The latter, building, has its former, dwelling, as its goal" (BDT, 347). In the foregoing, it is possible to see that the word *building* is invoked both as a noun (a physical site or structure) and a verb (the act of erecting a structure). Heidegger, however, wishes to distance himself from such a view, which he labels as a means-end schema (347): building as a means to the end of dwelling. Facially, it is not the case that such a view is necessarily false; rather, it requires clarification because it is incomplete or simplistic. Thus, Heidegger immediately writes that "not every building is a dwelling," that is, "not [strictly] dwelling places," and provides as examples stadia and railway stations (347). While it might be true that a railway station is not the home of many—in the sense that one does not call it and others like it home—Heidegger does admit that there is a relation between such sites and dwelling. This is because "these buildings are in the *domain* of our dwelling. That domain extends over these buildings and so is not limited to dwelling places" (347; emphasis added). To bring clarity

Dwelling in Ontological Homelessness   103

to this distinction, Heidegger explains that "[t]he truck driver is at home on the highway, but he does not have his lodgings there; the working woman is at home in the spinning mill, but does not have her dwelling place there; the chief engineer is at home in the power station, but he does not dwell there. These buildings house man" (347–348).

Heidegger appears to draw a distinction between the housing of people in a physical site and what it means to be (at) home. If this distinction is further extended, it is also possible to claim that a physical structure (including, perhaps, a house) might house one, but it does not necessarily ensure that one is (at) home. Importantly, this would mean that to be (at) home (to *not* be homeless) is a status or condition that is constituted by much more than a physical structure such as a house. To put this differently, to be (at) home and to live and be in a house (even if one owns it rather than merely rents it) are two fundamentally different statuses or conditions. The point to underscore is this: one can own and be in a house (or some other sort of shelter) and still be homeless. Thus, to take the example Heidegger provides, the truck and the road might not carry with them the everyday belongings of the truck driver, his lodgings as Heidegger puts it (e.g., food, clothes, family, and other personal goods), but they do, in some way at least, ensure that the truck driver is at home even though he does not live, at least for the most part, in/on the truck or on the road. As such, to be (at) home—which perhaps at this point can be read as "to be in oneself"—does not necessitate that one is at home in one's house. One is technically at home even though one is far from the physical structure or site of home. Extended to a logical conclusion, this means that a physical structure, in particular, a house, is an *insufficient* condition for home.

The other examples Heidegger provides—namely, the working woman in the spinning mill and the engineer in the power station—highlight another point. Heidegger says that both the woman and the engineer are at home in their respective sites of employment. The condition of being (at) home in these two sites is similar to the first example of the truck driver on the road, but there is a difference in how dwelling is conceptualized. This concerns a negation not of lodging, but of dwelling itself. That is, both the woman and the engineer are (at) home even though they *do not* dwell in these sites. If it is the case that one can be at home without dwelling in that site, then, there arise two important matters that need attention, which, however, can only be raised at this point and returned to later for more extensive treatment. The first concerns the relation between lodging and dwelling, specifically, whether these are one and the same. The answer, unequivocally, is no, but this can only be asserted at this point. The second concerns the word *dwell* (and its relation dwelling), and what it means (the first of two questions, recall, that Heidegger poses to explore dwelling vis-à-vis being).

Prior to engaging with these matters, another issue, raised earlier, requires attention. This concerns Heidegger's point that the sites in question—the road, the spinning mill, and the power station, among others—are in the *domain of dwelling*, and that the domain extends over buildings. By *domain*, Heidegger seems to be referring to areas or territories and claiming that these fall within the purview of dwelling: they are concerned or occupy themselves with dwelling but are farther reaching than specific and commonly thought of sites of dwelling (e.g., houses). Thus, the truck driver and engineer in their respective sites highlight that dwelling takes place in sites beyond the home or house, and this is why the truck driver is (at) home on the road even though the truck driver's house is physically sited elsewhere. This example aids Heidegger in seeking to answer the question "What is to dwell?" (BDT, 347) and, as well, the meaning of dwelling. This involves, as noted, debunking the presupposition that a specific structural site (e.g., a house) ensures dwelling is possible. As noted, these matters have only been provisionally addressed thus far, and attention now turns to their fuller consideration.

Heidegger writes that "He [man] inhabits them [buildings/sites] and yet does not dwell in them, if to dwell means solely to have our lodgings in them" (BDT, 348). If there is any uncertainty or ambiguity surrounding the preceding discussion, this statement clearly elucidates that a site alone (e.g., a house) is not a sufficient criterion for dwelling. To put this conversely, the material structure or site is insufficient for dwelling (in this sense, recall, as developed in the previous section, that such a material structure is an insufficient condition for being (at) home, which already speaks to the relation between dwelling and home, which will come to bear as the chapter progresses). How true this is, is evinced in the implication that Heidegger focuses upon: simply because one stores one's belongings (what he calls lodgings) in a specific, settled, site (e.g., a house), does not mean that one dwells (in that site). This would mean, and as briefly alluded to, that dwelling, lodging, and inhabiting are not the same, and should not be treated as such. Heidegger means something very precise and specific by dwelling. This is brought remarkably to light in the following which is as direct as it is sobering: "In today's housing shortage, even this much is reassuring and to the good; residential buildings do indeed provide lodgings; today's houses may even be well planned, easy to keep, attractively cheap, open to air, light and sun, but—do the houses in themselves hold any guarantee that *dwelling* occurs in them? Yet, those buildings that are not dwelling places remain in turn determined by dwelling insofar as they serve man's dwelling" (348; emphasis in original).

It is unequivocal that buildings provide lodging, and partly at least, lodging entails not merely sorting and storing things (and inhabitants themselves), but is also related to other issues, such as health (e.g., ventilation). While Heidegger does not explicitly say this—because it is implied—there is no doubt that buildings are vitally important, essential in fact, to the well-being of humans. After acknowledging the import of buildings as such, Heidegger is even willing to admit that buildings *may* be conducive to(ward) dwelling.

Dwelling and lodging, as such, might be related, but they are not the same. Heidegger underscores this difference to ensure that dwelling is viewed differently from the status quo, which equates dwelling to/with a material structure (again, recall the definition of the term as found in the *Oxford English Dictionary* in the first note of this chapter). The final sentence of the above quoted passage, where Heidegger is explicit that buildings that might not be conducive to dwelling (because they are not viewed as dwelling places) are nevertheless *determined* by dwelling because they serve the dwelling of beings (e.g., the power station or the truck on the road) clearly evidences this. Thus, Heidegger is admitting that building and dwelling do, in fact, go hand-in-hand, though not as traditionally maintained. That is, if the building-dwelling nexus is viewed as a means-end relationship (building serves as the means to the end of dwelling), then, the essence of dwelling is lost. "[D]welling," Heidegger says, "would in any case be the end that presides over all building. Dwelling and building are related as end and means. However, as long as this is all we have in mind, we take dwelling and building as two separate activities, an idea that has something correct in it. Yet at the same time by the means-end schema we block our view of the essential relations" (BDT, 348).

Building and dwelling, then, are related. However, to understand the essence of dwelling it is important to come to terms with the nature of the relation between building and dwelling. This relation does not—cannot—entail viewing building merely as a noun (as a structure). Instead, it is necessary to see that "building is not merely a means and a way toward dwelling—*to build is in itself already to dwell*" (BDT, 348; emphasis added). Heidegger alerts readers to the need to account for building not merely as a noun but also as a verb because it is only then that it is possible to appreciate that dwelling already precedes building, both in terms of a site and structure and the act of erecting such a structure. One builds because one dwells (and has already dwelled and will continue to dwell). This is why, as noted, building is an insufficient criterion or condition of dwelling.

To ground his claims, Heidegger undertakes an etymological analysis of the word *build* and asks: "[W]hat does *bauen*, to build, mean?" (BDT, 348). As he reads it, "[t]he Old High German word for building, *buan*, means to dwell. This signifies to remain, to stay in place" (348).[4] However, the meaning of the word *build* had undergone a significant transformation in the German language. As such, by the time Heidegger penned his essay, the link between building and dwelling had all but disappeared. To reintroduce this connection, Heidegger acknowledges that "[t]he proper meaning of the verb *bauen*, namely, to dwell, has been lost to us," and then claims that "a covert trace of it has been preserved in the German *Nachbar*, a neighbour. The *Nachbar* is the...near dweller, he who dwells nearby" (348–349). This allows Heidegger to (re)construct a certain permanence associated in the relation between dwelling and building, and in further underscoring this connection he writes that "to be sure, the old word *buan* not only tells us that *bauen*, to build, is really to dwell; it also gives us a clue as to how we have to think about the dwelling it signifies" (349). Thus, and to underline this point, Heidegger writes: "*Bauen* originally means to dwell" (349). Building, specifically the verb *to build*, as Heidegger reads its etymology, then, concerns dwelling: the two are inextricably linked. Dwelling, as Heidegger views it, and as noted in the previous discussion, concerns much more than lodging: it, in fact, speaks to the essence of being. In other words, not only does *bauen* mean to dwell, but "[w]here the word speaks in its original sense it also says how far the essence of dwelling reaches" (349; emphasis omitted). Dwelling, the essence of being, entails building (both sites and structures as well as the act of erecting these). This is, in some ways, what Heidegger means by the domain of dwelling.

After exploring the myriad derivatives of *bauen* and, with them, locating and connecting building and dwelling, Heidegger asks, "What then does *ich bin* mean? The old word *bauen*, to which the *bin* belongs, answers, *ich bin, du bist* mean I dwell, you dwell. The way in which you are and I am, the manner in which we humans are on the earth, is *buan*, dwelling. To be a human being means to be on the earth as a mortal. It means to dwell" (BDT, 349). What unfolds is crucial not only because it reiterates that building *is* dwelling, but, and more importantly for what is developed here, because it unequivocally states that to be (the being of beings, the meaning of existence) is to dwell, and to dwell, in complement, means to be. Dwelling and being, then, are inextricably linked. *To be* human, in other words, *is to dwell*. As this chapter progresses, it will become clear that, if to be is to dwell, then dwelling signifies homelessness. In other words, to dwell means or equals *to dwell in homelessness* (which is, as has been explicated, nothingness, an indeterminacy). As such, the sobering point is that not dwelling or refusing to dwell in homelessness results in not being, essentially negating being, negating existence.

In further elaborating upon the relation between dwelling and being, Heidegger, in a lengthy passage, explains:

> The old word *bauen*, which says that man *is* insofar as he *dwells*, this word *bauen*, however, *also* means at the same time to cherish and to protect, to preserve and care for, specifically to till the soil, to cultivate the vine. Such building only takes care—it tends to the

growth that ripens its fruit of its own accord. Building in the sense of preserving and nurturing is not making anything. Shipbuilding and temple-building, on the other hand, do in a certain way make their own works. Here building, in contrast with cultivating is a constructing. Both modes of building—building as cultivating... and building as the raising up of edifices...—are comprised with the genuine building, that is, dwelling. (BDT, 349; emphasis in original)

For Heidegger, building and dwelling are intimately connected given that dwelling precedes building: thus, one builds because one dwells, not the other way around: "We do not dwell because we have built, but we build and have built because we dwell, that is, because we are *dwellers*" (350; emphasis in original). Thus, and as Heidegger puts it pithily: "[b]uilding is really dwelling" (350). This also means that dwelling *is* being (or if dwelling is not being, then it is at least intimately tied to being). This latter point is evinced in the first sentence of the above quoted passage, where Heidegger says that building, dwelling, and being are linked, and intimately so (that is, man is insofar as he dwells, so that if one does not or cannot dwell, then, one is not). What is also clear from this is that Heidegger begins to read into, or discover in, the verb *to build* an element or ethic of caring and protecting (which has vestiges from his seminal *Being and Time*). That is, part of being, the preservation of the self, Heidegger claims, is met via the act of building and what materializes from it, namely, structures of buildings. This he calls "genuine building" (349) and locates it with dwelling. Thus, building, dwelling, and being are inextricably linked, and what is now necessary is to appreciate this connection, one which Heidegger underlines by noting what has been missing in the ontology of being: "[D]welling is not experienced as man's Being; dwelling is never thought of as the basic character of human being" (350).

Having demonstrated that building is, in fact, dwelling, and that dwelling and being are inextricably linked, Heidegger proceeds to explicate the concept of dwelling (recall this is the first of two questions posed; the second, the relation between dwelling and building, now clear). Thus, Heidegger asks: "[I]n what does the *essence* of dwelling consist?" (BDT, 350; emphasis added). After undertaking an etymological analysis of various words—which need not occupy attention here—he writes:

> To dwell, to be set at peace, means to remain at peace within the free, the preserve, the free sphere that safeguards each thing in its essence. *The fundamental character of dwelling is this sparing.* It preserves in its whole range. That range reveals itself to us as soon as we recall that human being consists in dwelling and, indeed, dwelling in the sense of the stay of mortals on the earth. (351; emphasis in original)

If there is a certain permanence about building (the edifice, for example, remains intact), then dwelling similarly has a certain permanence about it (think, again, in relation to the lingering noted earlier). Paul Harrison (2007, 634; emphasis in original), for example, locates this permanence as an immobility, noting that "there is something immobile within Heidegger's thought of dwelling, something that is already in place, of place, *before* the event of dwelling eventuates, something which cannot undergo displacement." This is unequivocally illustrated in Heidegger's comment that dwelling entails being at peace (see also Dauenhauer 1977, 194–195). If one understands being at peace as a certain restfulness—one is at peace with the result of being restful which is to say that one is okay or good with it—then, it is possible to see that the peace that is equated to/with dwelling refers, in some ways, to a sense of contentment (to be content with what transpires). In fact, it is much more than contentment that is meant by being at peace; that is, the equation of dwelling with peace captures a sense of fulfillment. If one is at peace with the result, for example, then, one is, in many ways, fulfilled by that result, even if that result is not what was originally desired. There is, then, some closure in the result, and this is what brings peace and, with it, fulfillment. This is perhaps why Harrison (2007, 630) notes that "Heidegger's thought of space is already in a movement of enclosure, is already informed by a protective, preservative, impulse." Thus, the peace that is equated with dwelling is said to be "set" and thus, one "remain[s]" in it. This suggests, as noted above, not simply the contentment and fulfillment that comes with dwelling but a certain permanence about it. Partly, as well, what brings peace is that the essence of dwelling is preserved in its core. This is what Heidegger has in mind when he claims that the "fundamental character of dwelling" is a "sparing" (BDT, 351; emphasis omitted; see also Dauenhauer [1977, 195], who says that "the fundamental characteristic of dwelling is saving"). That is, the essence or core of dwelling consists of peace, and this peace is, in circular logic, about the preservation of the core or essence. Since this preservation is secured and safeguarded, it is preserved and thus achieves a sense of permanence. To put it differently, being consists of dwelling and dwelling consists of sparing. What is spared, that is, preserved, is the core of what it means to be (human)—in this case, to be (set) at peace, a fulfilment of sorts of the being of beings (this setting at peace, as will become apparent shortly, requires things, which, among others, are to be found in erected structures such as buildings). This preservation and sparing—of recognizing that being is dwelling, and dwelling is making sense of the core of being—is what makes beings free.

Heidegger clearly articulates this point in his explication of sparing, which is here read as a preserving. This is a preservation of the whole range or spectrum of dwelling, which consists not merely in the structural components of the building, but in the act of building as well. Heidegger calls this the domain of dwelling and claims that it must be given its proper due to understand the essence of dwelling: "To free actually means to spare. The sparing itself consists not only in the fact that we do not harm the one whom we spare. Real sparing is something *positive* and takes place when we leave something beforehand in its own essence, when we return it specifically to its essential being, when we 'free' it in the proper sense of the word into a preserve of peace" (BDT, 351; emphasis in original). The crux of sparing, real sparing, is possible when the essence of something is left intact. Given that the essence of being is dwelling, setting dwelling at peace (via building, as will become apparent) spares and preserves its essence. It is fair to read Heidegger's notion of peace, then, as a sense of purity, though this purity will only emerge when the whole range of dwelling is accounted for; in this context, this accounting does not dismiss the structures of buildings but also does not grant to them primacy undeserving of them. Read in this way, the purity of dwelling and its relation to being can be brought to light.[5]

What is required, then, is to unpack how peace, that is purity, is kept intact, so that the essence of dwelling, and with it being, is spared, that is, preserved. To this end, Heidegger examines the place of buildings (e.g., a house) and the way such things permit dwelling to be kept in its essence. This requires explicating what Heidegger refers to as the fourfold.

The Fourfold: Dwelling and/in Things

The fourfold is a significant concept in Heidegger's mid-to-late scholarship and its import in making sense of the essence of dwelling cannot be underlined enough. The fourfold consists of the sky, the earth, divinities, and mortals (BDT, 351–352). The term itself—*the fourfold*—is as cryptic as it is abstruse, and its myriad interpretations and disparate readings only complicate matters. Pieter Tijmes (1998, 208), for example, reads the fourfold as "a modelling of reality in which heaven and earth on the one hand, mortals and gods on the other, are the elemental coordinates," and adds that it is "a closer articulation of the event of truth." Cecil Eubanks and David Gauthier (2011, 128–129) view the fourfold as a reflection of Heidegger's anti-subjectivist stance. Julian Young (2000, 201) appears to put it more straightforwardly: "[W]e live our lives on (a part of) the planet ('earth'), in a particular climate ('sky'), among human beings ('mortals'), and under the (appropriated or unappropriated) guidance of a given cultural tradition" (see also Dauenhauer 1997, 196, for a similar description). Acknowledging and accounting for the cumbersome and complicated nature of the term, this section explores the fourfold vis-à-vis dwelling.

Heidegger references the "simple oneness of the four we call the fourfold" (BDT, 352; emphasis omitted). This suggests that the fourfold should not be thought of as four different or unrelated entities, but rather as an inextricable connection of the four. As Tijmes (1998, 209) puts it, in "the four elements each element refers to the other three to emphasise the original unity." Thus, and to slightly reframe the above, the essence of one entity cannot be understood and made sense of without situating it in relation to the others, and this already presupposes, if not unity, then, at least a relation.

The relation between the fourfold and dwelling is revealed in how each is connected to beings. Beings, Heidegger says, "*are* in the fourfold by *dwelling*" (BDT, 352; emphasis in original), and this is because dwelling is *in* the fourfold. Heidegger calls this the domain of dwelling. As such, dwelling necessitates (that is, gives rise to) the fourfold. Thus it is now possible to see more clearly, as articulated previously, why building (as a noun) is an insufficient condition for dwelling: dwelling entails and presupposes a domain, namely, the fourfold. "Mortals," Heidegger writes, "dwell in the way they preserve the fourfold in its essential being" (352). This preservation or sparing, as noted, is what ensures that the meaning of existence is held intact: "To spare and preserve means to take under our care, to look after the fourfold in its essence" (353).

To this end, Heidegger poses two questions: "if dwelling preserves the fourfold, where does it [dwelling] keep the fourfold's essence?" and "How do mortals make their dwelling such a preserving?" (BDT, 353). Heidegger's immediate response is that "dwelling itself is always a staying with things. Dwelling, as preserving, keeps the fourfold in that with which mortals stay: in things" (353). That is, and as Dauenhauer (1977, 196) puts it, "the way mortals save the fourfold is by making things." Things, then, are clearly important. This appears to run counter to what has been propagated thus far, namely, that material structures such as houses are insufficient conditions for dwelling. To further probe the import of things vis-à-vis beings, attention now shifts to things and the making of things as the means by which beings dwell in the fourfold.

"Dwelling," Heidegger says, "preserves the fourfold by bringing the essence of the fourfold into things. But things themselves secure the fourfold *only* when they themselves *as* things are let be in their essence" (BDT, 353; emphasis in original). It is unmistakable that things are paramount to dwelling and the fourfold: if the fourfold is preserved by dwelling, it is because things preserve the essence of the fourfold; this means there is an important, essentially inseverable, relation between dwelling and things. Additionally, the ability of things to preserve the fourfold is only possible when things are left to their essences (or preserved in their essences).

To give colour to this, Heidegger draws upon a specific thing, a site and location, namely, a bridge. Before exploring this, there is a crucial matter that the foregoing points to which needs attention. Given the relation between dwelling, the fourfold, and things, Heidegger writes that "*[d]welling*, inasmuch as it keeps the fourfold in things, is, as this keeping, a *building*" (BDT, 353; emphasis in original). This means—simplifying Heidegger's sentence to make the obvious point—dwelling *is* (a) building. The significance of this can only be appreciated when considering that, for Heidegger, building *is* dwelling (one builds because one already dwells and has dwelt). What is visible now is the other side of this relation, namely, that dwelling *is* building. If dwelling is (a) building—referencing both noun and verb—then, it is possible to see and appreciate how and why it is a thing (a structure) capable of housing the fourfold. There is, as such, reciprocity between building and dwelling: building *is* dwelling as much as dwelling *is* building, and this is an inextricable connection and relation (think in terms of the title of Heidegger's essay—"Building Dwelling Thinking"—which eschews any separation of concepts via commas or semicolons). Yet, this does not mean that building (in terms of a structure) precedes dwelling; rather, dwelling necessitates building, which also means that building necessitates dwelling.

To explicate this, Heidegger asks, "In what way does building belong to dwelling?" (BDT, 353). "The answer to this question," he states, "will clarify...what building, understood by way of the essence of dwelling, really is" (353). To this end, Heidegger asks, "[W]hat is a built thing?" (354). He provides a bridge as an example of a built thing and notes that "[t]he bridge *gathers* to itself in *its own way* earth and sky, divinities and mortals" (355; emphasis in original). This involves, among other things, passage and movement between water and land (so that land and water are brought together); it also involves how water is gathered and collected from the sky and, as such, the bridge links mortals and the divine. Bernard Dauenhauer (1977, 190) aptly describes how a bridge ought to be viewed and why Heidegger invokes it:

There is no point to a bridge, no possibility of bridging, unless there is something in the distance, something far. Both in the showing of the bridge and in the actual crossing, that which is distant abides as the distant. Further, there is no point to a bridge unless the place from which one passes is somehow insufficient. To call this place insufficient is no denigration. Without it there could be neither bridge nor the distant place to which one is *en route*. And so, if there is to be a bridge, there must be some prior connection between the insufficient near and the far to which one passes.

It is not simply that the bridge gathers; it is that the act of gathering is engaged in the first place because of a specific necessity. This necessity, as Dauenhauer (1977) explicates, is because the present—both time and space (see BT, 134–148; see also Harrison 2007)—is somehow insufficient, that is, not fully whole or complete (Dauenhauer is hinting at the need to reach out into the essence). The bridge is a device which permits reaching out via the journeying of beings (Eubanks and Gauthier 2011, 141–143; Dauenhauer 1977, 194), essentially providing the platform for beings to leap ahead. The bridge, then, as will become apparent, is what Heidegger relies upon to help beings leap *into* dwelling in their journey homewards.

"To be sure," Heidegger writes,

> the bridge is a thing of its own kind; for it gathers the fourfold in such a way that it allows a *site* for it. But *only* something *that is itself a locale* can make a space a site. The locale is not already there before the bridge is...Thus the bridge does not first come to a locale to stand in it; rather, a locale comes into existence only by virtue of the bridge. The bridge is a thing; it gathers the fourfold, but in such a way that it allows a site for the fourfold. By this site are determined localities and ways by which a space is provided for. (BDT, 355–356; emphasis in original)

The bridge, as a thing, is of its own kind: this means that it gathers to itself and holds its essence (recall that for Heidegger, even things have essences that must be probed). When the bridge gathers the fourfold into itself, it allows a site for the fourfold. This can be thought of as the bridge storing—Heidegger also uses the term *housing*—the fourfold and taking it into its care. This means that the bridge is a location—Heidegger uses the term locale—because it stores or houses. The notion of location is important, though not fully developed at this point. For present purposes, and in passing, a location could be thought of as a site that is created by gathering things together, which, to draw upon Dauenhauer's (1977) explication, enables beings to leap forward in their travels. That is, the concept of location (like the concept of space) is, for Heidegger, a construct. This is why Heidegger says that it is not the location that precedes the bridge, but the bridge, as a thing, that creates a location through its gathering, in this case by gathering the fourfold. For Heidegger, spatial relations, via locations, are products of things gathered, and these things are buildings that are produced via building. Heidegger further underlines that "*[t]hings which*, as locales, *allow a site*" are called "*buildings*" (BDT, 356; emphasis added):

> They are so called because they are made by a process of building-construction. Of what sort this making—building—must be, however, we find out only after we have first given thought to the essence of those things which of themselves require building as the process by which they are made [e.g., a bridge]. These things are locales that allow a site of the fourfold, a site that in each case provides for a space. The relation between locale and space lies in the essence of these things as locales, but so does the relation of the locale to the man who lives at that locale. (356)

To put this straightforwardly, buildings, as structural constructs, are things, but they are buildings precisely *because* they allow locations—read, spatial relations—by bringing various things together via gathering (spatial relations permit the journeying of beings so they can leap forward). If one seeks to understand space and the relation between space and beings, then, Heidegger's essay reveals not the taken-for-granted matter about humans *and* spatial relations or humans *as* spatial relations, but how humans *become* and thus *are* spatial relations, in this case, via building buildings. This is emblematic of dwelling: humans, in other words, are dwellers, that is, they dwell. Dwelling, then, is constituted by spatial relations, a product of things, which are the result of the making of these very things via what Heidegger calls building.

Heidegger's essay is interesting because it contains an important and novel explication of space and place (BDT, 356–360) that builds upon and echoes his analysis in *Being and Time* (*BT*, 134–148). It is worth underlining that an examination of dwelling necessitates understanding the relation between beings and space, along with accounting for location (essentially spatial relations): "The spaces through which we go daily are provided for by locales; their essence is grounded in things of the type of buildings. If we pay heed to these relations between locales and spaces, between spaces and space, we get a clue to help us in thinking of the relation of man and space" (BDT, 358). After situating the matter in this way, Heidegger attends to the relation between man and space (the masculine reflecting the tenor of Heidegger's writing): "When we speak of man and space, it sounds as though man stood on one side, space on the other. Yet, space is not something that man faces. It is neither an external object nor an inner experience. It is not that there are men, and over and above them *space*" (358; emphasis in original). Two issues, not necessarily foregrounded in the above passages, need underlining. First, for Heidegger, as already noted, space and beings are inextricably linked and this linkage is cemented via building, both the act and the resulting product. This is evinced in Heidegger's claim that space is about neither an object nor an inner experience but a relation that is a product of the gathering that accrues via building. Second, and relatedly, the concept of space is not hierarchized, as it often is in other literatures that prioritize it, especially in terms of its constitutive capacity (e.g., Lefebvre 1974/1991). Rather, space and beings are equated and on the same level. If there is a hierarchical relation, it would flow from the premise that beings create space (not the other way around) via building, a building which is a product of their very being, that is, dwelling:

> Spaces, and with them space as such—"space"—are always provided for already within the stay of mortals. Spaces open up by the fact that they are let into the dwelling of man. To say that mortals *are*

is to say that in *dwelling* they [mortals] persist through spaces by virtue of their stay among things and locales. And only because mortals pervade, persist through, spaces by their very nature are they able to go through spaces. But in going through spaces we do not give up our standing in them. Rather, we always go through spaces in such a way that we already sustain them by staying constantly with near and remote locales and things. (BDT, 359; emphasis in original)

This means that space does not constitute beings, but beings constitute space, so that it is beings who sustain space. This sustaining, Heidegger reminds readers, is a product of things and locations—in other words, building. Thus, and importantly, "man's relation to locales and through locales to spaces, inheres in his dwelling. *The relationship between man and space is none other than dwelling*, thought essentially" (359; emphasis added). As such, it is via things, produced by/through building, that the meaning of beings, namely, dwelling, is shone.

In concluding his exploration of dwelling, Heidegger returns to the bridge: "The bridge," he writes, "is a thing of this sort" (BDT, 360), by which he is alluding to the birth of locations—essentially spatial relations between beings—via the making of things: "The locale allows the simple onefold of earth and sky, of divinities and mortals, to enter into a site by arranging the site into spaces. The locale makes room for the fourfold in a double sense. The locale *admits* the fourfold and it *installs* the fourfold. The two—making room in the sense of admitting and in the sense of installing—belong together" (360). A location, as a product of things, admits the fourfold, which means that it brings together (Heidegger uses the word *gathers*) the fourfold into one by making room (that is, space) for it. The word *admit* is illuminating in this regard. Admittance can be thought of in terms of something that requires permission or invitation. To be admitted into a play, for example, one requires a ticket; to go to a party, one requires an invite. As can be appreciated, then, the word *admit* can also refer to a particular siting (as in "to admit *into*"). Here, in admitting the fourfold, the fourfold is sited or housed in a place, and by gathering and making room for it, the fourfold can be cared for, that is, preserved and saved.

The notion of installation is equally illuminating because it suggests a certain permanence associated with things. If *to install* is to put together—and putting together leads to durability in terms of time, such as installing a dishwasher—then, what Heidegger appears to be saying is that things which give rise to locations admit the fourfold and keep it for an appreciable time. It is, then, not merely that things open the possibility for housing the fourfold, but that in/through things the duration of this housing is long lasting. A bridge, for example, gathers and keeps the fourfold so that it can care for it and preserve it. As such, in this context, caring and preserving refer to a duration. Or, to put this differently, the bridge becomes an emblem (but not just an emblem) of the ways that beings inhabit the earth, here in relation to dwelling, over the course of their lives. The bridge, then, makes clear the essence of being by permitting beings to journey along their path of dwelling, a point that Dauenhauer (1977, 196) articulates well: "Things, then, are bridges which gather together the fourfold and allow it to appear."

Heidegger underlines that "[a]s a double-space making [admitting and installing], the locale is a shelter for the fourfold or, by the same token, a house. Things like such locales shelter or house men's lives. Things of this sort are housings, though not necessarily dwelling-houses in the narrower sense" (BDT, 360). This passage begins to provide a view into Heidegger's claim that the truck driver or the engineer is at home in the truck and road or the power plant, even though they do not live there. It also begins to draw closer the connection between dwelling and home (and homelessness): The bridge shelters the fourfold by bringing it into its site. Such locations are dwellings because they shelter or house the lives of beings. The truck driver does not live in the truck or the road, but does, nevertheless, "live" on the road because he spends an inordinate amount of time there. A significant part of the truck driver's life is housed on the road, and this is why it can be said that he dwells there, even though he does not, as Heidegger says (explicitly distancing himself from the means-end schema), live there. This is why Heidegger claims that locations can be thought of as housings, but only if one broadens and refines the view of house and housing.

The exploration of locations vis-à-vis beings permits Heidegger to focus on the essence of dwelling: "To preserve the fourfold, to save the earth, to receive the sky, to await the divinities, to initiate the mortals—*this fourfold preserving is the simple essence of dwelling*. In this way, then, do genuine buildings give form to dwelling in its essence and house this essential unfolding" (BDT, 360; emphasis added). To reiterate, dwelling entails preservation and care (of the fourfold), and it is only via building(s) that this is accomplished. For Heidegger, "[b]uilding...is a distinctive letting-dwell" (360). Or, to put this differently, "[t]he essence of building is letting dwell." This is because "[b]uilding accomplishes its essential nature in the raising of locales by the joining of their spaces. *Only if we are capable of dwelling, only then can we build*" (361; emphasis in original).

Dwelling involves gathering the fourfold—the lengthy discussion hitherto is testimony to this. Yet, and perhaps somewhat surprisingly, this only speaks to a characteristic of/about dwelling. It does not speak to its essence. The preceding discussion has, however, prepared the way to now probe the essence of dwelling.

"Dwelling," Heidegger writes, "is the *basic character* of Being in keeping with which mortals exist" (BDT, 362; emphasis in original). Unsurprisingly, this means that the meaning of existence is tied to dwelling. To give colour to and unpack the essence of dwelling, Heidegger notes that "building belongs to dwelling and...receives its essence from dwelling. Enough will have been gained if dwelling and buildings have become *worthy of questioning* and thus have remained *worthy of thought*" (362; emphasis in original). What is novel here is not that building and dwelling go together or that building is a product of dwelling or even that building cannot be reduced to structures. These important points have already been canvassed in detail. Heidegger's intention at this point is to underline the connection between building and dwelling in relation to thought, both in terms of thinking and questioning. That is, building, dwelling, and thinking are all one and connected. This is why, as noted at the outset of this chapter, the title of Heidegger's essay is penned free of commas. Harrison (2007, 633; emphasis omitted) explains that "[t]he lack of commas...should give us (no) pause; Heidegger is claiming that these three are one and the same, to be said—have been said—in one and the same breath, by the same tongue, on the same ground." A lengthy passage in which Heidegger underlines the inextricable connection (and unity) between thinking, dwelling, and building illuminates this point:

> that thinking itself belongs to dwelling in the same sense as building, although in a different way, may perhaps be attested to by the course of thought here attempted. Building and thinking are, each in its own way, inescapable for dwelling. The two, however, are also insufficient for dwelling so long as each busies itself with its own affairs in separation instead of listening to each other. They are able to listen if both—building and thinking—belong to dwelling, if they remain within their limits and realize that the one as much as the other comes from the workshop of long experience and incessant practice. (BDT, 362)

For Heidegger, if building is dwelling, then, thinking is also dwelling. It is thinking that equips beings with the ability to engage in a clearing of sorts—to invoke the early-Heideggerian language of *Being and Time*—so that they can see and appreciate the state of their lives (see Young 2000, 191–192). Thinking about dwelling, for Heidegger, helps clear the fog that occludes visibility—here invoking the early-Heideggerian language from *The Fundamental Concepts of Metaphysics* (see also Ranasinghe 2020a). Heidegger wishes to give prominence to a habit of thinking (or a contemplative habit of mind, as Bertrand Russell [1935/1958, 5, 41–42] puts it) where what drives beings is a concern about the being of beings rather than merely being caught up in and being consumed by the world. This is aptly evinced, for example, in the incessant desire to counteract boredom (as discussed in chapter two) or in the overindulgence in and reliance upon technology which borders on addiction (something that is certainly more prevalent and relevant today than when Heidegger penned his thoughts on and concerns about technology; see QCT).

Returning to the building-dwelling nexus, this is why Heidegger insists on turning on its head the means-end schema that has plagued thinking about building—the starting point, recall, of his essay. In a lengthy passage—split in two here to ensure that the profundity of the point is not lost to the verbiage of the quotation—he writes:

> We are attempting to trace in thought the essence of dwelling. The next step on this path would be the question: *what is the state of dwelling in our precarious age?* On all sides we hear talk about the housing shortage, and with good reason. Nor is there just talk; there is action too. We try to fill the need by providing houses, by promoting the building of houses, planning the whole architectural enterprise. (BDT, 363; emphasis added)

After acknowledging the importance of the materiality of housing (including its shortage), Heidegger attends to the question of the state of dwelling in his age:

> However hard and bitter, however hampering and threatening the lack of houses remains, the *proper plight of dwelling* does not lie merely in a lack of houses...The proper dwelling plight lies in this, that mortals each search anew for the essence of dwelling, that they *must ever learn to dwell*. What if man's homelessness consisted in this, that man still does not even think of the *proper* plight of dwelling as *the* plight? Yet as soon as man gives *thought* to his homelessness, it is a misery no longer. Rightly considered and kept well in mind, it is the sole summons that *calls* mortals into their dwelling. (363, emphasis in original)

As such, while linked to buildings, dwelling is not exhausted in them. Rather, thinking is a key component of dwelling: to dwell is to think, to be a thinking being. One does not think because one dwells, but one dwells because one thinks. Thus, thinking is paramount to dwelling. To put this differently, one does not dwell if one does not/cannot think (recall the place of thinking in relation to being, developed in the previous chapter). This thinking, as Heidegger envisages it, is a thinking about the plight of being, that is, ontological homelessness. That is, whether beings are housed or not is irrelevant to whether they are homeless or not. The dwelling of beings, then, is a state of ontological homelessness: "to save the earth man must come back to his own proper essence. And that essence is to be a dweller" (Dauenhauer 1977, 194). Heidegger's quest is to ensure that beings are fully cognizant of this: the bridge, as an example of a thing, permits beings to leap ahead toward this cognizance and see their true essence. This is what Heidegger's essay sharply brings to light: the materiality of things or structures ought to be used as a starting point to think about the plight of humanity and the meaning of existence. They should not be the culmination of the essence of being, as Heidegger is at pains to outline. This requires, as Heidegger's essay shows, reimagining the essence of things. So doing helps illuminate the relation between dwelling, nothingness, and the indeterminacy of being.

Dwelling, Nothingness, and Being

Heidegger's essay on dwelling can be (and has been) read in myriad ways (cf. Young 2000; Harrison 2007; Rose 2012). This chapter has reread it to articulate the important relation between home—more specifically, being (at) home—and homelessness. Heidegger is unequivocal in saying that material structures that shelter, best represented in the house, are insufficient conditions for being (at) home. This is because a house does not and cannot ensure that dwelling takes place (even though it is perfectly suited, not to mention necessary, to shelter beings and things). This means, first, that dwelling and house—the material structure of shelter—while related, are not the same; and second, that there is a clear and visible link and relation between dwelling and home. It is, thus, worth probing the relation between dwelling and home in this rereading of Heidegger's essay. Once this relation is attended to, it will be possible to see and appreciate that while one can be housed (and thus firmly believe that one is (at) home), one can nevertheless be homeless, and profoundly so. One is—and will be—homeless if/when one does not/cannot dwell. It is dwelling, then, that provides the sufficient and necessary condition for being (at) home. On this front, it is worth underlining what has been raised earlier. If to be is to dwell, then, this dwelling pertains to dwelling in homelessness (chapters one and two read this homelessness as an indeterminacy labelled as nothingness). The grave and sobering point is this: not dwelling in homelessness (out of either ignorance or a refusal to do so) is tantamount to *not* being. As such, if profound boredom, the subject of chapter two, is thought about, its import becomes clearer now because putting it to sleep is tantamount to not dwelling in homelessness and this amounts to not being. Combatting profound boredom, then, is the very negation of being. Similarly, the failure to dwell in homelessness is the negation of being leading to inauthenticity and unfreedom. Dwelling shines light upon the indeterminacy of being, conceptualized here as nothingness. Chapters one and two conceptualized the nothingness of beings via the fundamental attunements of anxiety and profound boredom as found in Heidegger's early work. While Heidegger's middle and later work might not evince nothingness as explicitly and directly, this theme is still evident and highly relevant to Heideggerian thought as this and the preceding chapter demonstrate. The flow of the river Ister, discussed in chapter three, illuminates this: the direction of the flow, believed to be homeward, is flowing away—in fact, fleeing—from home, an image that aptly highlights the indeterminacy of being. Similarly, as this chapter explicates, sites and material structures that shelter and are crucial to everyday survival, such as houses, are the very things that might obscure the vision of beings, shielding them from seeing and recognizing their homelessness. As such, being human is an indeterminacy because even while beings are housed, they are homeless; and the entirety of their journeying in/through life, homeward as it is believed, is, in fact, a journeying away and against home, which is, in fact, against the very homelessness that is necessary to recapture and recoup home. Chapters three and four showed that beings are caught in a bind: the homelessness that constitutes their lives, which needs to be celebrated, embraced, and championed, is shunned for a homecoming that is thought to lead home; yet it is only seeing and appreciating their homelessness as an inescapable indeterminacy and a necessary condition for being (at) home that will, in fact, bring them home. To be (at) home is to be homeless, and to be in homelessness is the epitome of indeterminacy.

The indeterminacy of being has been read throughout this work as nothingness. As this chapter shows, dwelling illuminates the nothingness of beings. This is clear in Heidegger's use of the phrase no-thing, which appears frequently in his early work. Heidegger hyphenates *nothing* as *no-thing* to underline that being is no-thing (it is not a thing, like other entities). The concept of dwelling shines light on the no-thing, nothingness, of being. The house, recall, is paramount to survival. It is, a thing, a clearly marked structure, a building. Yet Heidegger wishes to distance himself from this means-end approach to shine light on the meaning of existence. In so doing, Heidegger distances himself from a thing (or things) and is thus embracing no-thing: home is to be found in no-thing, in this case, it is to be found in and through dwelling, and as repeatedly noted, this is dwelling *in* home-less-ness. The no-thing Heidegger embraces and underlines reveals that dwelling is an absolute condition for home(coming).

Conclusion

THIS BOOK HAS CONCERNED ITSELF with the key theme that animates the corpus of Martin Heidegger's writings, namely, the meaning of existence or what Heidegger refers to as the being of beings. Heidegger's engagement with this subject, as this book has sought to show through an exegetical analysis of several of Heidegger's texts from his early and middle-to-later phases, can be reread as a social philosophy. This is because the very essence of what it means to be human, which Heidegger probes via Dasein, cannot be extricated from the social world: Dasein is inherently social insofar as Dasein is in the world, and thus to meaningfully attend to Dasein and the meaning of existence is to understand that being-in-the-world grounds what it means to be. To that extent, this book resonates with the handful of scholars in the social sciences and sociology more specifically who argue that Heidegger's concern about the being of beings is certainly relevant if not important to an ontology of humanity. As such, this book has engaged with Heidegger's explication of the meaning of existence and, in so doing, has sought to further clarify, refine, and give colour to the being of beings.

Heidegger places significant importance on ontological homelessness. To be human is to be homeless. This is a homelessness that speaks at its core to the fact that beings are, by virtue of being human and in the world, separated and distanced from their essence or nature. Drawing upon the theme of homelessness, this book has sought to reread Heidegger's explication of being as one where the very nature of what it means to be human cannot be sited and located. This absence of site and location renders beings ontologically homeless: their very being is distanced and separated from their essence.

The distancing and separation of the self speaks to an indeterminacy of being which this book reads as nothingness. The meaning of existence, this book argues, is nothingness, a simultaneity of nothing and something. The term *nothingness* is meant to capture an absence or emptiness that is caused by something that is missing, that is, meant to be (there) but (apparently) not. In the same breath, however, this absence is, itself, something, though it is difficult, often impossible, for the subject to specifically detail what this something is. There is, then, an emptiness that constitutes the lives of subjects that is simultaneously both nothing and something. This indeterminacy goes with—that is, throughout—the lives of beings and constitutes them as they are in the world, as the moods of anxiety and boredom bring to light.

The homelessness of beings, as this book has repeatedly underlined, is not a sombre state and should not be looked upon as such. Rather, it reflects the nature of existence: being-in-the-world renders beings homeless; at the same time, it also—in reflecting the indeterminacy of life or, if one prefers, paradox—means that beings are (at) home, and can only be (at) home, *in* homelessness. In other words, homelessness is not simply the status or plight of beings as they are in the world but the very basis of being (at) home, or what has been referred to as authenticity. As such, to be home in homelessness, in the ontological sense, is fundamentally different from being home in the sense of being homeful (that is, sheltered). The latter speaks both to the separation and distancing from home and to the travels against home. To be home in homelessness, in the ontological sense, is to come to terms with and embrace the status of the being of beings: a perennial absence or emptiness that is simultaneously fulfillment, despite the recognition and acceptance that this missing-something, nothingness, is difficult to decipher. Fulfillment, in this sense at least, materializes in and through embracing this indeterminate nothingness in and through dwelling. Beings, then, are (at) home in dwelling, which is to say that they must learn to dwell in homelessness, where their essence is located.

Rather than further recapitulate what has been developed in this book, what follows seeks to bring further light and give colour to the arguments developed by examining two substantive matters that will put into perspective the core themes of the book. As such, this concluding chapter deviates somewhat from the template of a final and closing chapter in that it engages with substantive matters.

One way to think about the Heideggerian project and what is developed here is to return to the phenomenon of boredom, discussed in detail in chapter two. For the most part, boredom has been tied to—and defined as—an emotion, and this is especially so in the social sciences (particularly in sociology). From this perspective, boredom is understood to reflect the way in which humans both feel and interact with the world, and this is said to form a recursive relation or pattern in the way beings are and live. This is particularly relevant in the post-pandemic world, where boredom is claimed to have become an emotion constitutive of human beings especially in the way that it illuminates the dregs of life.

As such, there is a tendency to view boredom negatively, as something that ought to be overcome. Accordingly, the emotion of boredom is, with a handful of exceptions, focused upon precisely for what it is, an emotion, without any further engagement concerning what it might reveal about the essence of humanity. Heidegger's examination of boredom reveals that it is not something that is good or bad, but something that *is*—in fact, something that *already* is, which is to say that to be human is to be in/with boredom. In this sense alone, Heidegger provides a radically different and novel interpretation of boredom that probes the depths of the meaning of humanity: that humanity is constitutionally linked to time and how beings traverse and make sense of time (or what can be referred to as temporality) cannot be extricated from what it means to be human. Boredom, which already speaks to the relation of humans to time, speaks to what it means to be human. In other words, it is much more than an emotion and therefore cannot be merely reduced to an emotion. As such, arguments about whether boredom is good or bad are not only meaningless but, more importantly, misplaced: if to be human is to interact with time, then part of that interaction necessitates boredom, which is a processing of time and the concurrent expectations from/of time.

Thus, Heidegger's engagement with boredom, as chapter two shows, is an ontological engagement with the meaning of existence, which is to say that while it does not claim to bypass the emotional context or aspect of boredom, it does not situate its gaze strictly at this emotional level (or what could be called the ontical). Rather, ontological engagement with boredom, which pertains not to values but to the meaning of existence, clearly reveals the indeterminacy of being (think, for example, of the structural moments of boredom). This indeterminacy of being is read as nothingness. As such, boredom is perfectly situated to reveal the nothingness of being because while it has revealed and can reveal profound meaning vis-à-vis life, the desire to combat boredom and put it to sleep via what the world has to offer—and in some ways as the world demands—forecloses the possibility of revealing that boredom is part of the very essence of being (the very essence of the person's person, so to speak). Every effort to combat and circumvent boredom therefore distances and separates oneself from one's very self because the engagement that one has to the world (in how one interacts with and relates to time) is silenced. Hence, putting boredom to sleep is essentially akin to putting oneself to sleep, which is to say that it removes one's essence further from one's self because it fails to see, appreciate, and come to terms with the fact that boredom is not merely from without, but from the very core of within: combatting boredom is combatting one's very self. It is a failure to be in/with oneself, to dwell in one's homelessness.

As another example, consider the relation between house and home. Although it might be a contentious, perhaps even reductive, point, the social scientific (and especially sociological) literature on the home—specifically that which attempts to explicate the essence and meaning of home—can be used to illuminate several interesting aspects regarding the relation between house and home which bring to light the import of dwelling vis-à-vis being.[1]

There appears to be little doubt that the concept of home is a contested one (Meers 2023), which is to say that the complexities associated with coming to terms with its essence have created enormous difficulties in scholarship. That said, for present purposes, it is as important, as it is necessary, to underline that home and house have, for the most part, been conceptually differentiated: that is, a house, it is underscored, is not a home. Shelly Mallet's (2004) comprehensive review of the literature, now considered "influential" (Meers 2023, 600) for its, supposed, "sophisticated and scholarly analysis" (Blandy and Hunter 2009, 481), evidences this. Mallett (2004, 63; emphasis added) writes that "[h]ome *is place* but it *is also a space* inhabited by family, people, things and belongings—a familiar, if not comfortable space where particular activities and relationships are lived." This means that "the term home functions as a repository for complex, inter-related and at times contradictory socio-cultural ideas about people's relationship with one another" (84). Mallett's rendering of the literature is faithful to the concept of home as complex, complicated, and irreducible to one thing (or even a few things), specifically in relation to material structures, namely, houses and housing. This is why it is noted that the home is a space, by which Mallet is implicitly drawing upon (though she does not explicitly reference) the long tradition that locates space dynamically, as a discursive process, as a production, as an imagination, as multiplicities, and so on (see Lefebvre 1974/1991; De Certeau 1980/1984; Bachelard 1958/1994; Soja 1989, 1996; Harvey 2006). That said, Mallet is clear that home is a place. This already denotes that home needs to be located or sited in/on a particular site. This site, as will become apparent shortly, has been—whether by default or not—the house, and the literature, both before and in the wake of Mallet's review, tends to reproduce this. In other words, while home is not reduced to house/housing, the house is, at least in some ways, thought to be a necessary (but not sufficient) condition for home. As one example, consider that in one study, 90 per cent of the participants understood and imagined home "as a physical building, a house, [which was] transformed over time into a home" (Dupuis and Thorns 1996, 496).

There are exceptions to the foregoing, but they are in the minority. Joseph Rykwert (1991, 54) is clear that while a house requires a building, a home does not (see also Hollander 1991). His influential and nuanced etymological engagement of the concepts of house and home show that these concepts became fused in the consciousnesses of laypersons and even in the literature through the values of urban planners and utopians tasked in the nineteenth-century with designing and building houses (see Rybczynski [1986] for a historical analysis of the emergence of the home and its relation to the house). According to Rykwert, they promoted a vision of the house as home, or at least something that can be made into a home, so that house *is* home. Such a view is now entrenched into the psyche of society and, in some ways at least, reproduced in the literature (see Imrie 2004; Fox O'Mahony 2007, 170–176).

This is aptly illuminated in the equation Home = House + X (see Fox O'Mahony 2007, 139). This equation was first introduced in the mid-1990s (Meers 2023, 604) and has since become an "influential formulation" (601) in the way that house and home are conceptualized. It is undeniable that the equation conceptually separates house and home so that there is no doubt that a house is not a home. However, the equation does not necessarily distance house from home (or does not distance it enough), which is to say that the house is still an integral part of the home along with a range of other experiential factors that range from a variety of attachments to the home, be they cultural, emotional, or psychological (Fox O'Mahony 2007, 139, 145-145). In fact, as the equation stands, it would not be unfair to claim not only that it is the import of the house that is grounded, but that the house is the most important of the factors given the ambiguity surrounding what these other factors are or might be, their differing subjective attributes and attitudes, and the fact that their relative import to the home is not (and perhaps cannot be) easily assessed in juxtaposition to the tangible nature of the house (Fox O'Mahony 2007, 155-156). As such, while this equation unequivocally shows that a house alone cannot constitute a home because it lacks the X factor, the equation is equally clear that a home cannot be or exist without a house (or some form of material structure). In other words, while the house is not a sufficient condition for home, it is explicitly constructed as a necessary condition for it.

As one example, consider Luisa Schneider's (2022) ethnography of persons sleeping rough in Leipzig. Schneider is clear that her participants were quick and keen to note that they had a home despite not owning a house or having shelter (in the form of a rented space, for example). That said, for both Schneider and her participants, some place, that is, some site or structure, is necessary and important for making home. When, for example, participants were questioned about home, "they rarely name[d] a physical structure or geographical location" (Schneider 2022, 240). At the same time, they were, whether Schneider and the participants were cognizant of it or not, explicitly mentioning some site or structure: as in where they lived with their partners, for example, or where they raised their children, or their parents' place (240). Even disregarding or downplaying the fact that these "where-s" that Schneider's participants refer to are houses—theirs or their parents'—it is undeniable that the recollection of and nostalgia surrounding home is directly and palpably linked to a site and structure. In fact, when discussing a participant named Sara and her making of home, Schneider concludes that "[h]ome is then intimately tied to a sense of belonging and to the ability to shape" (244). For Sara, this belonging is to be found in a specific location: here, under a stairwell, where she and her boyfriend would sleep, spend time, and even store their belongings (244). The point, then, is that even when a house is not presented as a narrative of (making) home, it is undeniable that some site—not comparable to a house but certainly mimicking its functions—is pictured and imagined in the meaning and making of home. Thus, the house or some composite of it, as a site and symbol of a material structure, weighs heavily—reigns heavily, in fact—in the making and in the meaning of home in the psyche of everyday persons (e.g., Imrie 2004; Fox O'Mahony 2007, 131–241).

The importance of house to (the making of) home can be further appreciated by looking at the status of ownership. The literature is clear that people, especially in the western world, desire to own their houses. "The home," Peter Saunders (1989, 191) notes, "is the core of most people's lives, and to own that home is at the centre of most people's aspirations and values" (see also Dupuis and Thorns 1998, 1996; Saunders and Williams 1988, 86; Saunders 1989, 187). In fact, "notions of the ideal home reveal that people from diverse backgrounds express a consistent preference for a free-standing house with a yard and occupied by a single family" (Mallett 2004, 67; see also Porteous 1976), indicating not merely the desire to own, but that this desire is specifically tailored and most likely entrenched within a specific socio-cultural-historical ethic. As such, this desire for ownership speaks to both how much it is—and has been—ingrained into the psyche (see also Souralová and Žáková 2022, 1449; Fox O'Mahony 2007, 181–241).

Home, then, plays a significant role in identity formation, that is, in shaping and constituting the identity of beings. The extent to which this is entrenched is captured in the belief of the public that if a house is not owned, then it is impossible to lay claim to being (at) home, a belief that equally suggests that renters are housed and sheltered but not at home (see Fox O'Mahony 2007, 229–232, 173–176). Such a formulation again clearly resonates with the equation of the home being a product of both the house and other factors, which, as noted, grounds the house as a necessary (though insufficient) condition for/of home. Consider, for example, the comments of Margaret Thatcher, then Prime Minister of England, who stated in an address to the National Housebuilding Council in December 1984, "People who own houses do so not just for themselves, but for their children. They do so as members of a responsible society—part of the heritage derived from the past, glad to care for it and eager to give the next generation a bit of capital to give them a start. *I believe in home ownership because I believe in individual responsibility*" (quoted in Saunders and Williams 1988, 87; emphasis added).

This is a powerful statement about, even a reminder of, the place of ownership vis-à-vis beings and their identity. It is powerful not merely for what it conveys, but for what it demands. It is a demanding, even damning, statement and declaration that exhorts citizens to comport themselves in a particular manner. At its core, what it underlines is not simply that ownership means possession or even the capacity to transfer capital and wealth from generation to generation. Rather, it is unequivocal that ownership signals responsibility, which means that the failure to purchase, own, and care for a house is a sign that one is irresponsible. This is an irresponsibility not just toward oneself and one's family but toward the entire nation. There is, then, almost a contractarian ethic in Thatcher's statement (specifically in the mould of Thomas Hobbes [1651/1985]) that speaks to the "new Golden Rule" (Etzioni 1993, 1–11; 1996) of communal life where rights presuppose responsibilities.

There is no doubt that much has changed since Thatcher's pronouncements—the difficulty, even impossibility, of affording a house today aptly evidences this. What has not changed is the import of the house and ownership to the identity of being. What has also not changed is the place of the house to (the making of) home (see Imrie 2004; Fox O'Mahony 2007; Jenkins and Brownlee 2022; Souralová and Žáková 2022). This is visible not simply in the conceptualization of the house as a necessity *for* home, but also in the at times unnoticed conflation of the house and home (Imrie 2004, 745–746; Saunders and Williams 1988, 87; Dupuis and Thorns 1998). Equally, the conflation of dwelling and/with house/home, such that a so-called dwelling place, as some referred to it (e.g., Souralová and Žáková 2022, 1447; Haar and Reed 1996, 256; Colomina 1992, 127), becomes equivalent to home can, at times, also be noticed in the literature (see Pint 2013; Mezei and Briganti 2002), and this is so even in the otherwise sophisticated and nuanced analyses of Rykwert (1991, 56) and Hollander (1991, 44).

The literature on house and home engaged with above leads to a specific point about dwelling (as briefly noted, dwelling appears at times to be conflated with or confounded for house/home, even to the point that house is constructed as a necessary condition for/of dwelling). As developed in this book, however, especially in chapters three and four, dwelling is, for Heidegger, of profound import to the being of beings. As such, dwelling is (or equals) being, and this "being" refers to being in homelessness, which means that it is necessary to be with/in the indeterminate state of being, here called nothingness (essentially an unfinished—and perhaps unfinishable—state).

Heidegger, recall, explicitly separates dwelling and building as conceptual entities—they are related but are not the same. This means that building (as a noun: a structure or what is, in the literature, referred to as a dwelling place) is an insufficient category and condition for dwelling. In fact, though it is a contentious and certainly arguable point, Heidegger's position could be stretched to claim that building (the structure) is *unnecessary* for dwelling, though it is the former aspect (the insufficiency of building), not the latter (the irrelevance of building), that this book has sought to ground and give colour to. In claiming that building is not dwelling, Heidegger's point is that dwelling is no-thing (recall, again, his attempt, especially during the early phases of his scholarship, to underline the no-thing-ness of being, developed fully in chapters one and two). What is contented here is that accounting for dwelling sans structures and materiality steers the focus and conversation closer to the essence of what it means to be human (it is not that structures do not matter; it is that they ought to be located in their proper place to the essence of being). In other words, dwelling, in this ontological (not simply ontical) sense, shines light upon the as yet unfinished state or project of human life, an indeterminate state of nothingness, with all its possibilities still open and intact.[2]

This discussion of dwelling can be brought into a productive dialogue with the land claims of Indigenous people to animate Heidegger's philosophy of being vis-à-vis the social. There is a growing literature on Indigenous land claims, but this discussion will focus upon one text, namely, Robert Nichols' (2020) *Theft is Property!* Nichols' book is not engaged in a detailed manner nor subjected to a detailed critique. Rather, it is drawn upon to demonstrate how particular social, political, and normative matters can be buttressed via the Heideggerian ethic of dwelling.[3]

In narrating Indigenous land-claim disputes, Nichols draws heavily upon the concept of dispossession, namely, that Indigenous people have been dispossessed from/of their land. Given that dispossession is tied directly to land, it is, by extension, a reflection and representation of something material, that is, a thing or more commonly, property. Yet, as Nichols shows, land-claim issues framed around possession are already vested within a legal framework, and this raises agonistic issues regarding ownership, as inevitably occurred in such disputes, often to the detriment of Indigenous people. Thus, Nichols reads the dispossession of the land as theft because what occurred in and through myriad land treatises was that Indigenous people were dispossessed (or deposed) of their land.

Nichols (2020, 29) is quick to note that for many Indigenous people, dispossession has less to do with possession and more to do with "something like deracination or desecration." By deracination Nichols means uprooting, displacement and removal, which appear to tie the phenomenon directly back to property (being uprooted from land), whereas by desecration Nichols means a "degradation or defilement of some object of concern" (29), which, yet again, even if only implicitly, appears to invoke something material, in this case, land. Still, Nichols is certainly sensitive to the limitations of the legal-rights approach and claims that property is not about a set of things (for example, houses) but about a set of relations, one that is, however, premised upon exclusion (31)—a point, it should be noted, disseminated widely for many decades in many so-called "law and ..." fields, especially legal geography.

There is no denying that at the heart of the concept of dispossession, and regardless of what term is invoked, lies property (in this case, land). Even though Nichols' argument is framed around relations, *property* relations are at stake (Nichols 2020, 85–115). In the legal sphere, although property is viewed in terms of relations rather than things, these relations are premised upon and thus help further reproduce exclusion, as when a property owner has the right to exclude or remove another from his/her property (see Waldron 1991, 2000; Jenkins and Brownlee 2022; Essert 2022; Fox O'Mahony 2007). As such, these relations are framed such that at their core lie concerns that are essentially reduced to objects or things—here, land and property—and this core is animated by relations between contesting parties with the possibility of removal or exclusion. Dispossession, then, speaks to the very core of exclusion and removal that captures the history of Indigenous land. Accordingly, the concept of dispossession, as Nichols' text shows, does little to advance causes of justice that are already rooted and premised upon an unequal playing surface.

Heidegger's concept of dwelling, and specifically dwelling in homelessness, offers a different approach to such contentious issues. This is because dwelling explicitly concerns no-thing, and the indeterminate nothingness of being developed in this book's rereading of Heidegger can be usefully brought into dialogue with some of these pressing social and political issues. In other words, the concept of dwelling permits an appreciation of being—being-in-the-world—

without necessarily privileging things or people. At first glance, this appears counterintuitive, even contradictory, to what has been developed given the emphasis upon being-in-the-world from which Dasein cannot be extricated. The point is, however, to neither efface nor neglect beings or things, but to locate and contextualize them appropriately vis-à-vis the essence of being.

Rather than drawing upon property—and land—as a set of relations between different sets of parties, dwelling can be invoked to look at the relation of the self to itself (again, this neither effaces nor neglects the other, but locates one vis-à-vis the other). As such, it becomes possible to overcome the difficulties associated with/in land claim disputes in the settler-colonial context that Nichols alludes to. That is, the problem with the settler-colonial narrative vis-à-vis Indigenous land claims is that property was never stolen. Rather, it was freely and consensually transferred, and this transference produces and buttresses the relation between colonizer and colonized, which is grounded upon property. Framed in this way, the narrative of dispossession is both futile and meaningless to the colonized because the master narrative is that there was no dispossession to begin with: there was nothing to be disposed of. In dwelling—which, recall, does not equate property or land with a sufficient condition for dwelling (that is, being)—dispossession can be invoked as a meaningful category because it does not require dispossession from/of property or land, but dispossession of/from oneself. In other words, reading an Heideggerian ethic into landclaim matters requires acknowledgement of dispossession, but not via the contentious manner of legal and property rights. Rather, it requires acknowledgement of dispossession of the very essence of being, which need not be tied to legality. In and through dispossession, beings are stripped of their very essence and, as such, are unable to dwell in homelessness, that is, be (and become).

Returning to and drawing upon Nichols' (2014, 53–54) concept of depersonalization is helpful here. It is important to note that Nichols' work does not reduce dispossession to the material, that is, land and property. Rather, Nichols speaks of different grammars of dispossession in a recursive relation that references not merely material dispossession but also dispossession through theft of the interests and values of Indigenous people. This is best evinced in Nichols' discussion of Black Americans, where "another grammar of dispossession" aptly illustrates that "the primary locus of concern is not land, but the body, self, or person" (2020, 118), what can be broadly referred to as dignity, autonomy, or both. Nichols underlines the "violation of personal autonomy and/or bodily integrity" (118) in the very being of Black people. In fact, Nichols is quick to underline that while land (and property) is important, it is not the most important of the grammars of dispossession; rather, it is integrity and selfhood that are key (142).

As such, it is worth probing how selfhood and integrity (and what can also be referred to as dignity) can be salvaged and privileged via the discourse of dwelling. What is outlined here is not necessarily contra Nichols. Rather it draws inspiration from his endeavour while also seeking to avert specific historical lessons where rights-based claims tied directly or largely to property claims have not merely failed but have often been turned against the very claimant (something Nichols is aware of).

Depersonalization of dignity, of autonomy, and so forth helps situate and reveal, in Heideggerian language, what dispossession signifies: the personhood, essentially the dignity, of a person is removed or effaced from that person such that the person's very being, his/her dwelling (and a dwelling that is not solely tied to a thing) is rendered null. Dwelling in homelessness helps recover the essence of being because the place of things (land and property) is located in its rightful place and appropriately contextualized in relation to beings. In other words, land-claim issues surrounding Indigenous people and the state are reread not as a matter of land subject to legal procedures, which are then used against the very claimant, but as a matter of dwelling, of being, so that the dignity of humans—what in Heidegger's terms would loosely translate as authenticity (where the possibilities open to persons are left open and intact, thus rendering them free)—is preserved not in something but in peoples' very selves, so that they have vested in/with them the capacity to exercise their right to these very things. It is that capacity, then, not the things themselves, that dwelling preserves and in so preserving, authenticates the essence of being.

To put this into perspective, one attempt which draws specifically upon Heidegger's concept of dwelling and seeks to use this model to explicate the nature of land and the economy is worth briefly considering, even at the risk of further muddying matters with the introduction of yet another text. Todd Mei's (2017) *Land and the Given Economy* is an effort to examine "the being of land" (4), which is to say that it seeks to understand land in an ontological register. Land, for Mei, is "ontologically unique" (7), and he charts this uniqueness via the phenomenology of dwelling. In some ways, Mei's work runs counter to the rereading of Heidegger's notion of dwelling presented here largely because it (still) tends to reduce dwelling to the material, most concretely to land. It is, Mei notes, "land [that] allows us to recognize *how* we dwell" (115; emphasis in original), and adds that "land…is the basis of our existence" (115). As such, land becomes a necessary condition for dwelling. The foregoing should not necessarily be read as an explicit statement that land is the sufficient condition for dwelling, though there are times when Mei comes close to this. In underlining the need to understand land ontologically, Mei is definitive in saying that "[l]and provides for human existence not just materially but ontologically in the sense of constituting our existence and our understanding of what it means to exist" (91).

Despite what appear to be significant differences between what is articulated here and what Mei develops in his text, the intention is not to underline the points of departure as much as draw upon what can be culled for the purposes of edifying the present project, namely, the grounds for thinking of the essence of dwelling vis-à-vis the nature of being human. Mei's reading of Heidegger's view of shelter and sheltering is worth pursuing because Mei, too, claims that humans are homeless. Specifically, he claims that beings are homeless because they "have an *inappropriate* relation to land" (Mei 2017, 130; emphasis added). This aspect of inappropriateness, alluded to before, deserves further investigation even if what Mei might mean by "inappropriate" may be different from how it is understood in this book. An inappropriate relation, as suggested throughout this work without necessarily invoking this language, is one where the material is taken for the sufficiency of dwelling, so that, as noted, when particular rights-claims are funnelled into a legal channel that endorse property—which only knows the language or register of property—these very attempts backfire more so than not. Understanding the inappropriateness not merely of this strategy but of conceptualizing dwelling itself highlights the need to think about dwelling as something that is not tied to a thing (or things) but grounded into and as a way of thinking, and more broadly, a way of being. That way of thinking, as noted, is to retrieve and safeguard the essence of what it means to be human, which, as developed here in an exegetical rereading of Heidegger, is an indeterminate nothingness. Mei's (2017, 196) conclusion appears to come to this point (whether he is cognizant of this or not and whether he aligns himself with it or not, however, are different questions that need not be grappled with here): "land as the source of life becomes the source of death." As developed here, this hints at the very indeterminacy of being, an unfinished project that has been labelled nothingness. Giving primacy to dwelling as the essence of being without explicitly giving primacy to materiality or taking materiality as the sufficient condition of dwelling is the path toward understanding the essence of being human, an unfinished state or condition.

It is worthwhile returning to the relation between house and home discussed earlier to contextualize the place of dwelling to the being of beings. The house and home, recall, are conceptualized as separate entities, so that there is no ambiguity that the two are different (though, as noted, there is some slippage in the literature which, even if only unwittingly or unintentionally, tends to confound and conflate the two at times, and while this literature is in the minority, it is still appreciably noticeable). While house and home are separated conceptually, they are inextricably linked given the failure to distance the two, resulting in the house being constructed as a necessary condition for home (best evinced in the equation of Home = House + X, which has become quite influential in the scholarship on the home). As such, it is virtually impossible to conceive of home without house (and this inextricability tends to contribute to the conflation of house and home noted above). The import or implication of the necessity of house for home is significant and can be appreciated in law, where the concept of home is tied directly to rights, namely, in/of property. As such, the house (or land or shelter) becomes, yet again, not merely important but a necessary condition. In other words, the rights tenured to/with home cannot be meaningfully made sense of nor come to fruition unless the meaning of home is directly linked to property, in this case, a house or shelter (see Waldron 1991, 2000; Jenkins and Brownlee 2022; Essert 2022; Fox O'Mahony 2007). Thus, it is not merely in Indigenous land claim disputes that the close connection between home and property (or land) is witnessed, often, it should be underscored, to the detriment of those in the minority. In every act and definition of property, this appears to hold true.

This is aptly evinced in the plight of those who are materially without housing (see Desjarlais 1997; Ferrill 1991; Glasser 1988; Hopper 2003; Rossi 1989; Snow and Anderson 1993; Liebow 1993). As many commentators have noted, constructing home as requiring the materiality of house or shelter renders those who are on the streets homeless, regardless of any shelter they might have or seek to secure and regardless of whether they themselves might think of themselves, as sheltered and at home. In other words, this way of conceptualizing the phenomenon of material homelessness—which, in precise terms, is a phenomenon of houselessness or shelter-less-ness (or something akin to that)—forecloses any possibility of seeing and recognizing that people without material shelter might not necessarily view or label themselves as homeless. Or, to put this differently, it fails to see that homelessness is not directly related to the absence of housing (despite the now influential housing-first policy). Thus, in the legal sphere, the equation Home = House + X, eliminates ex ante the dignity from/of those who are on the streets because the fundamental meaning and conceptualization of home is grounded upon house/housing. Here, then, property rights become the spokesperson for those who are without housing. In the same way that Indigenous land-claims issues can only be maneuvered up to a point within the rights discourse of dispossession, so too the phenomenon of houselessness can only be maneuvered up to a point because at some point it will strip the essence of the very persons it seeks to help and will instead speak for them and their essence. In other words, the authenticity of the very being of these persons—which is tied as well to other areas such as freedom and dignity—is eviscerated (Schneider's [2022] ethnographic research, noted above, is a good example of this: while the intentions are laudable, even among her participants who sleep rough, the making of home is directly and primarily tied to a site, often a house, and this, no matter what her participants claim or believe, renders them homeless by official discourse that is grounded in the material).

Against this backdrop, the concept of dwelling, of dwelling in homelessness, comes to situate itself as a possible means of circumventing these issues. This is because it casts its attention not on the material, but on the essence of being, which is not to say that the material is irrelevant but rather that it is contextualized in its proper place. In accounting for the ontological dimensions of existence that cannot merely be tied to the ontical, dwelling functions not only as a recipe for coming to terms with the being of beings, here articulated as an indeterminate nothingness and an unfinished state, but also as a recipe for progressive change achieved by preserving the dignity of humanity by locating it within the meaning of existence. Thus, dwelling speaks to a status or, more precisely, dwelling *is* a status (not a thing). It is, however, not a status about/of rights and property (that is, a legal status) or a status of feelings and emotions tied to place (that is, a status of affect). Rather, it is a status of being human, of being in homelessness, in that unfinished or not fully materialized state that is here referred to as an indeterminate nothingness.

In that sense, the form of philosophical theorizing developed here, inspired by the Heideggerian project, can be extended to other areas of social life, a handful of which are noted in passing to whet the appetite for further reflections of this sort. One contemporary issue is the profound anxiety that appears to be enveloping humans, especially in the pandemic and post-pandemic world; such anxiety also appears to consume young persons, especially students. In the broader context, anxiety over climate change, especially that tied to land and its changing contours, is ripe for the type of investigation developed here. Another issue, as noted already, is boredom, specifically the attacks upon boredom led by corporate media platforms. This sort of exploration fits well with what has recently come to the limelight under the banner of "boredom studies" (Gardiner and Haladyn 2017). The growing refugee crises facing the world and its population can also be approached through this sort of reflection, especially in terms of what dwelling means in such contexts. Finally, the place of religion, especially Judeo-Christianity, in the meaning of existence is a subject of profound interest and importance to be taken up in a future project examining the clear parallels between being as an indeterminate nothingness and the core tenets of Christianity theology.

Notes

Introduction

1. Criminology is an insular discipline, and despite its claims to philosophical reflection, it is quite wary of philosophy given its affinity to science and the explanation of facts, and as such, has little interest in grappling with ideas. There are certainly exceptions, but they are in the minority. That said, philosophical investigation has enhanced the criminological endeavour in a variety of ways (see, e.g., Ranasinghe, 2014; 2022a; 2022b; 2023), and it is hoped that this will become an important trend in the discipline.
2. The same can be said of Anthony Giddens' (1984) seminal *The Constitution of Society*. A close reading reveals that what is really explicated is not ontological but ontical. This is evidenced, for example, in his conceptualization of ontological security, which is, however, at its core, a security that is tied to bodily control (see 50, 64). The implication of such theorization is seen, among others, in the studies that examine the meanings of home and home ownership, discussed in the concluding chapter, which equate home ownership to a security that is, in fact, ontical, despite being labelled as ontological (see Saunders and Williams 1988, 87; Saunders 1989, 187–188; Dupuis and Thorns 1998; on the notion of security generally, see Ranasinghe 2017, 2013a, 2013b).
3. This period includes his seminal *Being and Time*, considered a classic that spearheaded a revolution in philosophical thinking and garnered him fame and attention that was to shape and galvanize his philosophical career, as well as the *Fundamental Concepts of Metaphysics*. Each text

occupies a significant place in chapters two and three respectively. In fact, it is possible to speak of a phase even earlier than this one, where his work is distinctively different and grounded in theology, between about 1915 and 1923.

4. John Stuart Mill's (1859/2006) concerns about the erosion of rationality and individuality—a product of the social contract in the first place and, by extension, the censorship of speech—have parallels with what is outlined here. For Mill, the tyranny of the majority, the hold that the majority (read in terms of sheer numbers) has on the minority is as vast as it is profound, and this leads to the voices of the minority not only being displaced and silenced, but essentially being lost to or funnelled into the majority. This resonates with what Heidegger points to, namely, that in inauthenticity, Dasein loses itself in the they-self, which smothers and overwhelms the possibilities open to Dasein. The implications that this has for freedom in Heidegger's work are taken up elsewhere in this book, but these implications, too, have clear resonances with Mill, whose essay was a response to what he saw as the death of liberty given the tyranny of the masses.

5. The Black Notebooks (Heidegger 2016; 2017a; 2017b) have certainly brought renewed attention to this controversial subject on which there is now a substantial literature, itself quite divided about Heidegger's fascism and Nazism.

1 | Anxiety and the Revelation of Nothingness

1. There is an important and profound difference between being(s) (used interchangeably for both human being(s), that is, designating a person or persons as well as things and other entities) and being (often penned as Being to differentiate it from being(s) to underline its ontological inquiry about the meaning of existence). What follows uses being rather than Being when referring to being as an ontological status and inquiry, in relation to what it means to be, because of, and to draw upon and follow, Hubert Dreyfus' cautionary note: "If one writes Being with a capital B in English, it suggests some entity; indeed, it suggests a supreme Being, the ultimate entity," and for Heidegger, "being is not an entity" (1991, 11; see also Goodstein 2005, 287n9). Many translations, however, utilize Being rather than being, as evinced in the translation relied upon here.

2. There are other variations which are only mentioned in passing here as they are not germane to the present discussion. Where there exists a situation that is threatening but it is not proximally close enough, fear can become a source of alarm, but only when what is threatening "is proximally something well known and familiar" (*BT*, 181). In other

instances, where what is threatening "has the character of something altogether unfamiliar, fear becomes *dread*" (182; emphasis in original). Additionally, "where that which threatens is laden with dread, and is at the same time encountered with the suddenness of the alarming, fear becomes *terror*" (182; emphasis in original).

3. Though speaking in terms of psychological states, Freud (1916–1917/1974, 443) perhaps put it best: anxiety "relates to the state and disregards the object" while fear "draws attention precisely to the object."

4. Heidegger is clear that even though fear and anxiety are very closely related they need to be distinguished and, "for the most part," not only have they "not been distinguished from one another," but they have been confounded so that "that which is fear, gets designated as 'anxiety', while that which has the character of anxiety, gets called 'fear'" (*BT*, 230).

5. A more detailed explanation of the uncanny provided by Freud (1997/1919, 217; emphasis in original) helps make sense of the homelessness of the term that Heidegger, as will become apparent, draws attention to:

> In the first place, if psycho-analytic theory is correct in maintaining that every affect belonging to an emotional impulse, whatever its kind, is transformed, if it is repressed, into anxiety, then among instances of frightening things there must be one class in which the frightening element can be shown to be something repressed which *recurs*. This class of frightening things would then constitute the uncanny; and it must be a matter of indifference whether what is uncanny was itself originally frightening or whether it carried some *other* affect. In the second place, if this is indeed the secret nature of the uncanny, we can understand why linguistic usage has extended das Heimliche ["homely"] [brackets in original] into its opposite, das Unheimliche; for this uncanny is in reality nothing new or alien, but something which is familiar and old-established in the mind and which has become alienated from it only through the process of repression.

6. There is a wonderful passage in Fyodor Dostoevsky's (1868/2008) *The Idiot* which puts the temporality of being into perspective: Prince Myshkin is recounting a story about one of his friends who is on the verge of experiencing his death sentence come to fruition. The friend says that in the last five minutes he has, which he would seek make into an eternity, he would set aside the final two minutes to reflect upon his life. Myshkin says of his friend: then "came the two minutes he had set aside for thinking about himself; he already knew what he was going to think about: he kept wanting to imagine as swiftly and vividly as possible how on earth it could be that

now he existed and was alive and in three minutes' time he would merely be something—something or somebody, but who, though? And where? He thought he could resolve all this in two minutes" (64). Such profound questions, crises of sorts, are what Heidegger claims emerge when anxiety, as rare as it is, takes hold of beings who are faced with their temporality. As will become apparent, however, Heidegger does not mean mortality by the term death, as Gelven's reading appears to suggest, but rather the realization of the end of a certain way of thinking and being, the possibility of no more possibilities, as Haugeland (2013, 183) puts it.

7. There is an important difference between what Heidegger means by *death*, and what he refers to as *perishing* and *demise* (though there is a literature that erroneously conflates these). Perishing speaks to the cessation of the organic functioning of an organism, while demise, which is exclusive to humans, concerns the cessation of the ability of members of a normative community to participate in it (see Haugeland 2013, 180). What is common to both perishing and demise is that both are events that happen at particular—that is, specific—moments in time. Death, on the other hand, is not an event that transpires at a particular moment, but, as Haugeland says, is "a possible way to be (that is, a way of living)" (237). This means that in death, life continues and, thus, it is inappropriate to equate death to mortality. Death, in other words, speaks to the possibility that one can have no more possibilities.

Thus, for Heidegger, death is the realization of the limits of Dasein, and in that sense, has nothing to do with perishing or demise. It refers to a continuation of life fully aware of its limits. William Blattner (2013, 342) uses the term *existential death* to differentiate this concept from demise, or what is in common parlance referred to as death. In describing Heidegger's use of the term *death*, Iain Thompson (2013, 269, 271; emphasis in original) claims that Heidegger "calls death the possibility of an impossibility" because "[m]y projects collapse, and I no longer have a concrete self I can be, but I still *am* this inability-to-be. Heidegger calls this paradoxical condition [yet another paradox] revealed by anticipation 'the possibility of an impossibility' or *death*."

8. The reference to the word *naked* and imaginary of nakedness is from Heidegger himself: "Anxiety is anxious about naked Dasein" and "Dasein is taken all the way back to its naked uncanniness, and becomes fascinated by it" (*BT*, 393–394, 394).

2 | Profound Boredom

1. There is a voluminous literature on waiting, especially its relation to experiencing time (read: temporality) that is not canvassed here. For the

most part, and what is worth noting in relation to boredom, even if only in passing, is that waiting and boredom are treated as related but distinct (see Schweizer 2008, 1–2; Moran 2004, 218; Phillips 1993, 76–78; see also Bissell 2007; Gasparini 1995).

2. The authoritative text on civility, including its history, is Norbert Elias' (1939/1978, 1939/1982) two-volume *The Civilizing Process*. Lucien Febvre's (1930/1998) essay is insightful as well. See also Ranasinghe (2011, 2019a) for further expositions of civility.

3. It is worthwhile reflecting, even in passing, upon the interesting parallels between what Heidegger developed in *Being and Time* and the metaphysical essays penned by Georg Simmel during the twilight of his career. Heidegger appears to have formally or officially downplayed any influence Simmel may have had on his thinking and resultant scholarly output (Jalbert 2003, 260). There is, however, a literature that is beginning to chart the similar interests and trajectories between the two thinkers, a literature that is also unearthing the deep influence Simmel (may have) had upon Heidegger (Jalbert 2003, 260–261; Levine and Silver 2010, xxv–xxix). This is not the place to explore this relation, but the time is certainly ripe for further explorations of the way Simmel's sociology and philosophy may have influenced Heidegger's philosophy, thereby further buttressing the social dimensions of Heidegger's interests, concerns, and thoughts. This is especially visible in Simmel's (1918/2010) exploration of mortality, which has an uncanny resemblance to Heidegger's exploration of death, demise, and perishing (discussed in chapter one). The same is seen in Simmel's (1909/1994) discussion of the bridge which aids humans connect (to) things. In this context, the bridge represents the mental processes or exercises beings engage in. Simmel's discussion of the bridge has many parallels to Heidegger's discussion of the bridge, particularly the latter's exploration of the fourfold as a means by which beings come to, and are able to, dwell (discussed in chapter four).

4. In (and for) this section, when Heidegger speaks of profound boredom, it should be taken that he is referring to the profoundest form. It is important not to mistake and conflate the profoundest form of boredom for and with the profound boredom discussed in the previous section. The key is to think of gradations of boredom, ranging from superficial to profound, all related and thus not separate, but fundamentally different in terms of their constitutions.

3 | Ontological Homelessness and Revelation

1. The title *On Time and Being*—essentially an inversion of *Being and Time*—is immensely revealing as it captures how the change in form in

Heidegger's thinking, from the metaphysical to the poetic, charts a path for Dasein, which is largely homeless in Heidegger's early works, to find its way home.

2. Robert Mugerauer (2008, 194), for example, writes that *Being and Time* "was an effort to begin a homecoming for Dasein; but, according to Heidegger himself...this early attempt was not wholly successful." This is because Heidegger was still working within the history of metaphysics and had not yet fully branched into the poetic (see "Letter on Humanism" for Heidegger's own critique of *Being and Time*).

3. As articulated in chapter one, the term *uncanny* (or in German, *unheimlich*) was famously discussed by Sigmund Freud (1919/1997) in reference to a subject's familiarity with something from the past that causes fear or trepidation in the subject. Heidegger also uses the term *unheimlich*, which can be translated literally as "unhomely," as homeless. In this chapter, the uncanny is reread as a state of being distanced and separated from one's essence or from the nature of one's being.

4. In "Being Dwelling Thinking," discussed in detail in the next chapter, Heidegger is explicit and unequivocal that while material homelessness (the condition of lacking housing) is as vital as it is important, and is both a moral and an ethical matter, it pales in comparison to the oppressive effects of ontological homelessness.

5. This should not be confounded with what was noted in the previous section, that constitutively, humans are homeless; as such, it does not make sense to say that one is more homeless than another (even though a descriptor such as "most uncanny" does not help because it appears to evoke quantity). What is noted here does not speak to the degree of homelessness but the varying ways one is homeless.

4 | Dwelling in Ontological Homelessness

1. Such is the view that abounds definitionally. The *Oxford English Dictionary*, for example, defines *dwell* as to "live in or at a place" and *dwelling* as "a house or other place where someone lives." The ordinary meanings of *dwell* and *dwelling* are tied directly to material structures and sites. This is precisely what Heidegger wishes to move past. At the same time, language appears to permit some room for the manoeuvring Heidegger desires when it refers to "dwell on" as to "think, speak, or write at length about something." Here there is no reference to a site or structure, but it appears to capture a sense of lingering, the import of which will come to light as the chapter proceeds.

2. Bernard Dauenhauer (1977, 195–196) further breaks down the verb of building in Heidegger's thought as something that encompasses "two

fundamental, and equiprimordial, modes" (195): first, enclosing and caring via building, where the focus is upon cultivating; and second, building that constructs structures that are one's own, where the focus is upon making and fabricating. Dauenhauer claims that Heidegger focuses upon the latter, though one cannot speak of building without also accounting for the former—a point about which Heidegger is explicit. For a discussion of building as enclosure, see Harrison (2007).

3. A good and vivid example is Gaston Bachelard's (1958/1994) *The Poetics of Space*. Heidegger's call and exhortation is almost an anticipation of this line of thinking, which could also be found in times that preceded Heidegger's. See also Korosec-Serfaty (1984, 303), who writes that "dwelling is a total experience," which directly ties and links dwelling to the home, specifically (parts of) the house.

4. Recall the import of lingering found in the verb *dwell on* as found in the *Oxford English Dictionary*, which references a sense of remaining or staying but without necessarily tying it to a site or structure. This is precisely the path Heidegger wishes to pursue to reclaim the essence of dwelling by extricating it from a material structure. Recall, as well, the parallel between the lingering found here and that in the passage of time vis-à-vis profound boredom, as discussed in chapter two. In both cases, the lingering alluded to aids in coming to terms with the meaning of existence.

5. The use of the word *purity* is not meant to convey nor is it to be read, as some have, and rather problematically so, as indicative of Heidegger's nationalistic ethic and movement not just toward simplicity (as in the farmer), but also German purity (see Eubanks and Gauthier 2011; Harrison 2007; cf. Tijmes 1998, 206).

Conclusion

1. The literature is vast, perhaps exhaustive, and no effort is made to present it in a systematic manner, especially in what are final thoughts to this book. Instead, the focus is to present a few key themes that repeatedly emerge from this literature which help situate and give colour to what has been raised hitherto in a strictly theoretical manner. Neither is it claimed that this literature directly or even indirectly engages with Heidegger, though a handful of studies do, if only in passing (e.g., Fox O'Mahony 2007, 135); nor is the literature necessarily faulted for not engaging with Heidegger. Rather, the aim is to highlight how the social in Heidegger can be productively thought through and brought to life by examining aspects where Heidegger's scholarship might resonate with some subjects

pertaining to social life, as the example of boredom, recapitulated above, shows.
2. While there is no need to engage with this point here, as it is both contentious and requires detailed explication, possibly in the form of a book-length manuscript (the subject of a project currently being undertaken), it is worth highlighting the under-appreciated parallels between Heidegger's exposition of being and the human being in Christian theology, where both can be reread as speaking to an indeterminacy, an unfinished state, of what it means to be human (see Ranasinghe 2020b).
3. Nichols' book engages neither with Heidegger nor Heideggerian scholarship (save for a passing mention or two), but his (2014) previous book directly engages with Heidegger's early works, situating the concept of authenticity in relation to freedom. As such, Heidegger's concept of dwelling can be seamlessly translated into an exploration of the concepts of dispossession and depersonalization that Nichols (2020) reads as central to Indigenous land claims, though, it should be noted, Nichols makes no mention of dwelling, Heideggerian or otherwise.

Bibliography

Adorno, Theodor. c.1963/1998. "Why Still Philosophy?" In *Critical Models: Interventions and Catchwords*. Translated by Henry W. Pickford, 5-17. New York: Columbia University Press.

Adorno, Theodor. 1967/2003. "Author's Note." In *The Jargon of Authenticity*. Translated by Knut Tarnowski and Fredric Will, xvii-xx. London: Routledge.

Adorno, Theodor. 1973/2003. *The Jargon of Authenticity*. Translated by Knut Tarnowski and Fredric Will. London: Routledge.

Arendt, Hannah. 1969. "Reflections on Violence." *Journal of International Affairs* 23 (1): 1-35.

Aspers, Patrik, and Sebastian Kohl. 2013. "Heidegger and Socio-ontology: A Sociological Reading." *Journal of Classical Sociology* 13(4): 487-508.

Bachelard, Gaston. 1958/1994. *The Poetics of Space*. Translated by Maria Jolas. Boston: Beacon Press.

Barad, Karen. 2012. "What Is the Measure of Nothingness? Infinity, Virtuality, Justice." In *100 Notes—100 Thoughts*, edited by Bettina Funcke, no. 99, 4-17. Kassel, DE: dOCUMENTA (13) and Hatje Cantz.

Barad, Karen. 2017. "Troubling Time/s and Ecologies of Nothingness: Re-turning, Re-Membering, and Facing the Incalculable." *New Formations* 92 (1): 56-86.

Barbalet, Jack M. 1999. "Boredom and Social Meaning." *British Journal of Sociology* 50 (4): 631-646.

Barthes, Roland. 1973/1975. *The Pleasure of the Text*. Translated by Richard Miller. New York: Hill and Wang.

Barrow, John D. 2001. *The Book of Nothing*. London: Vintage Books.
Bauman, Zygmunt. 2000. *Liquid Modernity*. Cambridge: Polity Press.
Beckett, Samuel. 1931. *Proust*. New York: Grove Press.
Benjamin, Walter. 1936/1970. "The Storyteller: Reflections on the Works of Nikolai Leskov." Translated by Harry Zohn. In *Illuminations*, edited by Hannah Arendt, 83–109. London: Jonathan Cape.
Benjamin, Walter. 1938/2006. "The Paris of the Second Empire in Baudelaire." Translated by Howard Eiland. In *The Writer of Modern Life: Essays on Charles Baudelaire*, edited by Michael W. Jennings, 46–133. Cambridge, Massachusetts: The Belknap Press of Harvard University Press.
Ben-Dor, Oren. 2007. *Thinking about Law: In Silence with Heidegger*. London: Hart Publishing.
Berger, Peter L., and Thomas Luckmann. 1966. *The Social Construction of Reality: A Treatise in the Sociology of Knowledge*. New York: Penguin Books.
Bissell, David. 2007. "Animating Suspension: Waiting for Mobilities." *Mobilities* 2 (2): 277–298.
Blandy, Sarah, and Carolyn Hunter. 2009. "A Review of 'Conceptualising Home: Theories, Law and Policies.'" *European Journal of Housing Policy* 9 (4): 480–482.
Blattner, William. 2013. "Authenticity and Resoluteness." In *The Cambridge Companion to Heidegger's* Being and Time, edited by Mark A. Wrathall, 320–337. Cambridge: Cambridge University Press.
Blattner, William. 2021a. "Care (*Sorge*)." In *The Cambridge Heidegger Lexicon*, edited by Mark A. Wrathall, 137–144. Cambridge: Cambridge University Press.
Blattner, William. 2021b. "Temporality (*Temporalität, Zeitlichkeit*)." In *The Cambridge Heidegger Lexicon*, edited by Mark A. Wrathall, 727–728. Cambridge: Cambridge University Press.
Blattner, William. 2021c. "Time (*Zeit*)." In *The Cambridge Heidegger Lexicon*, edited by Mark A. Wrathall, 757–764. Cambridge: Cambridge University Press.
Bourdieu, Pierre. 1988/1991. *The Political Ontology of Martin Heidegger*. Translated by Peter Collier. Cambridge: Polity Press.
Bourdieu, Pierre, and Loïc Wacquant. 1992. *An Invitation to Reflexive Sociology*. Chicago: University of Chicago Press.
Brown, Richard. 1977. "The Emergence of Existential Thought: Philosophical Perspectives on Positivist and Humanist Forms of Social Theory." In *Existential Sociology*, edited by Jack D. Douglas and John M. Johnson, 77–100. Cambridge: Cambridge University Press.

Carman, Taylor. 2008. "Foreword." In Martin Heidegger, *Basic Writings*, revised and expanded ed., edited by David F. Krell, ix–xvii. London: Harper Perennial.

Carman, Taylor. 2013. "The Question of Being." In *The Cambridge Companion to Heidegger's* Being and Time, edited by Mark A. Wrathall, 84–89. Cambridge: Cambridge University Press.

Champetier, Charles. 2001. "Philosophy of the Gift: Jacques Derrida, Martin Heidegger." Translated by Constantin Boundas and Susan Dyrkton. *Angelaki: Journal of the Theoretical Humanities* 6 (2): 15–22.

Clark, Candace. 2002. "Taming the 'Brute Being': Sociology Reckons with Emotionality." In *Postmodern Existential Sociology*, edited by Joseph A. Kotarba and John M. Johnson, 155–182. New York: Rowman and Littlefield.

Close, Frank. 2009. *Nothing: A Very Short Introduction*. Oxford: Oxford University Press.

Corrigan, Paul. 1979. *Schooling the Smash Street Kids*. London: Macmillan.

Crewe, Don. 2009. "Will to Self-Consummation, and Will to Crime." In *Existentialist Criminology*, edited by Ronnie Lippens and Don Crewe, 12–50. London: Routledge-Cavendish.

Croissant, Jennifer L. 2014. "Agnotology: Ignorance and Absence or Towards a Sociology of Things That Aren't There." *Social Epistemology* 28 (1): 4–25.

Colomina, Beatriz. 1992. "The Split Wall: Domestic Voyeurism." In *Sexuality and Space: Princeton Papers on Architecture*, edited by Beatriz Colomina, 73–128. New York: Princeton Architectural Press.

Darden, Donna K., and Alan H. Marks. 1999. "Boredom: A Socially Disvalued Emotion." *Sociological Spectrum* 19 (1): 13–37.

Dauenhauer, Bernard P. 1977. "Heidegger, Spokesman for the Dweller." *The Southern Journal of Philosophy* 15 (2): 189–199.

Desjarlais, Robert. 1997. *Shelter Blues: Sanity and Selfhood among the Homeless*. Philadelphia: University of Pennsylvania Press.

de Certeau, Michel. 1980/1984. *The Practice of Everyday Life*. Translated by Steven Rendall. Berkeley: University of California Press.

Dostoevsky, Fyodor. 1868/2008. *The Idiot*. Translated and edited by Alan Myers. Oxford: Oxford University Press.

Douglas, Jack D. 1977. "Existential Sociology." In *Existential Sociology*, edited by Jack D. Douglas and John M. Johnson, 3–73. Cambridge: Cambridge University Press.

Douglas, Jack D., and John M. Johnson. 1977. "Introduction." In *Existential Sociology*, edited by Jack D. Douglas and John M. Johnson, vii–xv. Cambridge: Cambridge University Press.

Dreyfus, Hubert L. 1991. *Being-in-the-World: A Commentary on Heidegger's Being and Time, Division I*. Cambridge, Massachusetts: MIT Press.

Dreyfus, Hubert L., and Paul Rabinow. 1993. "Can There Be a Science of Existential Structure and Social Meaning?" In *Bourdieu: Critical Perspectives*, edited by Craig Calhoun, Edward LiPuma, and Moishe Postone, 35–44. Chicago: University of Chicago Press.

Dupuis, Ann, and David C. Thorns. 1996. "Meanings of Home for Older Home Owners." *Housing Studies* 11 (4): 485–501.

Dupuis, Ann, and David C. Thorns. 1998. "Home, Home Ownership and the Search for Ontological Security." *The Sociological Review* 46 (1): 24–47.

Edwards, Paul. 1989. "Heidegger's Quest for Being." *Philosophy* 64 (250): 437–470.

Edwards, Paul. 2004. *Heidegger's Confusions*. New York: Prometheus Books.

Elias, Norbert. 1939/1978. *The Civilizing Process*. Vol. I, *The Development of Manners: Changes in the Code of Conduct and Feeling in Early Modern Times*. Translated by Edmund Jephcott. New York: Urizen Books.

Elias, Norbert. 1939/1982. *The Civilizing Process*. Vol. II, *Power and Civility*. Translated by Edmund Jephcott. New York: Pantheon Books.

Emad, Parvis. 1985. "Boredom as Limit and Disposition." *Heidegger Studies* 1 (1): 63–78.

Erikson, Stephen A. 1966. "Martin Heidegger." *The Review of Metaphysics* 19 (3): 462–492.

Etzioni, Amitai. 1993. *The Spirit of the Community: Rights, Responsibilities, and the Communitarian Agenda*. New York: Crown Publishers.

Etzioni, Amitai. 1996. *The New Golden Rule: Community and Morality in a Democratic Society*. New York: Basic Books.

Eubanks, Cecil L., and David J. Gauthier. 2011. "The Politics of the Homeless Spirit: Heidegger and Levinas on Dwelling and Hospitality." *History of Political Thought* 32 (1): 125–146.

Essert, Christopher. 2022. "What Makes a Home: A Reply." *Law and Philosophy* 41 (4): 469–489.

Febvre, Lucien. 1930/1998. "History and Civilization: 'Civilisation: Evolution of a Word and a Group of Ideas.'" Translated by Folan, K. In *Classical Readings in Culture and Civilization*, edited by John Rundell and Stephen Mennell, 160–190. London: Routledge.

Feng, Wei. 2021. "Reframing Nothingness in the *Kunju* Adaptation of Eugène Lonesco's *The Chairs*." *ORBIS Litterarum* 76 (6): 311–320.

Ferrill, Lisa. 1991. *A Far Cry from Home: Life in a Shelter for Homeless Women*. Chicago: Noble Press.

Fisher, Cynthia D. 1993. "Boredom and Work: A Neglected Concept." *Human Relations* 46 (3): 395–417.

Fox O'Mahony, Lorna. 2007. *Conceptualising Home: Theories, Law and Policies*. London: Hart Publishing.

Freeman, Lauren. 2021. "Boredom (*Langeweile*)." In *The Cambridge Heidegger Lexicon*, edited by Mark A. Wrathall, 127–130. Cambridge: Cambridge University Press.

Freud, Sigmund. 1916–1917/1974. "Anxiety." Translated by James Strachey. In *Introductory Lectures on Psychoanalysis*, edited by James Strachey and Angela Richards, 440–460. Middlesex, England: Penguin Books.

Freud, Sigmund. 1919/1997. "The 'Uncanny.'" Translated by James Strachey. In *Writings on Art and Literature*, edited by Werner Hamacher and David E. Wellbery, 183–233. Stanford: Stanford University Press.

Fried, Gregory, and Richard Polt. 2000. "Translator's Introduction." In Martin Heidegger, *Introduction to Metaphysics*, translated by Gregory Fried and Richard Polt, vii–xix. New Haven: Yale University Press.

Gardiner, Michael E. 2012. "Henri Lefebvre and the 'Sociology of Boredom.'" *Theory, Culture and Society* 29 (2): 37–62.

Gardiner, Michael E. 2017. "Postscript: Not Your Father's Boredom: Ennui in the Age of 'Generation Meh.'" In *Boredom Studies Reader: Frameworks and Perspectives*, edited by Michael E. Gardiner and Julian Jason Haladyn, 234–246. London: Routledge.

Gardiner, Michael E., and Julian Jason Haladyn. (eds). 2017. *Boredom Studies Reader: Frameworks and Perspectives*. London: Routledge.

Gasparini, Giovanni. 1995. "On Waiting." *Time and Society* 4 (1): 29–45.

Gelven, Michael. 1989. *A Commentary on Heidegger's* Being and Time. Rev. ed. DeKalb, Illinois: Northern Illinois University Press.

Genz, Henning. 1999. *Nothingness: The Science of Empty Space*. Translated by Karin Heusch. Reading, Massachusetts: Helix Books.

Giddens, Anthony. 1984. *The Constitution of Society: Outline of a Theory of Structuration*. Cambridge: Polity Press.

Glasser, Irene. 1988. *More than Bread: Ethnography of a Soup Kitchen*. Tuscaloosa: University of Alabama Press.

Goodstein, Elizabeth S. 2005. *Experience without Qualities: Boredom and Modernity*. Stanford: Stanford University Press.

Gusman, Simon. 2018. "To the Nothingness Themselves: Husserl's Influence on Sartre's Notion of Nothingness." *The Journal of the British Society for Phenomenology* 49(1): 55–70.

Green, Ronald. 2011. *Nothing Matters: A Book about Nothing*. Winchester, U.K.: Iff Books.

Haar, Sharon, and Christopher Reed. 1996. "Coming Home: A Postscript on Postmodernism." In *Not at Home: The Suppression of Domesticity in*

Modern Art and Architecture, edited by Christopher Reed, 253–273; 290–292. London: Thames and Hudson.

Harrison, Paul. 2007. "The Space between Us: Opening Remarks on the Concept of Dwelling." *Environment and Planning D: Society and Space* 25 (4): 625–647.

Harvey, David. 2006. "Space as a Keyword." In *David Harvey: A Critical Reader*, edited by Noel Castree and Derek Gregory, 270–293. Oxford: Blackwell Publishing.

Haugeland, John. 2013. *Dasein Disclosed: John Haugeland's Heidegger*. Edited by Joseph Rouse. Cambridge, Massachusetts: Harvard University Press.

Heidegger, Martin. 1924/2005. *The Concept of Time*. Translated by William McNeil. Malden, Massachusetts: Blackwell Publishing.

Heidegger, Martin. 1927/1962. *Being and Time*. Translated by John Macquarrie and Edward Robinson. New York: Harper and Row Publishers.

Heidegger, Martin. 1929/2008. "What Is Metaphysics?" In *Basic Writings*, revised and expanded ed., edited and translated by David F. Krell, 93–110. London: Harper Perennial.

Heidegger, Martin. 1929–1930/1995. *The Fundamental Concepts of Metaphysics: World, Finitude, Solitude*. Translated by William McNeill and Nicholas Walker. Bloomington: Indiana University Press.

Heidegger, Martin. 1935/2000. *Introduction to Metaphysics*. Translated by Gregory Fried and Richard Polt. New Haven: Yale University Press.

Heidegger, Martin. 1942/1996. *Hölderlin's Hymn "The Ister."* Translated by William McNeill and Julia Davis. Bloomington: Indiana University Press.

Heidegger, Martin. 1943/2002. "Nietzsche's Word: 'God is Dead.'" In *Off the Beaten Track*, edited and translated by Julian Young and Kenneth Haynes, 157–199. Cambridge: Cambridge University Press.

Heidegger, Martin. 1944–1945/2011. *Introduction to Philosophy—Thinking and Poetizing*. Translated by Phillip Jacques Braunstein. Bloomington: Indiana University Press.

Heidegger, Martin. 1947/2008. "Letter on Humanism." *Basic Writings*, revised and expanded ed., edited by David F. Krell, translated by Frank A. Capuzzi and J. Glenn Gray, 217–265. London: Harper Perennial.

Heidegger, Martin. 1953/2008. "The Question Concerning Technology." In *Basic Writings*, revised and expanded ed., edited by David F. Krell, translated by William Lowitt, 311–341. London: Harper Perennial.

Heidegger, Martin. 1954/1993. "Overcoming Metaphysics." In *The Heidegger Controversy: A Critical Reader*, edited by Richard Wolin, translated by Joan Stambaugh, 67–90. Cambridge, Massachusetts: The MIT Press.

Heidegger, Martin. 1954/2008. "Building Dwelling Thinking." In *Basic Writings*, revised and expanded ed., edited by David F. Krell, translated by Albert Hofstadter, 347–363. London: Harper Perennial.

Heidegger, Martin. 1962/2002. *On Time and Being*. Translated by Joan Stambaugh. Chicago: University of Chicago Press.

Heidegger, Martin. 2016. *Ponderings II–VI: Black Notebooks 1931–1938*. Translated by Richard Rojcewicz. Bloomington: Indiana University Press.

Heidegger, Martin. 2017a. *Ponderings XII–XV: Black Notebooks 1939–1941*. Translated by Richard Rojcewicz. Bloomington: Indiana University Press.

Heidegger, Martin. 2017b. *Ponderings VII–XI: Black Notebooks 1928–1939*. Translated by Richard Rojcewicz. Bloomington: Indiana University Press.

Hobbes, Thomas. 1651/1985. *Leviathan, or, The Matter, Forme, and Power of a Common-Wealth Ecclesiasticall and Civill*. Edited by C.B. Macpherson. London: Penguin Books.

Hopper, Kim. 2003. *Reckoning with Homelessness*. Ithica, New York: Cornell University Press.

Hollander, John. 1991. "It All Depends." *Social Research* 58 (1): 31–49.

Imrie, Rob. 2004. "Disability, Embodiment and the Meaning of Home." *Housing Studies* 19 (5): 745–763.

Jalbert, John E. 2003. "Time, Death, and History in Simmel and Heidegger." *Human Studies* 26 (2): 259–283.

Jenkins, David, and Kimberlee Brownlee. 2022. "What a Home Does." *Law and Philosophy* 41 (4): 441–468.

Johnson, John M., and Joseph A. Kotarba. 2002. "Postmodern Existentialism." In *Postmodern Existential Sociology*, edited by Joseph A. Kotarba and John M. Johnson, 3–14. New York: Rowman and Littlefield.

Käufer, Stephan. 2005. "The Nothing and the Ontological Difference in Heidegger's *What Is Metaphysics?*" *Inquiry* 48 (6): 482–506.

Käufer, Stephan. 2021. "Authenticity (*Eigentlichkeit*)." In *The Cambridge Heidegger Lexicon*, edited by Mark A. Wrathall, 71–77. Cambridge: Cambridge University Press.

Klooger, Jeff. 2013. "The Guise of Nothing: Castoriadis on Indeterminacy, and Its Misrecognition in Heidegger and Sartre." *Critical Horizons* 14(1): 1–21.

Korosec-Serfaty, Perla. 1984. "The Home from Attic to Cellar." *Journal of Environmental Psychology* 4 (4): 303–321.

Kotarba, Joseph A. 2002. "Preface." In *Postmodern Existential Sociology*, edited by Joseph A. Kotarba and John M. Johnson, vii–x. New York: Rowman and Littlefield.

Krell, David F. 2008. "General Introduction: The Question of Being." In Martin Heidegger, *Basic Writings*, revised and expanded ed., edited by David F. Krell, 3–35. London: Harper Perennial.

Kuhn, Reinhard. 1976. *The Demon of Noontide: Ennui in Western Literature*. Princeton, New Jersey: Princeton University Press.

Lefebvre, Henri. 1974/1991. *The Production of Space*. Translated by Donald Nicholson-Smith. Oxford: Blackwell Publishing.

Levine, Donald N., and Daniel Silver. 2010. "Introduction." In George Simmel, *The View of Life: Four Metaphysical Essays with Journal Aphorisms*, edited and translated by John A.Y. Andres and Donald N. Levine, ix–xxxii. Chicago: University of Chicago Press.

Liebow, Elliot. 1993. *Tell Them Who I Am: The Lives of Homeless Women*. New York: The Free Press.

Lumsden, Simon. 2015. "At Home with Hegel and Heidegger." *Philosophy Today* 59 (1): 7–21.

Mallett, Shelly. 2004. "Understanding Home: A Critical Review of the Literature." *The Sociological Review* 52 (1): 62–89.

Macquarrie, John. 1965. *Studies in Christian Existentialism*. Montreal: McGill University Press.

Macquarrie, John. 1994. *Heidegger and Christianity*. New York: Continuum.

McKenzie, Jonathan. 2008. "Governing Moods: Anxiety, Boredom, and the Ontological Overcoming of Politics in Heidegger." *Canadian Journal of Political Science* 41 (3): 569–586.

McNeill, William, and Nicholas Walker. 1995. "Translators' Foreword." In Martin Heidegger, *The Fundamental Concepts of Metaphysics: World, Finitude, Solitude*, translated by William McNeill and Nicholas Walker, ix–xxi. Bloomington: Indiana University Press.

Mei, Todd S. 2017. *Land and the Given Economy: The Hermeneutics and Phenomenology of Dwelling*. Evanston, Illinois: Northwestern University Press.

Meers, Jed. 2023. "'Home' as an Essentially Contested Concept." *Housing Studies* 38 (4): 597–614.

Mezei, Kathy, and Chiara Briganti. 2002. "Reading the House: A Literary Perspective." *Signs: Journal of Women in Culture and Society* 27(3): 837–846.

Mill, John Stuart. 1859/2006. "On Liberty." In *On Liberty and The Subjugation of Women*, edited by Alan Ryan. London: Penguin.

Moran, Joe. 2004. "November in Berlin: The End of the Everyday." *History Workshop Journal* 57 (1): 216–234.

Mugerauer, Robert. 2008. *Heidegger and Homecoming: The Leitmotif in the Later Writings*. Toronto: University of Toronto Press.

Nielsen, Kelly, and Tad Skotnicki. 2019. "Sociology towards Death: Heidegger, Time and Social Theory." *Journal of Classical Sociology* 19 (2): 111–137.

Nichols, Robert. 2014. *The World of Freedom: Heidegger, Foucault, and the Politics of Historical Ontology*. Stanford: Stanford University Press.

Nichols, Robert. 2020. *Theft Is Property! Dispossession and Critical Race Theory*. Durham: Duke University Press.

O'Donoghue, Brendan. 2011. *A Poetics of Homecoming: Heidegger, Homelessness and the Homecoming Venture*. Newcastle upon Tyne: Cambridge Scholars Publishing.

Papacharalambous, Charis N. 2022. "Criminal Law Guilt and Ontological Guilt: A Heideggerian Perspective." *Law and Critique* 33(2): 149–173.

Pint, Kris. 2013. "Bachelard's House Revisited: Toward a New Poetics of Space." *Interiors* 4 (2): 109–124.

Phillips, Adam. 1993. "On Being Bored." In *On Kissing, Tickling and Being Bored: Psychoanalytic Essays on the Unexamined Life*, 68–78. Cambridge, Massachusetts: Harvard University Press.

Phillips, Scott W. 2016. "Police Discretion and Boredom: What Officers Do When There is Nothing to Do." *Journal of Contemporary Ethnography* 45 (5): 580–601.

Polizzi, David. 2011. "Heidegger, Restorative Justice and Desistance: A Phenomenological Perspective." In *Crime, Governance and Existentialist Predicaments*, edited by James Hardie-Brick and Ronnie Lippens, 129–155. Basingstoke: Palgrave Macmillan.

Porteous, Douglas J. 1976. "Home: The Territorial Core." *Geographical Review* 66 (4): 383–390.

Rae, Gavin. 2021. "The Equivocity of Being: Heidegger, Multiplicity, and Fundamental Ontology." *Human Studies* 44 (3): 351–371.

Ranasinghe, Prashan. 2010. "Re-conceptualizing Vagrancy and Reconstructing the Vagrant: A Socio-legal Analysis of Criminal Law Reform in Canada, 1953–1972." *Osgoode Hall Law Journal* 48 (1): 55–94.

Ranasinghe, Prashan. 2011. "Public Disorder and Its Relation to the Community-Civility-Consumption Triad: A Case Study on the Uses and Users of Contemporary Urban Public Space." *Urban Studies* 48(9): 1925–1943.

Ranasinghe, Prashan. 2012. "Jane Jacobs' Framing of Public Disorder and Its Relation to the 'Broken Windows' Theory." *Theoretical Criminology* 16 (1): 63–84.

Ranasinghe, Prashan. 2013a. "Discourse, Practice and the Production of the Polysemy of Security." *Theoretical Criminology* 17 (1): 89–107.

Ranasinghe, Prashan. 2013b. "'Undoing' Gender and the Production of Insecurity and Fear." *British Journal of Criminology* 53 (5): 824–842.

Ranasinghe, Prashan. 2014. "The Humdrum of Legality and the Ordering of an Ethic of Care." *Law and Society Review* 48 (4): 709–739.

Ranasinghe, Prashan. 2015. "Refashioning Vagrancy: A Tale of Law's Narrative of Its Imagination." *International Journal of Law in Context* 11 (3): 320–340.

Ranasinghe, Prashan. 2017. *Helter-Shelter: Security, Legality and an Ethic of Care in an Emergency Shelter*. Toronto: University of Toronto Press.

Ranasinghe, Prashan. 2019a. "The Aesthetics of the Hybridization of Civility: For Inclusion, Tolerance and an Ethic of Difference." *Ethnography* 20 (4): 463–482.

Ranasinghe, Prashan. 2019b. "Theorizing Anxiety and Its Relation to Fear (of Crime): An Heideggerian Inspired Polemic." *Manitoba Law Journal* 42 (4): 241–264.

Ranasinghe, Prashan. 2020a. "On Being, Nothingness and Ontological Homelessness: An Heideggerian Inquiry into Authenticity." *Cosmos and History: The Journal of Natural and Social Philosophy* 16 (1): 191–217.

Ranasinghe, Prashan. 2020b. "Theorizing Nothingness: Malaise and the Indeterminacies of Being." *Distinktion: Journal of Social Theory* 21 (3): 300–315.

Ranasinghe, Prashan. 2022a. "Friedrich Nietzsche, *On the Genealogy of Morals* and Criminology." *Theoretical Criminology* 26 (1): 75–90.

Ranasinghe, Prashan. 2022b. "The Pale Criminal, the Guilty Conscience, and the Constitution of Crime: Nietzsche Reading 'Raskolnikov.'" *Law and Literature* 34 (3): 291–312.

Ranasinghe, Prashan. 2023. "Cesare Beccaria and the Aesthetic Knowledge of *On Crimes and Punishments*." *Law and Critique* 34 (1): 127–144.

Ratcliffe, Matthew. 2013. "Why Mood Matters." In *The Cambridge Companion to Heidegger's* Being and Time, edited by Mark A. Wrathall, 157–176. Cambridge: Cambridge University Press.

Ratcliffe, Jerry H., Travis Taniguchi, Elizabeth R. Groff, and Jennifer D. Wood. 2011. "The Philadelphia Foot Patrol Experiment: A Randomized Controlled Trial of Police Patrol Effectiveness in Violent Crime Hotspots." *Criminology* 49 (3): 795–831.

Richmond, Sarah. 2007. "Sartre and Bergson: A Disagreement about Nothingness." *International Journal of Philosophical Studies* 15 (1): 77–95.

Rose, Mitch. 2012. "Dwelling as Marking and Claiming." *Environment and Planning D: Society and Space* 30 (5): 757–771.

Rossi, Peter H. 1989. *Down and Out in America: The Origins of Homelessness*. Chicago: University of Chicago Press.

Roy, Donald F. 1959. "'Banana Time': Job Satisfaction and Informal Interaction." *Human Organization* 18 (4): 158-168.

Russell, Bertrand. 1935/1958. *In Praise of Idleness and Other Essays*. London: George Allen and Unwin.

Rybczynski, Witold. 1986. *Home: A Short History of an Idea*. New York: Viking.

Rykwert, Joseph. 1991. "House and Home." *Social Research* 58 (1): 51-62.

Saunders, Peter. 1989. "The Meaning of 'Home' in Contemporary English Culture." *Housing Studies* 4 (3): 177-192.

Saunders, Peter, and Peter Williams. 1988. "The Constitution of the Home: Towards a Research Agenda." *Housing Studies* 3 (2): 81-93.

Schneider, Luisa T. 2022. "'My Home Is my People': Homemaking Among Rough Sleepers in Leipzig, Germany." *Housing Studies* 37 (2): 232-249.

Schweizer, Harold. 2008. *On Waiting*. New York: Routledge.

Schroyer, Trent. 1973/2003. "Foreword." In Theodor Adorno, *The Jargon of Authenticity*, translated by Knut Tarnowski and Fredric Will, vii-xvi. London: Routledge.

Scott, Susie. 2019. *The Social Life of Nothing: Silence, Invisibility and Emptiness in the Tales of Lost Experience*. London: Routledge.

Sheehan, Thomas. 2013. "The Turn: All Three of Them." In *The Bloomsbury Companion to Heidegger*, edited by Francois Raffoul and Eric S. Nelson, 31-38. London: Bloomsbury.

Simmel, Georg. 1903/1950. "The Metropolis and Mental Life." In *The Sociology of George Simmel*, edited and translated by Kurt Wolff, 409-424. New York: The Free Press.

Simmel, Georg. 1909/1994. "Bridge and Door." Translated by Mark Ritter. *Theory, Culture and Society* 11 (1): 5-10.

Simmel, Georg. 1918/2010. "Death and Immortality." In *The View of Life: Four Metaphysical Essays with Journal Aphorisms*, edited and translated by John A.Y. Andrews and Donald N. Levine, 63-97. Chicago: University of Chicago Press.

Slaby, Jan. 2021. "Ontology (*Ontologie*)." In *The Cambridge Heidegger Lexicon*, edited by Mark A. Wrathall, 551-559. Cambridge: Cambridge University Press.

Smith, Christian. 2010. *What Is a Person? Rethinking Humanity, Social Life, and the Moral Good from the Person Up*. Chicago: University of Chicago Press.

Smith, Christian. 2013. "Fellow Traveller in Theoretical Frontiers." *Contemporary Sociology* 42 (1): 12-16.

Snow, David A., and Leon Anderson. 1993. *Down on Their Luck: A Study of Homeless Street People*. Berkeley: University of California Press.

Soja, Edward W. 1989. *Postmodern Geographies: The Reassertion of Space in Critical Social Theory*. London: Verso.

Soja, Edward W. 1996. *ThirdSpace: Journeys to Los Angeles and Other Real-and-Imagined Places*. Cambridge, Massachusetts: Blackwell Publishing.

Souralová, Adéla, and Michaela Žáková. 2022. "My Home, My Castle: Meanings of Home Ownership in Multigenerational Housing." *Housing Studies* 37 (8): 1446–1464.

Spacks, Patricia Meyer. 1995. *Boredom: The Literary History of a State of Mind*. Chicago: University of Chicago Press.

Steinmetz, Kevin F., Brian P. Schaefer, and Edward L.W. Green. 2017. "Anything but Boring: A Cultural Criminological Exploration of Boredom." *Theoretical Criminology* 21 (3): 342–360.

Svendsen, Lars. 2005. *A Philosophy of Boredom*. Translated by John Irons. London: Reaktion Books.

Swedberg, Richard. 2011. "Thinking and Sociology." *Journal of Classical Sociology* 11 (1): 31–49.

Thiele, Leslie Paul. 1997. "Postmodernity and the Routinization of Novelty: Heidegger on Boredom and Technology. *Polity* 29 (4): 489–517.

Tijmes, Pieter. 1998. "Home and Homelessness: Heidegger and Levinas on Dwelling." *Worldviews: Environment, Culture, Religion* 2 (3): 201–213.

Thomson, Iain. 2013. "Death and Demise in *Being and Time*." In *The Cambridge Companion to Heidegger's* Being and Time, edited by Mark A. Wrathall, 260–290. Cambridge: Cambridge University Press.

Thomson, Iain. 2021. "Nothing (*Nichts*)." In *The Cambridge Heidegger Lexicon*, edited Mark A. Wrathall, 520–528. Cambridge: Cambridge University Press.

Tonner, Philip. 2018. *Dwelling: Heidegger, Archaeology, Mortality*. London: Routledge.

Wilson, James Q., and George L. Kelling.1982. "Broken windows: The police and neighborhood safety." *Atlantic Monthly* 249 (1): 29–38.

Waldron, Jeremy. 1991. "Homelessness and the Issue of Freedom." *UCLA Law Review* 39 (1): 295–324.

Waldron, Jeremy. 2000. "Homelessness and Community." *University of Toronto Law Journal* 50 (4): 371–406.

Winch, Peter. 1958. *The Idea of a Social Science and its Relation to Philosophy*. London: Routledge and Kegan Paul.

Young, Julian. 2000. "What Is Dwelling? The Homelessness of Modernity and the Worlding of the World." In *Heidegger, Authenticity and Modernity: Essays in Honor of Hubert L. Dreyfus*, edited by Mark Wrathall and Jeff Malpas, 187–203. Cambridge, MA: MIT Press.

Young, Julian. 2015. "Was There a 'Turn' in Heidegger's Philosophy?" In *Division III of Heidegger's* Being and Time*: The Unanswered Question of Being*, edited by Lee Braver, 329–348. Cambridge, MA: MIT Press.

Index

absence, xxvi–xxvii, 24–25. *See also* indeterminacy; nothingness
Adorno, Theodor, xvii, xli–l
   alienation, 18–19. *See also* inauthenticity
Antigone, 95–99
anxiety
   fear vs, 15, 20–23, 31, 147n4
   features of, 24, 30
   meaning of, 12–17
   nothingness and, 24–26
Aspers, Patrik, xx–xxi, xxii
attunements, fundamental
   definition, 35–36
   See also mood
authenticity
   criticism against, xliv, xlvi
   Dasein, xxxix–xli
   death leading to, xlvi–xlvii
   freedom, xl
   homelessness leading to, l, 28, 86, 128

jargon as, xliv, xlix
   See also ontology

Bachelard, Gaston, 40
Baudelaire, Charles, 61
be (at) home, 103–105, 123–125
being, xvi, xxvii–xxix, xxxiv, xliv, 2
   Being vs, 146n1
   See also authenticity; dwelling; homelessness; inauthenticity
being, brute, xxi–xxii
being of beings, xxvii, xxviii, 2, 6.
   See also homelessness; nothingness; turn, the
being-in-the-world. *See* Dasein
Benjamin, Walter, xxviii, 40, 61
Blattner, William, 148n7
Bollnow, Otto, xlix
boredom
   definition of, 34, 37, 73–74, 129
   essence of, 43, 47
   missingness, 43
   significance of, 40

167

structural moments of, 37, 42, 46–48, 58–60
temporality and, 36–44, 47, 50, 70–74
See also profound boredom; profoundest boredom; superficial boredom; time, passing
boringness, 40–41, 47
Bourdieu, Pierre, xviii, xlv
Brown, Richard, xxi
building
    dwelling and, 103, 106–109, 114, 121
    etymology of, 107–109
    See also thinking

Candace, Clark, xxii
care, 6, 13–14, 15, 113, 120
Carman, Taylor, xxviii, 3, 6, 8, 63
Champetier, Charles, 6
circularity, liii–liv
circumspection, 15
civility, 48, 149n2
criminology, xvi, 145n1

Dasein
    anxiety to reveal, 13, 20, 27
    authenticity, xxxix–xli
    boredom and, 39
    care of, 6, 13–14, 15
    definition, xxii–xxiv, 4
    fear and, 15–17
    moods, 11
    profound boredom, 13
    temporality of, 9
    See also ontic; ontology
Dauenhauer, Bernard, 113, 114, 116, 119, 150n2
death, xlvi–xlvii, 148n6, 148n7. *See also* authenticity

deep boredom. *See* profound boredom
Deleuze, Gilles, xxviii
depersonalization, xxxviii, 138
deracination, 137
desecration, 137
dialecticism, liv
dispossession, 136, 137, 138
Dostoevsky, Fyodor, 147n6
Douglas, Jack, xxi
dread. *See* anxiety
Dreyfus, Hubert, 5, 20, 27, 146n1
Durkheim, Emile, xviii, xxviii
dwelling
    be (at) home, 123–125
    building and, 103, 106–109, 114, 121
    domain of, 103, 105–106
    essence of, 109–112, 120
    in the fourfold, 112–114
    land-claim issues, 136–139, 140
    lodging vs, 106
    meaning of, xxxii–xxxiii, xxxvii, l, lii, 103, 150n1
    space and, 116–118, 131
    See also being; thinking

Edwards, Paul, xvii, xxxiv
ek-sistence, 80
Emad, Parvis, 66
emotion, human
    boredom, 36–44, 73–74, 129
    fear, xlii, 13–17
    sociology of, xxi–xxii
emptiness, li, 46–47, 53–56, 67, 100, 128. *See also* alienation; indeterminacy; nothingness
enigma, 83, 84, 86–87
entity. *See* being
epistemology, xv
Erikson, Stephen, xviii

Eubanks, Cecil, 112
everydayness, 8, 18. *See also* Dasein
existence, meaning of. *See* ontology
existential sociology, xxi–xxii

fallenness, xxxviii, 18
fascism, xviii, xlii
fear
    anxiety vs, 15, 20–23, 31, 147n4
    meaning of, xlii, 13–17, 90
fourfold, the, 112–114
freedom, xl–xli, 57. *See also* authenticity; homelessness
Freud, Sigmund, 20, 23–24, 147n3, 147n5, 150n3
Fried, Gregory, 5

Gauthier, David, 112
Gelven, Michael, liii, 8, 25, 30, 69
geography, xvi
Giddens, Anthony, 145n2
Green, Ronald, xxxv

Harrison, Paul, 110, 120–121
Haugeland, John, 72
Heidegger, Martin
    criticism of, xvii–xviii, xli–l, 7
    poetizing, 80–83
    the turn, xxix, xxxi, lii
Hölderlin, Friedrich, xxxi, 79
home
    equation, 132, 141
    identity due to, 134, 135
    See also dwelling; homelessness; nothingness
homecoming, 80, 86, 90, 99, 101, 125. *See also Antigone*
homelessness
    authenticity, xxxix–xli, 28

    being home in, 83, 135
    dwelling in, xxix, xxxi, xxxii–xxxvii, 143
    Ister (the river), 82–83, 87–89
    land and, 140–141
    material, xxv–xxvi, xlviii, 102, 142, 150n4
    ontological, xxv–xxvii, xlviii, 31, 81–83, 91–95, 127–128
    overcoming, 99, 100
    See also indeterminacy; nothingness; uncanny
house
    home vs, 132, 141
    nostalgia for, 133
    ownership of, 133, 134
houselessness, xxv. *See also* homelessness
humanistic sociology, xxi–xxii

ideology, xliii, xlvi
inauthenticity
    Dasein, xxxviii–xli, 28–29, 146n4
    journey towards, 85
    unfreedom, xl, 18–19
indeterminacy, 27, 51–52, 58–59, 63
indifference, 35, 65–68
inquiry, ontical. *See* ontic
inquiry, ontological. *See* ontology
Ister (river), 82–83. *See also* homelessness; journey

jargon, xlii, xliv
Jaspers, Karl, xxx
Johnson, Jack, xxi
journey, 84–87

Kohl, Sebastian, xx–xxi, xxii
Kotarba, Joseph, xxi
Krell, David, 5

land
  being of, 140
  claims, 136–139
  See also dwelling
language, conceptual, xxxi–xxxii
law, xvi
locale. *See* site
Lunsden, Simon, xviii

Mallet, Shelly, 131
Marx, Karl, xviii, xxviii
materiality, xxv–xxvi, xlviii, 102, 113, 122–123
McKenzie, Jonathan, 17
Mei, Todd, 140
metaphysics, xv, xxxi, 79
Mills, John Stuart, 146n4
mood
  anxiety, xxiii, 13–17
  boredom, xxiii, 34, 36–44
  definition of, 11–12
  disclosure through, 11, 13
  fear, 13–17
  See also emotion, human
mortals, 113, 122
Mugerauer, Robert, xvii, 4, 18, 80, 150n2

National Housebuilding Council, 134
Nazism, xviii, xlii
Nichols, Robert, xv, xxxviii, xl, xli, 136–137
Nielsen, Kelly, 18
Nietzsche, Friedrich, xxviii, xxxi, 79
nihilism, 80
non-homely, 92–93, 96–97
no-thing, xxxiv, 125

nothingness
  absence leading to, xxvi–xxvii, 24–25
  homelessness, xxxiv, 29–30, 31, 81–83
  indeterminacy as, 27, 31, 35, 52, 100, 130
  meaning of, 25
  vs nothing, xxxiv–xxxvi, 47, 48, 65
  See also temporality

O'Donoghue, Brendan, xviii
ontic
  definition of, xix
  importance of, 6, 8
  inquiry, xxix, 3, 130
  limitation of the, xix–xx
ontology
  authenticity, xliii
  beings, xxvii
  criticism of, xli–l
  Dasein and, 8–9
  definition of, xx, xxviii, xliii
  fundamental, xvi, xxviii, liii, 3, 6–7
  homelessness, xxv–xxvii, 31, 81–83, 91–93, 127–128
  as ideology, xliii
  inquiry, xix–xx, xxix, 3, 130
  jargon, xlii, xliii, xlix
  See also nothingness

paradox, 24, 28, 96, 128
paranoia, xlii, xlv, xlvi
phenomena, 8
poetizing, 80–83. *See also* thinking
Polt, Richard, 5
preservation. *See* sparing

profound boredom
   agency in, 56–57
   Dasein leading to, 52
   indeterminacy due to, 51–52, 58–59
   structural moments of, 53–60
   superficial vs, 50–53, 54–55, 56
   temporality in, 70–74
profoundest boredom
   Dasein disclosed through, 63–64, 67–69
   definition of, 62
   passing time, 64
   structural moments of, 65–70
projection, 19–20. *See also* authenticity; inauthenticity; understanding
property. *See* home; land

Rae, Gavin, xxix
Ratcliffe, Matthew, 22
Rykwert, Joseph, 131, 132

Sartre, Jean-Paul, xxxv
Saunders, Peter, 133
Schneider, Luisa, 132–133
Scott, Susie, xxxv
shelter, xxvi, xlv, xlviii–xlix, l, 119
Shroyer, Trent, xliii
Simmel, Georg, 61, 149n3
site, 83, 87, 97, 115–116, 131
Skotnicki, Tad, 18
Smith, Christian, xx
social reality. *See* ontology
sociology, xvi–xvii
   existential, xxi–xxii
   Heidegger in, xvi, xviii–xix, xx–xxii
   humanistic, xxi–xxii
socio-ontology, xx

Sophocles, 90
space, 116–118, 131
sparing, 111–112, 113. *See also* building; dwelling
superficial boredom
   passing time, 44–45, 47–48
   profound vs, 50–53, 54–55, 56
   structural moments of, 46–48
Swedberg, Richard, xxii

technology, 18, 82
temporality
   boredom and, 36–44, 47, 70–74, 129
   significance of, 9
   time vs, 38
Thatcher, Margaret, 134
they-self, xxxviii, 18, 28, 82
Thiele, Leslie Paul, 5
things. *See* materiality
thinking, 2, 81–83, 121–122. *See also* building; dwelling
Thompson, Iain, 148n7
Tijmes, Pieter, 112
time, passing, 38, 44–45, 48–49. *See also* temporality
turn, the, xxix, xxxi, lii, 79

uncanny, 23–24, 30, 90–93, 96, 147n5, 150n3
understanding, 17
unfreedom, xl, xli, xlix, 55, 57, 99. *See also* inauthenticity
unhomely, 92–95, 96–98

Weber, Max, xviii, xxviii
Winch, Peter, xxxv

Young, Julian, xxx, 112

www.ingramcontent.com/pod-product-compliance
Ingram Content Group UK Ltd.
Pitfield, Milton Keynes, MK11 3LW, UK
UKHW042335230126
467268UK00003B/224